Transitional Justice in Law, History and Anthropology

Transitional justice seeks to establish a break between the violent past and a peaceful, democratic future, and is based on compelling frameworks of resolution, rupture and transition. Bringing together contributions from the disciplines of law, history and anthropology, this comprehensive volume challenges these frameworks, opening up critical conversations around the concepts of justice and injustice; history and record; and healing, transition and resolution. The authors explore how these concepts operate across time and space, as well as disciplinary boundaries. They examine how transitional justice mechanisms are utilised to resolve complex legacies of violence in ways that are often narrow, partial and incomplete, and reinforce existing relations of power. They also destabilise the sharp distinction between 'before' and 'after' war or conflict that narratives of transition and resolution assume and reproduce.

As transitional justice continues to be celebrated and promoted around the globe, this book provides a much-needed reflection on its role and promises. It not only critiques transitional justice frameworks but offers new ways of thinking about questions of violence, conflict, justice and injustice. It was originally published as a special issue of the *Australian Feminist Law Journal*.

Lia Kent is a Fellow in the School of Regulation and Global Governance at the Australian National University. Her research is concerned with questions of peacebuilding, transitional justice, reconciliation and memory, with a geographic focus on Timor-Leste.

Melissa Demian is a Senior Lecturer in Social Anthropology at the University of St Andrews, UK. She is a specialist in the anthropology of law with particular reference to Papua New Guinea, and has published on topics ranging from property and land disputes to customary and constitutional law.

Transitional Justice in Law, History and Anthropology

Edited by
Lia Kent and Melissa Demian

Routledge
Taylor & Francis Group
LONDON AND NEW YORK

First published 2020
by Routledge
2 Park Square, Milton Park, Abingdon, Oxon, OX14 4RN

and by Routledge
52 Vanderbilt Avenue, New York, NY 10017

Routledge is an imprint of the Taylor & Francis Group, an informa business

British Library Cataloguing in Publication Data
A catalogue record for this book is available from the British Library

ISBN 13: 978-0-367-27819-9

Typeset in Times New Roman
by RefineCatch Limited, Bungay, Suffolk

Publisher's Note
The publisher accepts responsibility for any inconsistencies that may have arisen during the conversion of this book from journal articles to book chapters, namely the inclusion of journal terminology.

Contents

Citation Information

The chapters in this book were originally published in the *Australian Feminist Law Journal*, volume 42, issue 1 (June 2016). When citing this material, please use the original page numbering for each article, as follows:

Chapter 1
Introduction: Transitional Justice in Law, History and Anthropology
Lia Kent
Australian Feminist Law Journal, volume 42, issue 1 (June 2016), pp. 1–11

Chapter 2
Court in Between: The Spaces of Relational Justice in Papua New Guinea
Melissa Demian
Australian Feminist Law Journal, volume 42, issue 1 (June 2016), pp. 13–30

Chapter 3
Sounds of Silence: Everyday Strategies of Social Repair in Timor-Leste
Lia Kent
Australian Feminist Law Journal, volume 42, issue 1 (June 2016), pp. 31–50

Chapter 4
Women Lawyers and the Struggle for Change in Conflict and Transition
Anna Bryson and Kieran McEvoy
Australian Feminist Law Journal, volume 42, issue 1 (June 2016), pp. 51–73

Chapter 5
Justice Claims in Colonial Contexts: Commissions of Inquiry in Historical Perspective
Jennifer Balint, Julie Evans and Nesam McMillan
Australian Feminist Law Journal, volume 42, issue 1 (June 2016), pp. 75–96

Chapter 6
Whose Reparation Claims Count? Gender, History and (In)justice
Natalia Gerodetti
Australian Feminist Law Journal, volume 42, issue 1 (June 2016), pp. 97–118

Chapter 7
Civil Society and Gender-Based Violence: Expanding the Horizons of Transitional Justice
Nicola Henry
Australian Feminist Law Journal, volume 42, issue 1 (June 2016), pp. 119–136

Chapter 8
'They Say That Justice Takes Time': Taking Stock of Truth Seeking in Peru, Argentina and Serbia
Olivera Simic
Australian Feminist Law Journal, volume 42, issue 1 (June 2016), pp. 137–161

Chapter 9
Prosecuting the Khmer Rouge Marriages
Maria Elander
Australian Feminist Law Journal, volume 42, issue 1 (June 2016), pp. 163–175

Chapter 10
The Transitional Heart: Writing Poetry on War, Grief and the Intimacy of Shared Loss
Robyn Rowland and Mehmet Ali Çelikel
Australian Feminist Law Journal, volume 42, issue 1 (June 2016), pp. 177–195

Notes on Contributors

Jennifer Balint is Associate Professor in Socio-Legal Studies in the School of Social and Political Sciences at the University of Melbourne, Australia. Her work addresses the constitutive role of law, with a focus on genocide and other state crime.

Anna Bryson is a Senior Lecturer in the School of Law at Queen's University Belfast, UK. Her research interests span the fields of oral history and transitional justice. Her recent publications focus on the role of oral archives in giving voice to victims and dealing with the past.

Mehmet Ali Çelikel is Professor and Head of the Department of English Language and Literature at Pamukkale University, Turkey.

Melissa Demian is a Senior Lecturer in Social Anthropology at the University of St Andrews, UK. She is a specialist in the anthropology of law with particular reference to Papua New Guinea, and has published on topics ranging from property and land disputes to customary and constitutional law.

Maria Elander is a Lecturer in Criminology and Law at La Trobe Law School at La Trobe University, Australia. Her research is primarily in the broader field of international criminal justice, and engages with theories in cultural and feminist legal studies.

Julie Evans is Associate Professor in Criminology in the School of Social and Political Sciences at the University of Melbourne, Australia. She researches the intersections between law, history, race, and colonialism.

Natalia Gerodetti is a Senior Lecturer in, and Course Director of, Sociology in the School of Social Sciences at Leeds Beckett University, UK. She has an interest in socio-historical and socio-legal dimensions around eugenics and gender and sexuality politics.

Nicola Henry is Associate Professor and Principal Research Fellow in the Social and Global Studies Centre at RMIT University, Australia. Her research has mostly focused on sexual violence and the law in both international and domestic contexts, with more recent work on civil society and transitional justice, as well as on digital technologies and sexual violence.

Lia Kent is a Fellow in the School of Regulation and Global Governance at the Australian National University. Her research is concerned with questions of peacebuilding, transitional justice, reconciliation and memory, with a geographic focus on Timor-Leste.

Kieran McEvoy is Professor of Law and Transitional Justice in the School of Law, and a Senior Research Fellow at the Senator George J. Mitchell Institute for Global Peace, Security and Justice, at Queen's University Belfast, UK. He has conducted research in over a dozen conflicted or transitional countries on topics including politically motivated prisoners, ex-combatants, victims, amnesties, truth recovery, human rights, restorative justice, and the role of lawyers in conflict and transition.

Nesam McMillan is a Lecturer in Global Criminology in the School of Social and Political Sciences at the University of Melbourne, Australia. Her interdisciplinary research explores how events of mass harm, and their global significance, are culturally negotiated.

Robyn Rowland is an Irish-Australian, living between both countries. She regularly visits and works in Turkey. She has published thirteen books, ten of poetry. She has published and read in Australia, Ireland, Japan, Bosnia, Serbia, Austria, Turkey, Canada, India, New Zealand, Portugal, the UK, the USA, Greece, and Italy.

Olivera Simic is a Senior Lecturer at the Griffith Law School at Griffith University, Australia, and Visiting Professor at the UN University for Peace, Costa Rica. Her research engages with international law, gender, crime, and transitional justice from an interdisciplinary perspective.

INTRODUCTION

Transitional Justice in Law, History and Anthropology

*Lia Kent**

1.0 Introduction

It has become almost axiomatic to suggest that societies emerging from protracted periods of conflict need to find ways to 'come to terms with' past human rights abuses. In recent decades, a set of mechanisms and tools known as 'transitional justice' has been developed with the goal of assisting states to confront the wrong-doings of repressive predecessor regimes. These mechanisms seek to ascribe individual criminal responsibility for past acts, enact punishment, provide opportunities for truth-telling, produce historical records of conflict and deliver reparations to victims. At its core, transitional justice works discursively to establish a break between the violent past and a peaceful, democratic future, and is based upon compelling frameworks of resolution, rupture and transition.

Over the past two decades, transitional justice, both a field of interdisciplinary scholarship and as practice, has seen an extraordinary rise. There has been a proliferation of war crimes courts and tribunals around the globe and a growing number of truth commissions. Transitional justice is now firmly entrenched as part of peacebuilding interventions that seek to promote stability, liberal democracy and a market economy in post-conflict societies, and has become 'an article of faith as a catalyst for reclaiming societies in political and social imbalance and dysfunction'.[1]

This Special Issue on *Transitional Justice in Law, History and Anthropology* unsettles many of the assumptions of transitional justice theory and practice by critically reflecting on the analytical frameworks of justice and injustice; history and record; healing, transition and resolution its proponents take for granted. Drawing together contributions from the disciplines of law, history and anthropology, Melissa Demian and I seek to open up critical conversations around these frameworks by exploring how they operate across time and space, as well as disciplinary boundaries. We adopt a broad view of transitional justice, recognising that a range of related mechanisms have been used in different geographical locations to respond to different reports of historical injustice. We acknowledge, too, that what are now termed 'transitional justice mechanisms' join a list of many other legal and quasi-legal mechanisms

*As guest editors of this Special Issue, Melissa Demian and I extend our sincere thanks to Judith Grbich, Karen Crawley and Olivia Barr for their support for this Special Issue, and to the anonymous referees and contributors.

[1] Mutua Makau 'Transitional Justice: Does it have a Future?' (2015) 9(1) *International Journal of Transitional Justice* 1 at 1.

and processes, including Royal Commissions, Boards of Inquiry, magistrate courts, truth and reconciliation commissions, criminal courts (international, national and 'hybrid') and local village courts. A common thread running through this Special Issue is that these mechanisms are utilised by governments and, increasingly, international bodies such as the United Nations, in an attempt to resolve complex legacies of violence in ways that are often narrow, partial and incomplete, and reinforce existing relations of power.

Of particular interest to us are the closely linked concepts of resolution and transition. The concept of resolution, which is underpinned by an assumption that conflict is resolvable and that the law is the prime vehicle for achieving this resolution, is consistently reproduced from very large scale institutions (such as truth commissions, national and international tribunals) to small scale ones, such as local magistrate courts and village courts. This narrative is undoubtedly 'seductive'[2] because it reinforces an idea that straightforward solutions can be found to complex historical and political problems. Yet, by foreclosing other, more nuanced, ways of thinking about those problems, and about what 'justice' may entail, it is also deeply problematic. For instance, narratives of resolution can paper over the extent to which transitional mechanisms do not always 'resolve' interpersonal disputes but may, at times, aggravate them. They may also render invisible the many other reasons why people engage with such mechanisms, for instance, to publicly shame family members or reconfigure relationships.[3]

The concept of transition, by contrast, is commonly applied to nation states, where it is embodied in the suggestion that states will be able to 'move on' from violent pasts by undergoing a linear transition from conflict to peace and liberal democracy. Here it helps to enact what Ruti Teitel refers to as a ritual of 'bounded change', a political rite of passage that, by representing and responding to certain forms of past violence, and relegating them to the 'past', announces a shared narrative of the future.[4] As the work of Claire Moon has suggested, the narrative of transition is a progress narrative that has a clear beginning (conflict) and a clear end (peace or reconciliation), evolves 'as *if* in a linear and developmental trajectory' and has now come to appear natural or universal.[5] It is a narrative that is undoubtedly convenient for fragile, post-conflict political elites seeking to consolidate new regimes, enable stable governance and construct new narratives of national identity and unity. It is also useful to post-conflict 'interveners' who may be seeking to downplay their own nation states' contributions to colonial-era harms and reconstruct themselves as 'saviours' in its aftermath.[6] Yet, just as this imagining of liberal societal progress remembers and responds to certain

[2] McEvoy Kieran 'Beyond Legalism: Towards a Thicker Understanding of Transitional Justice' (2007) 34(4) *Journal of Law and Society* 411.

[3] See, for example, Demian Melissa 'Court in Between: The Spaces of Relational Justice in Papua New Guinea' (2016) 42(1) *Australian Feminist Law Journal* 13.

[4] Teitel Ruti *Transitional Justice* Oxford University Press Oxford & New York 2000 p 229–30.

[5] Moon Claire *Narrating Political Reconciliation* Lexington Books London 2008 p 6.

[6] See, for example, Nesiah Vasuki 'The Trials of History: Losing Justice in the Monstrous and the Banal' in Buchanan Ruth and Zumbansen Peer (eds) *Law in Transition: Human Rights, Development and Transitional Justice* Hart Publishing Oxford & Portland Oregon 2014 p 305; Orford Anne

aspects of the past, it forgets others. Overlooked, for instance, are the underlying economic, social and institutional legacies that affect the ability of many so-called post-conflict states to become stable democracies. Many of these are legacies of colonialism. The narrative of transition also works to bolster the post-conflict peace-building 'industry' which, worryingly, tends to assume that external experts can implement solutions to conflict that embody universal values without regard to the specificities of local contexts.

That narratives of resolution and transition too often reinscribe, rather than disrupt, gendered power relations, is also apparent. What is easily eclipsed in the narrative of progression from conflict/violence to liberal democracy is that definitions of violence are deeply gendered, and tend to ignore the 'everyday' violence experienced by women in the private sphere. It also becomes easy to overlook the extent to which the achievement of liberal democracy does not necessarily equate to improvements in all areas of women's lives.[7] Obscured, for instance, is the structural violence and discrimination against women that, in many societies, is rooted in pre-conflict power relations and leads to the continued subordination of women following the formal end of conflict.[8]

This Special Issue seeks to destabilise the sharp distinction between 'before' and 'after' war or conflict that narratives of transition and resolution assume and reproduce. We also aim to examine the ways in which these narratives can become smokescreens that obfuscate the continuation of past injustices into the present. Yet, we acknowledge, too, that official attempts to enact rituals of bounded change that herald a new beginning are seldom completely successful or all-encompassing. As a number of contributions to the Special Issue show, these attempts often come up against, and are unravelled by, the counter efforts by victims of injustice or their supporters to keep the past alive. All of this is a reminder that there are no bright lines between the past and the present, and that closure can be ephemeral or elusive.

2.0 Overview of Articles

Broadly speaking, the contributions to this Special Issue adopt one of three analytical approaches to the investigation of transitional justice frameworks of resolution and transition. Each approach contributes to the project of unsettling these frameworks by analysing them from a slightly different angle. The first set of articles seek to 'ground' transitional justice by exploring how it operates across diverse geographic

'Muscular Humanitarianism: Reading the Narratives of the New Interventionism' (1999) 10(4) *European Journal of International Law* 679.

7 See, for example, Buckley-Zistel Susanne and Zolkos Magdalena 'Introduction' in Buckley-Zistel Susanne and Stanley Ruth (eds) *Gender in Transitional Justice* Palgrave Hampshire & New York p 8; Bell Christine and O'Rourke Catherine 'Does Feminism Need a Theory of Transitional Justice? An Introductory Essay' (2007) 1(1) *International Journal of Transitional Justice* 23; Franke Catherine M 'Gendered Subject of Transitional Justice' (2006) 15 *Columbia Journal of Gender and Law* 813.

8 See, for example, Sigsworth Romi and Valji Nahla 'Continuities of Violence against Women and the Limitations of Transitional Justice: The Case of South Africa' in Buckley-Zistel Susanne and Stanley Ruth (eds) *Gender in Transitional Justice* Palgrave Hampshire & New York p 115.

sites and is experienced by different actors. The second set of articles shows that transitional justice needs to be situated as part of a political and historical continuum rather than seen as something new. The third set of articles looks beyond state-centred and legalistic approaches to consider how transitional justice might be conceptualised in more creative, more expansive ways.

2.1 *Grounding Transitional Justice: Sites, Voices, Relations*

Transitional Justice is often viewed as a universal set of discourses, mechanisms, tools and practices that can be applied uniformly around the globe. The opening set of articles unsettles these assumptions by paying close attention to the ways in which transitional justice 'travels'. By examining the lived experiences of transitional justice in diverse locations (from Papua New Guinea to Timor-Leste, from Cambodia to South Africa) and amongst diverse actors (village court participants, 'ordinary' people and female lawyers), these articles help to show how orthodox assumptions about transition, resolution, justice, injustice and agency are both unravelled and ascribed new meanings within in specific local contexts.

The opening article in the Special Issue, by Melissa Demian,[9] works to problematise narratives of resolution through a finely grained case study of Papua New Guinea's (PNG) village courts. Instigated at PNG's independence, the village court system was intended to provide ordinary people with access to the legal system, and provides a highly public forum in which a wide range of grievances may be brought for general debate. Demian draws on long-term ethnographic observations to suggest that many of the cases managed by the courts 'very patently do not produce "peace" and indeed may lay the groundwork for future conflict'.[10] What kind of justice is being enacted in the village courts, she asks, 'if not the "peace" of closure, completion and non-conflict'?[11]

Focusing on two types of cases that are commonly brought to the village court — adultery accusations and sorcery accusations — Demian suggests that, while there is rarely an identifiable conclusion or resolution to such cases, the 'having-out of problems in the open space of the court' often appears to be an end in itself.[12] The village court can also provide an important mechanism of public shaming. Intriguingly, Demian also describes the way in which different people with an interest in a case will deliberately occupy different spatial positions during the court hearings. To explain the significance of these observations, Demian brings into conversation two different conceptions of justice: relational justice, drawn from anthropology; and spatial justice, drawn from legal theory and expounded by Andreas Philippopoulos-Mihalopoulos.[13] She suggests that what is occurring in the PNG village court cases is the interpellation of spatial justice with relational justice. What she means by this is that 'people in PNG bring relations that have run into trouble into view in the space they create, through both the disposition of their bodies and of their speech,

[9] Demian above note 3.
[10] At 19.
[11] At 17.
[12] At 28.
[13] Philippopoulos-Mihalopoulos Andreas *Spatial Justice: Body, Lawscape, Atmosphere* Routledge Abingdon 2015.

in the village court'.[14] In this sense, the village courts may offer an ongoing and open-ended justice, rather than a justice of closure.

There are a number of synergies between Demian's article and the second article, by Lia Kent,[15] which similarly brings ideas of relationality — so often overlooked by the individualised focus of liberal transitional justice mechanisms — to the fore. With a geographic focus on Timor-Leste, Kent's article destabilises the juxtaposition of 'speech' versus 'silence' that is central to the discourse and practice of transitional justice, in particular, the work of truth commissions. This juxtaposition, which suggests that silences must be 'broken' in order for both individuals and societies to 'move on' constructs silence in a negative light: as a marker of absence, pathology or repression.

Through a close reading of some of the 'everyday' ways in which East Timorese people are seeking to rebuild their lives in the aftermath of the 24-year Indonesian occupation, Kent shows how problematic this interpretation of silence can be. While acknowledging that silence is often associated with repression, shame and humiliation, Kent suggests that it might also, at times, be essential to the maintenance of critical relationships, the protection of reputations and the achievement of a better life for children in a context of enduring patterns of violence, poverty and stigmatisation. The apparent absence of verbal, public discussion about the past conflict also indicates that individuals and communities are working with its legacy in other ways, by for instance participating in ritual or community life. These rituals and practices, which underscore the centrality of embodied and relational forms of communication in the Timor-Leste context, show that individuals, families and communities are engaging in an enormous amount of *work* to negotiate the legacies of the conflict, suggesting that silence should not be equated with absence. Resonating with Demian's observations of the PNG village courts, Kent also suggests that everyday strategies of social repair in Timor-Leste are *ongoing*, and that, while 'tentative forms of "closure" and resolution may be possible, individuals, families and communities remain engaged in a dialogue with the past, rather than making a complete break with it'.

The third article, by Anna Bryson and Kieran McEvoy,[16] which is similarly informed by rich empirical material, examines the experiences of female 'cause lawyers' in conflict and transitional societies. Focusing on the cases of Cambodia, Chile, Israel, Palestine, Tunisia and South Africa, and drawing on detailed interviews with female cause lawyers, the authors explore the ways in which these lawyers seek to 'make a difference' amid broader structural constraints. Bryson and McEvoy compellingly examine the personal, familial and relationship toll of involvement in cause lawyering and show how this intersects in complex ways with questions of gender. The comments of their interviewees illustrate the paradoxical effects of 'transition' for women, showing how, even though times of transition may allow for new ideas and opportunities to emerge, that newness can equally hide 'deep pitfalls of structural

[14] Demian above note 3 at 30.

[15] Kent Lia 'Sounds of Silence: Everyday Strategies of Social Repair in Timor-Leste' (2016) 42(1) *Australian Feminist Law Journal* 31.

[16] Bryson Anna and McEvoy Kieran 'Women Lawyers and the Struggle for Change in Conflict and Transition' (2016) 42(1) *Australian Feminist Law Journal* 51.

and entrenched gender discrimination'.[17] All of this means that the '"opportunities" arising for female lawyers during times of conflict and transition do not automatically translate into wider material gains for women in the legal profession — or indeed wider society'.[18]

Nonetheless, many of the stories highlighted by Bryson and McEvoy are inspiring, and suggest that despite the significant structural constraints upon their work, women exercise agency. What emerges from these narratives presented here is that these women cause lawyers are deeply invested in activism, and are at the 'very heart of the social and political struggles of their respective societies'.[19] While at times they may be 'complicit in propping up and perpetuating deeply gendered processes, accommodations and structures'[20] they also use the law and legal settings as a space to engage in contests over political power. By highlighting the creativity and energy of women cause lawyers, Bryson and McEvoy's piece stands as a powerful corrective to the narrative of 'women as victims' that informs much transitional justice and research and practice.

2.2 *Political and Historical Hauntings*

The next set of articles continue to destabilise orthodox transitional justice assumptions by attending not only to questions of geography and space, but also to questions of time. By adopting an historical lens, these articles help to illuminate the ways in which past injustices continue to resonate in the present, and draw links between 'modern' transitional justice mechanisms and a much older set of legal and state tools (among them Commissions of Inquiry). By honing in on the ways in which historical injustices continue to haunt established liberal democracies, these articles also help to unsettle what Anne Orford refers to as the assumption that 'massive human rights violations are an exceptional problem confronting states transitioning from authoritarianism or dictatorship to democracy'.[21]

The article by Jennifer Balint, Julie Evans and Nesam McMillan draws links between the mechanism of the truth commission and the broader history of Commissions of Inquiry.[22] Focusing on the Commissions of Inquiry into the Morant Bay Rebellion in Jamaica (1865), the Rwandan genocide (1998) and the Coranderrk Aboriginal Reserve in Australia (1881), they explore how inquiries have been employed by colonial and former colonial powers to manage social and political controversies linked to colonialism and its legacies. Their analysis suggests that Commissions of Inquiry often operate in ways that limit legal and political recognition of the underlying inequality of colonial relations, deflecting attention

[17] Ní Aoláin Fionnuala 'Advancing Feminist Positioning in the Field of Transitional Justice' (2012) 6(2) *International Journal of Transitional Justice* 1 at 3.
[18] Bryson and McEvoy above note 16 at 72.
[19] At 73.
[20] At 73.
[21] Orford Anne 'Commissioning the Truth' (2006) 15 *Columbia Journal of Gender and Law* 851 at 854.
[22] Balint Jennifer Evans Julie and McMillan Nesam 'Justice Claims in Colonial Contexts: Commissions of Inquiry in Historical Perspective' (2016) 42(1) *Australian Feminist Law Journal* 75.

from the need for broader structural reform and, instead, legitimating state authority and reproducing colonial relations. This is accomplished, in part, through the deployment of a particular 'politics of time', one that silences 'modes of relating to the past that do not accord with the commission's vision of societal progress and repair through reconciliation'.[23]

Yet, as Balint, Evans and McMillan show, this story is not only one of injustice and circumscribed possibilities. Despite their limits, Commissions of Inquiry can also open up spaces for structural injustices to be brought to the fore and put on record. For instance, even though the Coranderrk Inquiry that took place in 1881, in Victoria, Australia (concerning the management of the Coranderrk Aboriginal station) had very circumscribed terms of reference, due to the courage of Aboriginal witnesses and some Europeans, a deeper story of structural injustice was able to be told. Even in the context of deliberately circumscribed legal processes, 'people come to law to lay claims and to provide their testimony of lived realities'. Whether these claims are heard, however, is 'dependent on the political and social frameworks in which they are situated'.[24]

Natalia Gerodetti's article focuses on the issue of reparations for historical wrongs, asking the question 'whose reparations claims count'.[25] Specifically, she considers past 'eugenics' policies and measures that were enacted within established democracies, including the involuntary sterilisation of women. These policies were framed within a prominent progress narrative of their time, a 'utopian' narrative that drew on discourses of rationality, reason and science, and was aimed at improving the 'gene pool of the national collective'.[26]

Gerodetti compares and contrasts the ways in which the Swedish and Swiss governments have, in recent years, addressed claims for reparations emerging from cases of involuntary sterilisation, and draws out their gendered implications. The Swedish government has been quick to respond to claims that, between 1934 and 1976, over 60,000 people had been sterilised by either force or persuasion — the majority of whom were women — by decreeing that compensation claims could be launched. Nonetheless, underpinning this swift response was, according to Gerodetti, a 'wish to atone quickly and move on from the uncomfortable history' which was difficult to reconcile with Sweden's image of itself as a 'caring welfare state'.[27] This has led to an emphasis on compensation rather than a more thorough grappling with the legacies of the past. The Swiss government, by contrast, has adopted a far more legalistic approach. In 2004, a proposal for compensation was rejected by Parliament, a move that was underpinned by an argument that it was wrong to 'judge the past according to today's measures'.[28] According to Gerodetti, this legalistic interpretation obscures the extent to which 'the responsibility for the victims of the past is a question

[23] Bevernage Berber 'Writing the Past Out of the Present: History and the Politics of Time in Transitional Justice' (2010) 69(1) *History Workshop Journal* at 116.
[24] At Balint, Evans and McMillan above note 22 at 90.
[25] Gerodetti Natalia 'Whose Reparation Claims Count? Gender, History and (In)justice' (2016) 42(1) *Australian Feminist Law Journal* 97.
[26] At 116.
[27] At 107.
[28] At 113 citing AB 2004 N 246 Mathys SVP.

of the present'.[29] It also means that those women who were subjected to coerced sterilisation continue to experience 'a threefold form of injury: first, a coerced sterilisation; second, a life managing womanhood without motherhood; and third, a present government that rejects them by neither issuing a clear apology nor a symbolic gesture of compensation'.

2.3 *Transitional Justice Beyond Law: Art and Civil Society*

The final set of articles and praxis notes further the project of unravelling orthodox transitional justice assumptions by exploring how questions of injustice and justice might be understood in less legalistic, less state-centric ways. By examining the roles played by civil society and arts initiatives in resisting premature closure on the violence of the past, and the attempts by war crimes trials to go beyond traditional representations of harm, they help to show that more creative, expansive and open-ended conceptions of transitional justice might be possible.

The subject of Nicola Henry's article is civil society tribunals — sometimes known as 'people's tribunals' or 'people's courts' — as a transitional justice mechanism.[30] Civil society tribunals have operated to address various past harms in different geographical locations, yet, as Henry rightly notes, due to the state-centric focus of transitional justice scholarship, there has been scant scholarly attention to their role and impacts. This is unfortunate because, as Henry suggests, these tribunals, including women's courts, can make a powerful contribution to the field of transitional justice. Henry draws a number of examples, including the Women's Tribunal that was established by civil society groups in 2000 to examine the experiences of the so-called 'comfort women' of the Second World War. This tribunal brought international attention more broadly to the prevalence and impacts of wartime sexual violence.

Henry argues that civil society tribunals might be seen as an example of Nancy Fraser's 'counter publics' in that they actively seek to articulate alternative discourses on the past, and fill in the gaps left by formal justice processes.[31] While acknowledging that civil society tribunals may reproduce some of the problems of conventional justice measures, Henry nonetheless suggests that they also hold the potential to investigate underlying causes of gender-based violence, provide a space for victim-survivors to tell their stories in a non-adversarial context and consider both individual and collective forms of responsibility. For these reasons, more scholarly attention to civil society tribunals is needed.

Olivera Simic similarly approaches the question of transitional justice through a broader lens by considering the role of the arts and artists in transitional justice.[32]

---

[29] At 113 citing Schürer Stefan *Die Verfassung im Zeichen historischer Gerechtigkeit. Schweizer Vergangenheitsbewältigung zwischen Wiedergutmachung und Politik mit der* Geschichte Chronos Zürich 2009 p 301.

[30] Henry Nicola 'Civil Society and Gender-Based Violence: Expanding the Horizons of Transitional Justice' (2016) 42(1) *Australian Feminist Law Journal* 119.

[31] Fraser Nancy 'Transnationalizing the Public Sphere: On the Legitimacy and Efficacy of Public Opinion in a Post-Westphalian World' (1997) 24(4) *Theory, Culture and Society* 7.

[32] Simic Olivera '"They Say Justice Takes Time": Taking Stock of Trust Seeking in Peru, Argentina and Serbia' (2016) 42(1) *Australian Feminist Law Journal* 137.

Simic focuses on three case studies, the Dah Theater in Serbia, the work of Gustavo Germano in Argentina and the Grupo Cultural Yuyachkani in Peru which, in different ways, are working to raise awareness about past atrocities through grassroots art and theatre projects. All these projects are concerned with the issue of missing persons; they all call for keeping memories alive and underscore the need to know the truth about victims' fates. Art, Simic suggests, can 'transcend the temporal limits of legal justice'.[33] It can 'work against the notion that transition can be "over"'[34] and serve as a reminder that 'wounds are still open and healing is not yet over'.[35] Another valuable aspect of the arts is that it can 'reach much wider and more diverse audiences than legal justice'.[36] The artists discussed by Simic seek, in different ways, to keep the memory of past violence alive, and defy denial and official silence; they resist official attempts to delimit attention to the past and herald new beginnings.

The short but insightful praxis note by Maria Elander hones in on some of the challenges faced by war crimes trials in attempting to 'do justice' to complex experiences, events and suffering.[37] Elander focuses on a case that will soon be considered by the Extraordinary Chambers in the Courts of Cambodia (ECCC), the tribunal set up through an agreement between the United Nations and the Cambodian government to prosecute crimes committed during the Khmer Rouge period.[38] 'Case 002' includes a trial segment on the 'regulation of marriages' (the so-called 'forced marriages' that were instigated by the Khmer Rouge regime). As she suggests, the stakes in this case are high. Specifically, the case is viewed as an opportunity for the ECCC to contribute to an evolving — and until recently, neglected — body of law on sexual and other gender-based crimes in times of conflict. Elander also highlights a number of interesting, and potentially promising, aspects of the charges, which depart from the ways in which sexual and gender-based crimes are generally treated by international criminal law. For instance, both persons in the imposed relations — i.e. the male and female spouse — are considered victims, which takes the emphasis away from an exclusive focus on women as victims. In addition, there is a suggestion that communities as well as individuals may have suffered due to the ways in which the marriages ruptured important societal bonds and undermined traditional marriage rituals.

Despite these promising elements, which push the boundaries of traditional legal representation of sexual and gender-based crimes, Elander remains concerned about whether the case will produce a sufficiently nuanced account of the marriages. What she finds worrying is that, within the ECCC Closing Order, the consummation of the marriage — in other words, the sexual act, comes to dominate the description of the crime of 'the regulation of marriage', suggesting that the case may ultimately result in a 'narrow focus on the injured and sexualised body'. All of this means that

[33] At 145.

[34] At 145 citing Bell Vikki 'Contemporary Art and Transitional Justice in Northern Ireland: The Consolation of Form' (2011) 10(3) *Journal of Visual Culture* 324 at 325.

[35] Simic above note 32 at 145.

[36] At 148.

[37] Elander Maria 'Prosecuting the Khmer Rouge Marriages' (2016) 42(1) *Australian Feminist Law Journal* 163.

[38] *Prosecutors v Nuon Chea, Ieng Sary, Khieu Samphan and Ieng Thirith (Closing Order)* (ECCC Trial Chamber Case No. 002 15 Sep 2010) ('*The Closing Order*').

the forthcoming trial segment should be watched closely, and with an awareness of the impossibility of the law to fully recognise the 'complex relations and the multifaceted suffering imposed through these marriages'.[39]

Given the commitment of this Special Issue to disrupting linear narratives of resolution and transition, it is fitting that the final praxis note is original poetry by Robin Rowland coupled with Turkish translations by Mehmet Ali Çelikel on the experiences of both Australians and Turks during the Canakkale/Gallipoli campaigns of the First World War.[40] In addition to sharing some of her poetry, including some previously unpublished poems, Rowland reflects on the difficulties she faced in creating a book of poetry on the First World War[41] and how, during intense periods of work she 'had to stop to recover from the onslaught of that story; the loss, the horror, the stupidity, the waste'.[42] She found it hard to let go of 'all the voices that have disappeared into the earth'.[43] As she writes, 'I felt I knew many of them, and wanted them here still'.[44] A number of poems from the book are also reproduced, in both English and Turkish, reflected on companion pages, which powerfully convey something of the complex effects of the First World War on a wide range of individuals, among them Allied troops, Turks, women and children. Collectively these poems help to tell a more nuanced and multifaceted narrative of the Gallipoli story than the one that has entered into Australian mythology in the form of the ANZAC legend.[45] In this sense, Rowland's poetry resonates with Simic's observations about the significance of arts initiatives; it works to forestall the relegation of the Great War to mythology, and to keep the memories of its personal and enduring effects alive in the public sphere.

3.0 Conclusion

While the articles in this Special Issue are diverse, and are grounded in different disciplinary approaches, what they share is a commitment to looking beyond the transitional justice frameworks of resolution and transition to new ways of thinking about questions of violence, conflict, injustice and justice. Several of the contributors suggest there may be other, more creative ways of responding to conflict that hold potential for moving beyond the constraints of the resolution narrative. For Balint, Evans and McMillan, this requires taking into account broader structural injustices that are often occluded by Commissions of Inquiry (and indeed, other mechanisms of transitional justice). For Kent, it entails unsettling the presumed link between public

[39] Elander above note 37 at 174.

[40] Rowland Robyn 'The Transitional Heart: Writing Poetry on War, Grief and the Intimacy of Shared Loss' (2016) 42(1) *Australian Feminist Law Journal* 177.

[41] *This Intimate War Gallipoli/Çanakkale 1915 — İçli Dışlı Bir Savaş: Gelibolu/Çanakkale 1915*, Turkish translations Mehmet Ali Çelikel, Five Islands Press (Australia) and Bilge Kültür Sanat (Turkey) 2015.

[42] Rowland above note 40 at 180.

[43] At 180.

[44] Ibid.

[45] See Rhoden Clare '"Poppy-Hunters, Poppy-Picking": Review of Robyn Rowland, This Intimate War: Gallipoli/Canakkale 1915' (2015) 19(2) *Text: Journal of Writing and Writing Courses.*

disclosure and both individual healing and societal reconciliation, and paying more attention to 'everyday' acts of social repair. For Demian it is about letting go of a preoccupation with peace and embracing an ongoing and open-ended idea of justice. For Henry and Simic, it is about broadening understandings of what constitutes transitional justice to encompass the roles and possibilities of civil society and arts initiatives. For Bryson and McEvoy, it is about recognising the paradoxical effects of transition for women while at the same time acknowledging their agency. For Elander, it requires acknowledging the limitations of the law in fully capturing complex experiences of suffering and trauma.

As transitional justice continues to be celebrated and promoted around the globe, critical reflections on its role — and promises — are timely and necessary. Legal and quasi-legal institutions are too easily seen as holding the capacity to resolve complex legacies of conflict, as providing a solution to trauma arising from it, or as the obvious safeguard against future violence. Rarely discussed are the ways in which such institutions can also perpetuate and even exacerbate the underlying conditions that foster violent conflict, mask the myriad ways in which violence continues into the present and delimit possibilities for justice and redress. We hope that this Special Issue helps to promote critical reflection on these questions.

Court in Between: The Spaces of Relational Justice in Papua New Guinea

*Melissa Demian**

Abstract. This article considers local-level disputing in Papua New Guinea by bringing two theories into play: spatial justice, borrowed from the 'geographical' turn in legal theory, and relational justice, from the anthropology of law. Disputes negotiated by means of the country's village courts system are sometimes characterised by metropolitans as institutions that dispense peace instead of justice. I argue, through a comparison of contemporary and historical examples from local disputing processes, that village courts do exercise a form of justice, but it is not a justice of closure or peace. Rather, it is the justice of opening the space of relations between disputing parties, as a technique of recognising the ongoing potential of such relations.

What is the purpose of highly localised disputing systems, if not to afford reconciliation between the specific parties concerned? What are the public goods emergent from such disputing systems, and who is the beneficiary of such goods? I open with these questions in response to a remark made by a senior legal official from Papua New Guinea (PNG), at a workshop in the national capital of Port Moresby in early 2015, in which the research team of which I am a member was presenting preliminary findings from our three-year project on the country's village courts system. 'The purpose of village courts,' this official said, 'is peace, not justice.' He repeated the assertion several times over the course of a lengthy meditation on the place of village courts in PNG's legal landscape. The village courts are for peace, not justice. While I make no claims to knowing exactly why he insisted upon this distinction, it had obvious resonances with the 'harmony ideology' that Laura Nader once drew out as a key feature in the missionary phase of the colonial era,[1] and that Michael Goddard later identified as an anxious discourse running through both colonial and

*With profound thanks to Olivia Barrand Lia Kent, as well as three anonymous reviewers for AFLJ, for their feedback on this article. This work was supported by the United Kingdom Economic and Social Research Council [grant number ES/J012300/1].

[1] Nader Laura *Harmony Ideology: Justice and Controlina Zapotec Mountain Village* Stanford University PressS tanford 1990.

anthropological accounts of dispute management in PNG.[2] In line with these observations, the peace in the equation of 'peace not justice' appeared not only to signify the absence of violence — a desideratum that remains stubbornly elusive in some parts of the country — but the absence of any form of conflict at all.

Further to this, one of the moves the 'peace not justice' distinction also effected was a conceptual distancing of the village courts from the country's district and national courts, which operate according to an adversarial system that would be familiar to any participant in the Anglophone legal tradition. The village courts are quite different. Instigated at PNG's independence in 1975, they were intended to provide access to the legal system to ordinary Papua New Guineans without the interference of a formally educated and trained legal profession. Lawyers are explicitly disallowed from any involvement in the village courts. The magistrates, clerks and 'peace officers' who oversee the courts are local men (and occasionally women) appointed because they are deemed to command the respect of their communities and hold knowledge of local practices useful to the resolution of disputes. They have no formal training in the law beyond any workshops that might have been offered to them at the provincial level, and the only legal code applied to cases is that found in the village court Magistrates' handbook — which they may or may not have read, depending on their literacy level in English or in Tok Pisin, the national *lingua franca*. Disputing by means of the village courts is free, in accordance with the principle of their accessibility to all Papua New Guineans, but the jurisdiction of these courts is strictly limited. They cannot, for example, hear cases involving murder, damage to government property or land disputes. The fines and compensation orders they may levy are capped. A court hearing can only be adjudicated by an odd number of magistrates, normally three to five. Where only a single magistrate, or an even number, are present, they cannot adjudicate but must instead mediate the cases brought to them.

A single court sitting tends to hear as many cases as have been brought to the magistrates since the previous sitting, and accordingly a sitting may last for just a few hours or for an entire day — or even longer, as in one type of case I will describe below. Village courts across the country vary greatly in the formality with which they proceed. Some adhere strictly to the rituals of higher court procedure, to the limits placed on them by the village courts handbook and to the documentation of cases in the form of summonses issued and orders recorded in the clerks' notebooks at the conclusion of cases. Others adhere to few if any of these formalities. In towns and other more cosmopolitan areas of the country, there tends to be a greater emphasis on documentation to record the actions of the village court; in the remote rural area with which I have the most experience, documentation is almost entirely absent apart from the most perfunctory notes made by village court clerks. In a locality where everyone speaks the same language and most relationships are those of kinship and other 'small-scale' affiliations, court sittings and their outcomes are a matter of public knowledge retained in local memory. Apart from the presence of the Papua New Guinean flag and the seating of magistrates in chairs to elevate them above the disputants who are seated on the ground, courts in this locality are largely informal

[2] Goddard Michael *Substantial Justice: An Anthropology of Village Courts in Papua New Guinea* Berghahn Books New York 2009.

affairs, where anyone can speak to any case in which they have even a passing interest. The village court is in other words a highly public forum in which grievances of all kinds may be brought for general debate as well as for specific outcomes. Whether those outcomes are necessarily the ones sought by people bringing a grievance is a subject to which I will return shortly.

In practice, many if not all village courts around the country exceed some aspects of their jurisdiction in one way or another, an issue which is sometimes pointed to — again by metropolitans — as evidence that the courts are 'failing' or at least going off-script, raising questions of whether they are still actually part of the legal system. With such anxieties about village courts adhering to their formally recognised capacities in circulation, it is not difficult to see how a metropolitan legal official might imagine that what the village courts are practising cannot possibly be considered to fall under the category of justice. It is much more straightforward to say that they dispense peace: a public good with which no one could possibly take issue. But is it the same public good in which those who are actually taking their conflicts to the village court see themselves as participating?

I argue that village court disputants and magistrates regard themselves very much as participating in the seeking of justice, and that the 'peace' imagined by the legal official in Port Moresby is a far more problematic proposition than it might appear. This article has been composed under the influence of two avenues for thinking about justice as a social condition, one from anthropology and one from legal theory. The anthropological avenue has to do with asking what kind of justice might be pursued in societies where it is social relationships rather than individual persons or even groups of people that are imagined to be rights-bearing entities, capable of being damaged and in need of restitution; this has been referred to as relational justice.[3] The legal, or legal-geographical, avenue is that of spatial justice, the notion that space and social relationships are mutually constituted, such that any consideration of creating equity in relations in and through space must be qualified by how those relations are generative of the very space in which they are conducted. I come to this set of ideas through the work of Andreas Philippopoulos-Mihalopoulos, who has suggested that:

> Space is not just the question 'how would this judgment/legal text/legal act be formed over there?', but significantly, 'why is this judgment/legal text/legal act expected to be formed in this way here?' The result is a law that keeps on questioning itself, not in eternal undecidability but in continuous acknowledgment of its own limitations: the law can only do that much, and even that is uncertain. Space is law's mirror on which the irresolvable paradox between its universality and particularity is thrown into relief. Spatiality is an ethical position.[4]

I am attempting to bring these two sets of ideas into dialogue with each other because they have an important analytical positioning to offer any consideration of what

[3] Robbins Joel 'Recognition, Reciprocity, and Justice: Melanesian Reflections on the Rights of Relationships' in Clarke Kamari Maxine and Goodale Mark (eds) *Mirrors of Justice: Law and Power in the Post-Cold War Era* Cambridge University Press Cambridge 2009 p 171.

[4] Philippopoulos-Mihalopoulos Andreas 'Spatial Justice: Law and the Geography of Withdrawal' (2010) 6(3) *International Journal of Law in Context* 201 at 209.

putatively peripheral dispute-management systems — such as village courts in PNG — are actually doing when the state's back is turned, so to speak. I am interested in the idea of spatiality as an ethical position because not only does it allow us to confront the universal/particular conundrum that perennially faces anthropologists of law as well as other legal theorists, but also allows us to be explicit about where the putative gatekeepers of law perceive its limits to be — for example, in the dispensing of peace, not justice — and how some people engaged in processes they deem legal exceed or redraw those limits in the social spaces they open up for themselves. The ethics of space is reminiscent of Iris Marion Young's political philosophy of difference, wherein any 'justice' claimed to be achievable by treating persons as undifferentiated in their experience, perspective or social positionality is simply another form of oppression.[5] Young proposed instead a concept of justice based on the ideal of city life 'as a vision of social relations affirming group difference. As a normative ideal, city life instantiates social relations of difference without exclusion'.[6] The problem with holding up cities as exemplars of the recognition of difference as a technique of justice is, firstly, that not all cities are places of mixing between different social groups, and indeed many cities of the postcolony in particular retain the infrastructural and architectural features of their segregationist histories.[7] More importantly, a rigorous application of spatial justice as a justice of relationships — which, in line with both Young and Philippopoulos-Mihalopoulos, is a justice founded in differentiation rather than commonality — should be applicable at any scale on which social relationships are conducted, precisely because of its sensitivity to modes of differentiation that occur at a 'micro' level, that is, in the 'face-to-face' societies classically favoured by anthropology. This would include gender, a form of differentiation with which universalist readings of justice continue to struggle.

Furthermore, I am interested in the historicity of these relational spaces, and how people reflect on their own legal practices through the lens of past relationships, such as, in this case, relationships with the dispensers of colonial legal regimes. For again, while the concept of spatial justice has thus far been applied to urban contexts,[8] there have to date been few attempts to extend it beyond the metropole. This is curious, given the political potential of the concept for opening up discussion of the legal postcolony in ways that circumvent the categorical distinctions with which such discussions are normally burdened, such as customary law/imposed law, traditional/modern and indeed peace/justice, which is implicit in the legal official's assessment of village courts as being in some way incompletely integrated into the metropolitan legal system. This very assertion is itself an artefact of how something identified as a 'legal system' was introduced to rural Papua New Guineans during the colonial era.

---

[5] Young Iris Marion *Justice and the Politics of Difference* Princeton University Press Princeton 1990.
[6] As above at 227.
[7] Caldeira Teresa P R *City of Walls: Crime, Segregation, and Citizenship in São Paulo* University of California Press Berkeley 2001; Demian Melissa 'Making Women in the City: Notes from a Port Moresby Boarding House' 42 *Signs: Journal of Women in Culture and Society* (forthcoming).
[8] See, for example, Dikeç Mustafa 'Justice and the Spatial Imagination' (2001) 33 *Environment and Planning A* 1785; Soja Edward W *Seeking Spatial Justice* University of Minnesota Press Minneapolis 2010; Bengtsen Peter 'Just Gardens? On the Struggle for Space and Spatial Justice' (2013) 39(2) *Australian Feminist Law Journal* 79.

Finally, a word about the methods that brought me to these questions in the first place. I am an anthropologist with a 20-year relationship with the Suau-speaking population living in southeastern PNG where the examples presented later in this article were collected. They were collected in the course of a particular project on village courts, but my interest in the country's legal system and legal conundrums spans over a decade of ethnographic research in the country. So the question of relational justice stems from my own relationship to PNG as a fieldsite in general and to the Suau region in particular. My tools for approaching these questions are the ethnographer's tools of long-term residence, use of the local language, immersion in local relationships and some more formal techniques such as the recording of court cases and interviewing of court officials. But as with the porous nature of the village courts themselves, it is in informal discussions with these officials, with disputants and with members of my host community that the 'real' use and purpose of the courts have emerged. And it is the non-linear, non-teleological nature of village court disputes themselves that have led me to ask what kind of justice is being enacted there, if it is not the 'peace' of closure, completion and non-conflict.

1.0 The Justice of Relations

I begin with the notion of relational justice. The term as I employ it here is borrowed from the anthropologist Joel Robbins, although ideas about the distributed, transitive, multi-constituted or, in older works, 'communal' nature of the concepts of justice and rights in PNG have long been in circulation in the literature on legal developments within the country.[9] Robbins takes up the topic out of a specific concern with the presumed incompatibility between the classic relativist (or particularist) position of much anthropological literature and the set of humanist (or universalist) values that inform both the academy that anthropologists work in and often our own political convictions as well. He has suggested that we eschew attempts to play relativism off against universalism, and instead, as he puts it, 'play the universalist game'.[10] But by this he does not mean we embrace uncritically those elite, post-Enlightenment and post-war values promoted as 'global' by powerful international institutions originating almost exclusively in Western Europe and North America. Instead, he suggests that anthropologists get into the business of finding what he calls 'candidate universals', that is, values that are present but latent or backgrounded in the late modern capitalist milieu, but fully expressed or foregrounded in some of the non-European environments in which anthropologists work.

One candidate universal proposed by Robbins is what he identifies as relational justice. As he explains:

---

[9] Lawrence Peter 'Law and Anthropology: The Need for Collaboration' (1970) 1(1) *Melanesian Law Journal* 40; Fitzpatrick Peter *Law and State in Papua New Guinea* Academic Press London 1980; Demian Melissa 'Custom in the Courtroom, Law in the Village: Legal Transformations in Papua New Guinea' (2003) 9(1) *Journal of the Royal Anthropological Institute* 97; Strathern Marilyn *Kinship, Law and the Unexpected: Relatives Are Always a Surprise* Cambridge University Press Cambridge 2005.

[10] Robbins above note 3 at 173.

> What makes this kind of justice unusual in terms of globally diffused models of justice and rights is that it treats relationships, rather than individuals or groups, as the most important bearer of rights. Specific relationships have a right to be realized and to flourish, and legal processes and protestations of injustice dwell on the injuries done to, or the unmet needs of, relationships.[11]

I would draw the reader's attention to Robbins's insistence that relationships rather than individuals *or groups* are in some places the focus of attention on the just composition of society. His formulation, drawn from the ethnographic work he and others have conducted in PNG, seeks to circumvent the individual rights/group rights contrast that has dogged most of the history of legal anthropology. Relational justice is not 'communal justice'; rather, it affects the flourishing of both groups and individuals by means of the relationships that compose persons simultaneously as singular and plural in form. I appreciate and emphasise this element of Robbins's argument because it undermines an argument implicit in much policy-related discussion of the Pacific in general and PNG in particular: that where 'group rights' or 'communal justice' are emphasised, it is women who lose out. The presumed incompatibility between the interests of women and those of the kinship and ethno-political entities of which they are members also implies that this problem can be resolved through political and legal engagement with 'women' conceived as a *sui generis* social category existing in a relational vacuum, and through a legal emphasis on the rights of the autonomous individual. The latter strategy is obviously a precondition for the former. Indeed, as Goddard has noted, a widespread discourse of discriminatory practices against women in the village courts within the international aid and development industries has not only circulated for decades in the absence of any kind of rigorous research, but has also proven highly resistant to abundant evidence to the contrary.[12] I submit that the power and persistence of this discourse derives precisely from the underlying notion that women's interests are fatally compromised by the relational value in Papua New Guinean and other Melanesian societies. It is only, as the standard narrative goes, by promoting women's rights as human rights — that is, including women as beneficiaries of a set of 'universal' values — that they will fully be able to assert interests imagined to be at odds with their incorporation into wider social groups.[13]

The liberatory potential offered by the concept of relational justice is precisely its potential to move discussions of what happens in PNG conflict management forums away from the group rights:individual rights::men's interests:women's interests analogy. Instead, relational justice shifts the questions one might ask of conflict and dispute management away from the notion that group rights countervail individual rights — with the gendered analogy this seems always to imply — and toward an

[11] As above at 174.
[12] Goddard above note 2 at 85 and 255.
[13] See Demian Melissa 'On the Repugnance of Customary Law' (2014) 56(2) *Comparative Studies in Society and History* 508 at 522 for a discussion of an iconic case in the National Court of Papua New Guinea in which the humanity of a woman, and what this meant and didn't mean in terms of how her kin could regard her as a clan resource, was precisely the issue at hand. The same case, *In re Miriam Willingal* [1997] PGNC 7, is discussed in Strathern above note 9 at 111.

exploration of what might actually be occurring in the field of social relationships in a forum like the village court.

My interest in relational justice stems from certain types of cases I have observed in the village court which very patently do not produce 'peace' and indeed may lay the groundwork for future conflict. In these cases, nothing remotely resembling a cessation of conflict is established; they represent the very antithesis of 'indigenous jurisprudence' as it is sometimes represented in restorative justice circles and experimented with as a quasi-state institution.[14] I have in mind both the fairly low-stakes example of an adultery accusation and the quite high-stakes example of a sorcery accusation. Despite their very different content, the structural similarities between these types of case in the part of PNG where I have observed them are striking. Similar too are the outcomes to both kinds of case, which are so predictable in their moral configurations as to seem almost scripted or choreographed. And key to these outcomes is that nobody leaves the court sitting particularly happy with them, in the sense that suspicion and other negative feelings persist, accusations may or may not be resolved and the stage for future conflict remains set. Nonetheless, people bring such cases to the village court with tremendous regularity, implying that they achieve something in the act itself of bringing them to this forum. I will take each example in turn.

2.0 Adultery

Adultery cases in the part of PNG where my primary research is conducted are nearly always brought by women, and are almost never only about adultery.[15] Adultery, which was in fact classed as a criminal offence under the colonial-era *Native Regulation 1939 (Territory of Papua)*, has by now become an organising framework for a whole range of marital grievances including domestic violence, whose legal and moral categorisation are much less clear in the Papua New Guinean public consciousness.[16] In practical terms, this means that a case which will appear in the minimal records kept by village court clerks as an 'adultery' case may also involve drunkenness or violence, locking the wife out of the house, use of love magic to entice the wife away from her family in the first place and

[14] See, for example, Cohen Amy J and Gershon Ilana 'When the State Tries to See Like a Family: Cultural Pluralism and the Family Group Conference in New Zealand' (2015) 38(1) *PoLAR: Political and Legal Anthropology Review* 9.

[15] This is on the mainland of Milne Bay Province at the southeastern extremity of the country. The local language is Suau, the dominant church denomination Protestant and the inheritance system, unusually for much of PNG but in common with the rest of this province, is matrilineal. Land claims are nonetheless largely the purview of men who stake claims on behalf of their wives or sisters. See Demian Melissa '"Land Doesn't Come from Your Mother, She Didn't Make it with Her Hands": Challenging Matriliny in Papua New Guinea' in Lim Hilary and Bottomley Anne (eds) *Feminist Perspectives on Land Law* Routledge-Cavendish New York 2007 p 155.

[16] Domestic violence was recently criminalised in PNG under the *Family Protection Act 2013 (Papua New Guinea)*. There have been public awareness campaigns to communicate the contents of the Act, and most village court magistrates I have spoken to are aware of it. However, wife-beating is still regarded as entirely appropriate by many Papua New Guineans, especially among both men and women of the senior generation.

Figure 1. Testifying in an adultery case, Isuisu Village, Milne Bay Province, PNG, 2015. Photograph by Melissa Demian.

comparable acts of aggression or disrespect. The actual accusation of adultery will be embedded among these other causes for grievance by a wife, and unless the husband's girlfriend becomes pregnant, there is unlikely to be much in the way of evidence that adultery has actually taken place. Instead, an aggrieved wife will marshal witnesses to report generalised suspicious behaviour on the part of her husband, along the lines of: 'He was seen walking away from so-and-so's hamlet at night when he had no business being there.' Figure 1.

Given that every single adultery case I have ever recorded has proceeded along these lines, it is worth asking what these cases are 'really' about, as a strategy on the part of the women who bring them. At the beginning of such cases the wife will often ask for her husband to be penalised in some way or in severe cases she may ask to divorce him. In the latter instance village court magistrates must remind the fractious couple that they cannot grant divorces, which is indeed outside their jurisdiction under the *Village Courts Act 1989*, and that a divorce can only be agreed between the two families involved. In cases where the woman has asked for her husband to be penalised, he will only in very extreme instances (such as domestic violence) be asked to kill a chicken or pig for her to show his contrition. But more often than not, once wife, husband and all their witnesses have spoken, the bulk of the court hearing will be taken up by lectures on the correct nature and conduct of a marriage from the magistrates, the pastor and any other senior persons of note in attendance. The disputing parties may also be chastised for allowing their ill will to escalate into a court hearing instead of working out the problem themselves with the help of their families or church elders. Critically, there is very rarely an identifiable conclusion to such cases, especially if no form of compensation has been ordered; the magistrates may at best be able to extract a promise from both husband and wife to take the marital project a little more seriously. But as often as not the case will end with either the husband or the wife departing the scene in a highly emotive state. Nobody has been satisfied, except insofar as an errant husband has been publicly shamed, and a marital conflict has been momentarily deprived of energy. But there has not been a 'resolution' of any kind. Indeed, many of these cases appear largely to set the scene for future conflict, as my second example will demonstrate in a far more serious and ramifying social register.

3.0 Sorcery

Throughout PNG, concerns about sorcery and witchcraft saturate people's everyday lives — which is to say, any death, major illness or misfortune is likely to give rise to speculation as to who might be responsible. High-profile murders of accused sorcerers have dominated media reports from PNG in recent years.[17] But most of my own research has been conducted in a part of the country where sorcery accusations are dealt with 'well', that is, through the forum of the village court rather than by means of vigilante violence. This is not to say sorcery cases are not regarded as presenting hazards to those involved, especially to the magistrates who may be future targets of the accused sorcerer's ire, but the fact that they are dealt with at all in the village courts is indicative of the fact that sorcery is regarded in this part of PNG as a social problem with a social solution. But like adultery, sorcery cases rarely conclude with anything identifiable as a *resolution*, with most of the parties involved leaving the court hearing often still quite angry or frightened by the events that led up to the hearing.

Also in common with adultery cases, a sorcery accusation is not so much 'about' sorcery as it is about the history of relations gone wrong between two families. In the background of the accusation may be a land dispute, a disappointed lover, a promise not kept, a debt not paid, any combination of these and more. Insofar as a sorcery case involves a forensic process, it is a process of discovering not who the sorcerer is — this is already known at the beginning of the case — but why he or his lineage has a grievance against the lineage in which one or more deaths has occurred. Once this process is complete, signalled by the confession of the accused sorcerer and a detailed account of how and when the grievance arose (it may be years or even decades in the past), the magistrates can order compensation. But this is not unidirectional compensation in terms of simple reparations for damage done: it is paid in two directions, and in exactly equal amounts. That is, not only must the accused sorcerer and his family

[17] These murders have been highlighted by some journalists and academics as particularly grievous instances of 'gender-based violence'; see, for example, George Nicole 'Beyond "Cultural Constraint": Gender, Security and Participation in the Pacific Islands' in Davies Sara E Nwokora Zim Stamnes Eli and Teitt Sarah (eds) *Responsibility to Protect and Women, Peace and Security: Aligning the Protection Agendas* Martinus Nijhoff Leiden 2013 p 155; Clark Helen 'Sorcery and Sexism in Papua New Guinea' *The Diplomat* 2 June 2015 <http://thediplomat.com/2015/06/sorcery-and-sexism-in-papua-new-guinea/> Accessed 2 June 2016. Such narratives erase the fact that both the ethnographic record and the case law document how sorcery accusations and murders resulting from them target men as frequently as women. See Jorgensen Dan 'Preying on Those Close to Home: Witchcraft Violence in a Papua New Guinea Village' (2014) 25(3) *The Australian Journal of Anthropology* 267; *State v Toropo* (No. 2) [2015] PGNC 119; *State v Mathias* [2011] PGNC 228; *State v Latuve* [2013] PGNC 207; *State v Martin* [2008] PGNC 29. One could conceivably make the argument that 'sorcerer' is a gender in itself, as sorcerers are commonly understood to be either incompletely human or entirely non-human, marked as a distinct category of person from fully human men and women. But this is not the argument being made in claims that sorcery-related murders are a form of gender-based violence, coded as violence against women.

pay compensation to the family of the person or persons he is supposed to have killed, but that family also must pay him.

The idea, magistrates told me, is to instantiate 'peace and reconciliation' between the two lineages. The phrase is a recent one in their repertoire, reproduced faithfully in English, the dominant second language in the province where I work. And on the face of it, it appears to underscore the point made by the elite Papua New Guinean I mentioned at the beginning of this article: that the purpose of village courts is the establishment of peace, not justice. But this formulation does a certain violence of its own to what happens at the conclusion of many village court cases and sorcery cases in particular. I wish to be very clear that the outcome of these cases may be the absence of violence, but neither is it necessarily the presence of peace. Nobody ever forgets that the case happened, and these are families in small, heavily interconnected communities who must deal with each other on a daily basis for the rest of their lives. While village courts do not operate on the basis of precedent, people will refer to them in conversation outside the court if, in the future, further problems unfold between the families involved. And not only families but institutions, such as local schools and businesses acting in a family-like capacity, have sometimes become enrolled as actors in village court cases and their aftermath, such as in the payment of compensation.[18] So village court cases can become integrated into what the anthropologist Nancy Munn has referred to as the 'event history' obtaining between families, indexed retroactively as a source of causality when violence or sorcery accusations do precipitate out of the normal run of relations.[19] In other words a sorcery accusation is itself a form of violence, a visible response to the invisible actions of the sorcerer, that the accuser knows can potentially set in train a grim sequence of events. On occasion I have heard village court magistrates chastise complainants who appeared to be making oblique sorcery accusations, warning them to think carefully before saying what they appeared to be saying. A presumed death by sorcery can be strategically ignored, but an accusation of sorcery cannot, precisely because speech of this kind often contains an implicit call to action, as I will discuss further in the next section.

It is these processes of the folding and unfolding of events in people's memories, and the management of the danger of physical violence or other forms of ill will that might manifest in the field of social relationships, that have led me to explore what the concept of spatial justice might offer to my consideration of what is happening in the village courts, if peace is not the condition being established by these courts. In other words, I am trying to follow Philippopoulos-Mihalopoulos' lead in thinking about spatial justice as more than just another iteration of social justice.[20] It would be very easy to discuss, for example, how under-resourced the village courts are, how magistrates and other village court officials feel unsupported by their provincial governments, how they would like any level of government at all to show respect for the

[18] Houghton Eve *Whose Case Is It Anyway?* Paper presented at the State of the Pacific Conference, The Australian National University, Canberra, 7–9 September 2015.

[19] Munn Nancy 'Constructing Regional Worlds in Experience: Kula Exchange, Witchcraft and Gawan Local Events' (1990) 25(1) *Man* 1.

[20] Philippopoulos-Mihalopoulos Andreas 'Law's Spatial Turn: Geography, Justice and a Certain Fear of Space' (2010) 7(2) *Law, Culture and the Humanities* 187.

work they do by supplying them with uniforms, badges, training workshops, stipends that actually reach their bank accounts and police who actually enforce the imprisonment orders they issue. These are all real and pressing concerns for the village courts and I do not mean to diminish them. But it is insufficient to say that the relation of the village courts to the rest of PNG's legal apparatus, especially village courts in remote rural areas such as the one where I have conducted most of my research, is the perpetually frustrated or abjected relation of a periphery to a metropole. It is also my aim to draw attention to what happens to relations in the space of a village court sitting itself, to consider what form of justice is being created there, specifically in the absence of the 'peace' envisioned in the metropole.

In order to do so, I will introduce in the following section the institution that preceded village courts as the embodiment of a metropole-periphery relationship. This is critical to my project of demonstrating not only how the relational justice practised in Papua New Guinean village courts is not a uniquely Papua New Guinean version of justice, but one that became foregrounded through a specific manifestation of the relationship between coloniser and colonised. As such it illustrates Young's principle of 'asymmetrical reciprocity' or the impossibility of one subject actually assuming the perspective of another, particularly under conditions of structural inequality,[21] for the metropole in this case was Australia, and the embodiment of Australian law was the figure of the *kiap* or patrol officer.

4.0 Asymmetrical Reciprocity: Papua New Guineans Imitating Australians Imitating Papua New Guineans

In the Enlightenment tradition, law mediates between a people and the state, regardless of the form taken by that state, is in theory accountable to the people whose interests it is meant to serve and is institutionally connected to the state whose interests it enforces. But the colonial era was only just gaining momentum in the eighteenth century, and many Enlightenment writers still imagined colonised peoples to be existing in a state of nature. What none of them anticipated was how European colonial systems would introduce their own social forms or the ways in which those social forms were introduced. Take, for example, the introduction of a legal system in colonial Papua and New Guinea, which was, as Sinclair Dinnen and John Braithwaite have noted, undifferentiated from a policing system: 'Throughout most of the colonial period, policing was an integral part of an overall system of administration marked by a lack of institutional differentiation'.[22] As they go on to observe, this lack of differentiation was in part a pragmatic response to the difficulty of governing a dispersed and diverse population across a geographically challenging terrain. But it also had particular effects in relation to how this population may have seen itself being governed by those seeing themselves doing the governing. Young's attentiveness to the issue of perspective, and its role in moral judgments, is key here.

[21] Young Iris Marion 'Asymmentrical Reciprocity: On Moral Respect, Wonder, and Enlarged Thought' (1997) 3(3) *Constellations* 341.

[22] Dinnen Sinclair and Braithwaite John 'Reinventing Policing through the Prism of the Colonial Kiap' (2009) 19(2) *Policing and Society* 1 at 4.

One of the more interesting assumptions behind the presumed contemporary workings of the village courts is the assumption of what they have failed to emulate, that is, the country's district and national courts, or perhaps the African 'native courts' whose composition inspired the formation of the village courts in PNG. But one of the things I would like to suggest is that the excesses of jurisdiction of which the village courts are accused are an artefact of their being modelled on the total jurisdiction of the dispute management system that immediately preceded them in the colonial era. These were the patrol officers of the Australian territorial administration, or *kiaps* as they are known in Tok Pisin, derived from the German *Kapitan*. *Kiaps* were an attempt to introduce law in the absence of a state. Although *kiaps* had in their own imaginations the power of the Australian government whose laws they were enforcing, they shared this imaginary only partially with the people they were charged with introducing to the rule of law. And when the independent PNG state introduced the village courts in 1975, it in turn imagined a clean break with the colonial past, a system of law available to all citizens. The conceptual framework for the village courts was invariably influenced by local-level courts in other recently decolonised Anglophone jurisdictions, notably in sub-Saharan Africa, although early reports on how such a system might work were at pains to distinguish the proposed system from the African model because a 'dual legal system' for PNG was unpalatable to the territorial administration in Canberra at the time.[23] But what no one in Port Moresby seems to have recognised was that many grassroots Papua New Guineans regarded the courts as a continuation or inheritor, in imperfect or diminished form, of the *kiap* system.

Kiaps were responsible for introducing and then exercising the authority of the Australian administration over rural PNG populations. Their brief was to 'pacify' these populations by bringing local warfare and vengeance killing to an end, assert 'law and order' through hearing disputes and punishing malefactors and implement techniques of governmentality such as census-taking, corvée labour and taxation. One of the striking features of *kiaps* was the way in which they combined within their persons both the administrative and legal capacities of the government. This ultra-pragmatic approach to colonisation and its efficiency at carrying out the 'civilising mission' was a source of both pride within the Australian administration and recognition that it was ultimately unsustainable. As an influential Minister for Territories from 1951 to 1963 noted, the idea that the *kiap* system required separate institutions to replace it stemmed from 'the need to ensure that the courts and the police and the prisons were not regarded simply as instruments to serve the ends of orderly administration' but to serve the nation-building project in PNG.[24] Nonetheless, the pragmatism that concentrated and embodied an entire legal regime in the person of the *kiap* served, again in Philippopoulos-Mihalopoulos' terms, to render the law invisible, while simultaneously generating an environment saturated with law, a 'lawscape'.[25] Mobilising the *kiap* across the landscape of PNG recreated this landscape as a

[23] Goddard above note 2 at 43–45.

[24] Hasluck Paul *A Time for Building: Australian Administration in Papua and New Guinea 1951–1963* Melbourne University Press Melbourne 1976 p 176.

[25] Philippopoulos-Mihalopoulos Andreas 'Atmospheres of Law: Senses, Affects, Lawscapes' (2013) 7 *Emotion, Space and Society* 35.

lawscape, from the colonial administration's perspective at least, precisely by means of the relationship the *kiap* generated between the administration and the people it sought to govern.

As Robert Gordon has observed, not only did *kiaps* execute the requirements of the administration, they *were* the administration in the eyes of many PNG communities and arguably in their own view as well.[26] A significant component of the *kiap* narrative of efficacy was that they were seen as disinterested or neutral adjudicators of disputes, in large part because they dispensed a form of law (usually as outlined in their Standing Instructions but occasionally invented on the spot) that was both unknown and unknowable to the populations with whom they worked. In other words, they perceived themselves as standing outside the numerous local systems they were supposed to bring within a single, universal system of 'law and order'. Their externalised position permitted them a perspective that they felt Melanesians did not and indeed could not share: this was the source of their authority. But even as 'the image of "impartiality" enjoyed by expatriate *kiaps* was maintained through this "unknowable" quality',[27] *kiaps* were at the same time engaged in a project of demonstrating both to their superiors in Australia and to their subject populations that these populations were knowable, and therefore governable, through a very particular form of engagement.

This form, Neil Maclean has argued, was mimetic.[28] *Kiaps* were concerned to exert the power of something called law over Melanesians through concealing the content or nature of that law, or rather, presuming that law existed at a level or order of experience unknowable to most if not all Melanesians. The most effective way to do this was by attempting to replicate what they thought Melanesians *would* understand as law. Normally, and particularly in the Highlands populations which were the last to be 'pacified' (a process that was by no means ever completed), this meant a focus on the ritual exchange of gifts, glossed as 'compensation'. For the *kiaps*, compensation appeared to be the local alternative to warfare to which they could appeal in order to achieve the cessation of war, making it the preferred form in which many *kiaps* attempted to resolve disputes. But Maclean takes a cue from Marilyn Strathern's observation that in PNG Highlands political systems, warfare, talk and gift exchange are all perpetually convertible into one another.[29] Drawing upon this insight, he argues that what the *kiaps* accomplished instead of 'pacification' was the misrecognition of how these conversions are achieved. By requiring Highlands big men to pay compensation — to the government as well as to their enemies — they appeared to be attempting to foreclose on the possibility of future warfare.

I would extend Maclean's argument further by suggesting that the connection established by *kiaps* in imitating what they thought Highlanders were doing points to a colonial assumption that the Highlands mix of talk, ritual exchange and

---

[26] Gordon Robert 'The Decline of the Kiapdom and the Resurgence of "Tribal Fighting" in Enga' (1983) 53(3) *Oceania* 205.
[27] As above at 216.
[28] Maclean Neil 'Mimesis and Pacification: The Colonial Legacy in Papua New Guinea' (1998) 11(1) *History and Anthropology* 75.
[29] Strathern Marilyn 'Discovering "Social Control"' (1985) 12(2) *Journal of Law and Society* 111.

warfare were *already segregated from each other*, such that choosing one (say, exchange) determined how to move from each form of action to the other in a teleology: from warfare to exchange and finally to talk, that is, to 'peace'. *Kiaps* embodied the capacity to effect these transformations precisely because of their own undifferentiated persons; they were empowered by the colonial administration to execute any and all duties necessary to impressing local populations with the administration's authority. *Kiaps* were able to use their undifferentiated capacities to perform the mimetic experiment in conversion. In other words, if they did what they thought they saw Highlanders doing, they could direct the flow of conversion from one form of action to another. They could do this precisely because, as undifferentiated agents of an undifferentiated system, only they could elicit the differentiation of action to be effected within the social worlds encompassed by that system. The end point of the experiment, if successful, would be the integration of those worlds into a world of law.

A word about convertibility, however. Among the problems with *kiap* claims to know Papua New Guineans by means of imitating them was an incompatibility of hierarchies. The *kiaps* made the mistake of assuming any form of action could be converted into any other form of action that was observable on the level of experience they sought to encompass, and furthermore, that this conversion could be effected in a unilineal, 'evolutionary' fashion. Highland Papua New Guineans never recognised this unilineal flow, because conversion in this particular mix is always too precarious, too subject to transformation into one of its other forms: talk can at any time turn into fighting, which can at any time turn into compensation, which can in turn produce either more talking or more fighting, and so on. The encompassing lawscape which *kiaps* embodied and into which they sought to bring all efficacious action never appeared to Highlanders or indeed any other Papua New Guineans in the same way. If there are any encompassing systems to be found at all in PNG, they are in local cosmologies, the forms of ritual action emergent from these cosmologies and the hierarchies of exchange that they engender.[30] Law simply became one way or style among others of conducting social relations, and when the village courts were introduced and *kiaps* phased out, the courts were incorporated into this existing style.

I have now left law in an unacceptable position from the point of view of a state, whether colonial or postcolonial. The epoch of the *kiaps* is long past, and the singular figure of the *kiap* has since become divided into any number of legal and administrative actors, including judges, magistrates, legal officers, police and other agents of state law. The problem for these agents is that they are differentiated in a way that *kiaps* were not, and each brings a perspective to their relations with other legal subjects that cannot be totalising in the way the perspectives of the *kiaps* had the potential to be. So a judge, for example, is confined by the Constitution and other statutes, as well as the norms and conventions of the judicial profession, within her relationship to law. Insofar as any judge can be an innovator, she can only do so in terms of the

[30] Iteanu André 'Levels and Convertibility' in Barnes R H de Coppet Daniel and Parkin R J (eds) *Contexts and Levels: Anthropological Essays on Hierarchy* JASO Occasional Papers 4 Oxford 1985 p 91.

interpretation of precedents and of existing legislation, and her decisions may be subject to appeal within that same system of interpretation.

What was an advantage for *kiaps* — being 'outside of the system' — is a distinct disadvantage for judges, who are constrained to make choices about what it means to be outside a system or not. While both *kiaps* and judges act as translators or interpreters of the law for a population that may have radically different notions of what the law is or does, judges are trying to translate between bodies of colonial, constitutional and customary law that they must imagine to be functioning in analogous ways. *Kiaps* were trying to do the work of differentiation by means of interpretation, but their interpretation was one that was constantly open-ended: they could and did make up the law in the very act of trying to communicate to subject communities what the law was. Judges in PNG may occasionally appear to be 'making up the law' in cases where custom is pleaded,[31] but this is only a secondary effect of the fact that custom does not have the status of law but only of evidence once it has travelled 'up' the legal system to the district and national courts.

In the village courts of the present day, few effects of the differentiation within the legal system instigated at PNG's independence have been felt, and many village courts attempt to operate in the manner of the *kiaps*, as if they were still undifferentiated, if not especially powerful, agents of the state. For while Australia officially withdrew its colonial governance of PNG in 1975, many Papua New Guineans declined to recognise this withdrawal as the conclusion of a relationship. The colonial lawscape had been instantiated by means of the undifferentiated persons of the *kiaps*, and its transformation into the differentiated form of the village courts, for grassroots Papua New Guineans, was and is by no means a complete one — or even one to which they ever acquiesced in the first place.

Instead, disputants in these courts continue to recognise differentiation within social relationships themselves: between families disputing over land; between sorcerers and proper human beings; and between wives and husbands. These are forms of differentiaton with which many universalising legal regimes, including that to which PNG is an inheritor, are deeply uneasy. 'Normative judgment', as Young wrote:

> is best understood as the product of dialogue under conditions of equality and mutual respect. Ideally, the outcome of such dialogue and judgment is just and legitimate only if all the affected perspectives have a voice. If it were possible for agents to reverse perspectives with one another in making moral judgments, this condition that all voices and perspectives should be represented might not be necessary.[32]

But it is not possible for such a reversal or exchange of perspectives to occur. The outcome of such experiments in PNG was, for example, *kiaps* mimicking what they thought Highland Papua New Guineans did in order to 'stop' warfare, when what Highlanders were actually doing was establishing conditions *both* for the cessation *and* the future potential for warfare. Or in a more contemporary example, as one

[31] Demian Melissa 'Fictions of Intention in the "Cultural Defense"' (2008) 110(4) *American Anthropologist* 432.
[32] Young above note 21 at 360.

Local Level Government Councillor in my fieldsite in PNG declared to disputants at the commencement of a court sitting in 2015: 'We are talking to the law!'. The law has its own, differentiated perspective on how disputes should be conducted, just as families, schools, businesses, God and individual men and women are assumed to have. The fundamental asymmetry of all these subject positions means that the establishment of equity between them is not ultimately possible, but the establishment of equity in relations between them is.

5.0 Revealing the Space of Relational Justice

There is a dyad of moral-aesthetic values found in many parts of PNG, if not the entire country, and elaborated in a number of ways in the area where I work. This dyad is the contrast between that which is hidden or concealed from view, and that which is revealed or conducted in the view of others. Both have their place in the run of everyday life, and relationships in a state of conflict that are under negotiation through the village courts are, again in the specific locality with which I am most familiar, negotiated out in the open. Village courts in this coastal region are always conducted on the beach, during the daytime, under the shade of a tree but in plain sight of any onlookers and participants who care to come. It is a public forum in the most profoundly democratic sense of the term: anyone who is present can speak in the village court, and although officials often draw a pair of 'boxes' in the sand to indicate where the different sides of a dispute must sit, speakers might situate themselves on the dividing line between the two boxes to indicate that they do not have an interest in speaking for one side or the other, or alternatively they might make a show of querying the magistrates as to where they ought to sit. Even people with an interest in the case will select with care their physical placement in relation to the primary disputants. For example, one woman in her twenties appeared deliberately to have situated herself and her young children outside the boxes but directly behind her mother who was involved in a land dispute, in order to berate her mother from her own position of perceiving that her interests and the interests of her children had been sidelined or disregarded in the case. In this matrilineal corner of PNG, a person who feels she has not been given enough land by her lineage must take it up with her mother and mother's brothers. Failing that, the village court is a useful tool with which to publicly shame family members into doing the right thing by their descendants.

The authority of the state is represented as faithfully as court officials are able to make it, normally by placing one or more PNG flags next to the chairs where they sit, and occasionally by emulating the rituals of opening a court hearing that they may have observed in the district courts, such as by having participants stand and bow at the beginning and end of the hearing. But in most of the country the state is functionally absent, a fact to which court officials will sometimes allude. They do not necessarily assume the weight of the state upon themselves or upon the other officials present; most magistrates I have observed in action continually exhorted disputants to try to solve their problems themselves before taking the drastic step of bringing them before the court.

But it is precisely this having-out of problems in the open space of the court that appears to be an end in itself. This is most starkly demonstrated in the adultery

Figure 2. A young man accused of destroying the local water pipeline in an attitude of shame, bottom right. Siloa Pota Village, Milne Bay Province, PNG, 2015. Photograph by Melissa Demian

cases mentioned earlier, especially those brought by younger women whose expectations of marriage are observably distinct from those of their mothers' generation in this extremely youthful country. Accusing a husband of paying illicit attention to another woman is an effective way of pointing out that his care and support are insufficiently focused upon his wife or their children. And if he has also been assaulting his wife or otherwise acting in a manner opposed to how she may have hoped or expected him to treat her when they married, then she may ask the court to sanction him in some way.

I would argue that even in cases where no such sanction against the husband is ordered, the women who bring them have received some measure of what they needed from the court: to declare publicly that their marriages are unsatisfactory and to shame their errant husbands. Shame is another powerful moral-aesthetic value in PNG, expressed bodily through a lowered head, downcast eyes, trembling and especially tears. If seated on the ground, one may also draw one's fingers through the sand or soil in further mortification. Shame is the embodied acknowledgement of wrong action and the wrong treatment of one's relationships. If, as I am arguing, women bring adultery cases to the village court to shame their husbands, I do not mean merely that they wish to make a spectacle of them. I mean more critically what Philippopoulos-Mihalopoulos refers to when he says that:

> justice finds its space in the movement of escape, of *withdrawal*: withdrawing from judgement, from justice itself, from one's own justice, and away from the space of the other's claim. *Spatial justice is the movement of taking leave.*[33] Figure 2

This leave-taking, as I understand it, is not one of abjuring responsibility for the claims of another, but precisely the opposite: it is to *acknowledge* that claim, to open the space of the relation between the other and one's self as another, so that both positions are

[33] Philippopoulos-Mihalopoulos above note 4 at 213, emphasis in original.

observable, not only by those persons involved in a dispute, but by all witnesses present in the space of the court. The only way to achieve relational justice is through its instantiation in spatial justice — a concept that has perhaps been a long time coming for legal anthropology, by virtue of its own relations with other disciplines. Note, for example, that in this article I have appropriated a concept that legal theorists appropriated in turn from urban social geographers. Here I have tried to apply the concept to a 'small-scale' horticulturalist population in the way it conducts the legal process handed down to it from the metropole. I have tried to show that spatial justice 'works' as a concept there precisely because of the way that it is interpellated with relational justice, with the way people in PNG bring relations that have run into trouble into view in the space they create, through both the disposition of their bodies and of their speech, in the village court. What then happens may or may not result in peace, either between husbands and wives, or between families with longstanding grievances against each other. The result may be something more like what other observers of the village courts have called amity, or a 'sociality ... predicated upon on-going and self-assertive engagements: one in which people compelled each other into active participation in each other's pasts, presents and futures'.[34] Amity, at least defined in this way, is not quite the 'peace and reconciliation' hoped for in the independent metropole of Port Moresby or the colonial metropole of Canberra. But it points toward the possibility of releasing village courts from the obsession with 'peace', or with a teleology of converting all other forms of conflict into talk and resolution, that has been a feature of the Papua New Guinean lawscape since the colonial era. To take the notion of withdrawal seriously, one would have to consider that village courts offer an ongoing and open-ended justice, rather than a justice of closure. This is a justice of the space that disputants open between themselves and others each time they bring their conflicts to the village courts, and through the new perspective offered by the forum of the court itself, situated as it is in between persons and groups in a state of conflict, and in between those persons and groups and a state whose regard is perceived as having shifted permanently elsewhere.

Disclosure Statement

No potential conflict of interest was reported by the author.

[34] Errington Frederick and Gewertz Deborah 'Reconfiguring Amity at Ramu Sugar Limited' in Barker John (ed) *The Anthropology of Morality in Melanesia and Beyond* Ashgate Aldershot 2007 p 93 at 93.

Sounds of Silence: Everyday Strategies of Social Repair in Timor-Leste

*Lia Kent**

Abstract. Transitional justice discourse and practice is imbued with assumptions about the liberatory power of speech, and constructs silence as a marker of absence, pathology or continuing repression. This article unsettles these assumptions by examining some of the 'everyday' ways in which East Timorese people are seeking to rebuild their lives in the aftermath of the Indonesian occupation. Close attention to everyday strategies and practices of social repair brings to the fore the 'civil' and 'pragmatic' dimensions of silence, while also underscoring the significance of relational and embodied forms of communication in the Timor-Leste context. I conclude that, rather than viewing silence as a 'problem', more attention should be paid to its diverse meanings, and to the rich realm of everyday life in which they are embedded.

1.0 Introduction

Transitional justice is promoted around the globe as a means of assisting both individuals and nations to 'come to terms' with the legacy of violent conflicts. Built upon a compelling narrative of 'transition', both criminal trials and truth commissions work discursively to delineate the violent past from the peaceful present and mark a definitive sense of 'now' and 'then'. Central to this narrative is the idea of speech — that the verbalisation of painful memory and its public acknowledgement will contribute to both personal healing and national transformation. Speech is juxtaposed with silence, which is understood as the condition of subordination and repression in which human rights abuses take place, and which must be broken. The call for

---

*The fieldwork that forms the basis of this article was conducted in Timor-Lestein July 2011, June–July 2014 and July 2015, and was funded by an Australian Research Council Discovery Grant [DP 140202360].

transitional justice thus revolves around the imperative for societies to 'lift the lid of silence and denial' and 'effectively unsilence' painful and taboo subjects.[1] It is an imperative that has come to seem natural and universal.

The link between speech and individual healing and national transformation is powerfully embodied in the mechanism of the truth commission. The South African Truth and Reconciliation Commission (TRC), the commission that has done most to shape global discourse, mobilised around the mantra 'Revealing is Healing', promoting the idea that victims' statements about human rights violations would build a shared knowledge of the apartheid era that would, in turn, contribute to national unity.[2] These assumptions have infused the workings of many subsequent truth commissions, including that of the UN-sponsored Commission for Reception, Truth and Reconciliation (CAVR) that was established in Timor-Leste in 2002, in the aftermath of the 24-year Indonesian occupation and during the territory's transition to formal independence. The CAVR was described by the UN Special Representative of the Secretary General, Sergio Viera de Mello, as a 'vitally important initiative' that would provide the East Timorese with an 'official ear to listen to their grievances and acknowledge their pain'.[3] A key component of its work was a nationwide truth-seeking process that saw interviews conducted with victims of human rights abuses around the country and national public hearings which sought to place 'ordinary people at the centre of the national debate on healing, reconciliation and justice'.[4] In its final report, presented to the President and tabled in the parliament in 2005, the CAVR acknowledged the thousands of East Timorese who participated in its truth-seeking process, and made special note of the 'extraordinary courage' possessed by women who 'voluntarily came forward to tell their stories of sexual violence'.[5]

While the women, and men, who participated in the CAVR were undoubtedly courageous, what can be said of those who did not tell their stories in this institutional context? In this article I seek to unsettle the juxtaposition of speech against silence by reflecting on how some East Timorese people are seeking to rebuild their lives *outside* formal institutional contexts and in ways that may not elevate verbal speech over other forms of communication. In doing so, I draw upon the insights emerging from a growing body of social science and ethnographic scholarship that unsettles transitional justice assumptions about resolution through public disclosure.

Following a brief overview of emerging scholarship on silence and 'the everyday', the main body of the article focuses on case studies from Timor-Leste, which illuminate a range of diverse ways in which people are reconstructing life after years of conflict. I begin by drawing on interviews with a number of women who opt not to talk

---

[1] Doxtader Eric 'The Quietude of Transitional Justice: Five Rhetorical Questions' (2015) 6(1) *African Yearbook of Rhetoric* 23 at 35.

[2] Ross Fiona 'On Having Voice and Being Heard' (2003) 3(3) *Anthropological Theory* 325. See also Wilson Richard *The Politics of Truth and Reconciliation in South Africa* Cambridge University Press Cambridge 2001.

[3] Speech by Sergio Viera De Mello in Huang Reiko and Gunn Geoffrey 'Reconciliation as State-Building in East Timor' (2004) *Lusotopie* 19 at 30.

[4] Commission for Reception, Truth and Reconciliation (CAVR) *Chega!* CAVR Dili Timor-Leste 2005 Executive Summary p 33.

[5] As above at Part 7.7 p 5.

publicly or with their close family members about certain aspects of their pasts. I show how their silences, which arguably reflect the silencing power of hegemonic discourses and structures, can also be seen as a silence of pragmatism and as a silence of civility.[6] I then draw on the narratives of three individuals: Anna's, which highlights the revitalisation of rituals and practices surrounding the recovery and reburial of the bodies of those who died during the conflict, and Joao and Nuno's, which illuminate the efforts by East Timorese displaced in Indonesian West Timor to return to their families and communities. Collectively, these narratives bring to the fore the significance of embodied, relational and non-verbal ways of responding to the legacies of the Indonesian occupation. While not suggesting that efforts to improve official truth-seeking endeavours should be abandoned, the conclusion reflects on how, by paying greater attention to the realm of the everyday, it becomes clear that silence should not be pathologised or dismissed as absence, lack or avoidance.

2.0 Speech, Silence and the Everyday

The rise and celebration of transitional justice discourse and practice, and its related assumptions about the liberatory power of speech, has been accompanied by a robust critique. Not only has it been argued that the verbalisation of painful memories through a one-off process of public testimony may not contribute to healing,[7] but the universal applicability of the individualised, confessional model of healing promoted by transitional justice mechanisms (in particular truth commissions) has also been questioned.[8] Critiques have highlighted that speaking publicly may have negative personal and political consequences, especially for women who speak about sensitive, and often stigmatised, issues of sexual violence and in contexts where violence against women many be ongoing.[9] These dangers, which may lead some women to refrain from participating in truth commissions, are not always adequately recognised by those commissions. Fiona Ross's work on the South African TRC powerfully demonstrates this, and shows that the TRC's reading of the absence of women's testimony as a silence caused by 'reticence, propriety, or lack of education about rights', perpetuated an erroneous view that they were 'autonomous subjects with the capacity to choose freely how to engage in institutional processes'.[10] Similar observations have been made in relation to Timor-Leste where, it has been suggested that for a range

[6] Eastmond Marita and Selimovic Johanna Mannergren 'Silence as Possibility in Postwar Everyday Life' (2012) 6 *The International Journal of Transitional Justice* 502.

[7] See, for example, Hamber Brandon 'Does the Truth Heal? A Psychological Perspective on the Political Strategies for Dealing with the Legacy of Political Violence' in Biggar Neil (ed.) *Burying the Past: Making Peace and Doing Justice after Civil Conflict* George Town University Press Washington 2001 p 155.

[8] See, for example, Shaw Rosalind 'Memory Frictions: Localizing the Truth and Reconciliation Commission in Sierra Leone' (2007) 1(2) *International Journal of Transitional Justice* 183.

[9] See, for example, Ross Fiona 'An Acknowledged Failure: Women, Voice, Violence and the South African Truth and Reconciliation Commission' in Shaw Rosalind and Waldorf Lars (eds) *Localizing Transitional Justice: Interventions and Priorities after Mass Violence* Stanford University Press Stanford California 2010 p 69.

[10] As above at 75.

of reasons — including the stigma and shame associated with sexual abuse — many women refrained from participating in the CAVR.[11] There was limited support available for those who did speak publicly and some experienced negative social ramifications.[12] These critiques illuminate that speaking publicly of suffering depends critically on trust: trust in the capacity of the listener to attend to suffering, trust 'in institutions anticipated to assist' and 'in social relations and support networks'.[13] The extent to which these conditions of trust can be met is, in many contexts, questionable.

Further destabilising the juxtaposition of speech versus silence is the fact that transitional justice discourse and practice embeds its own silences. Even as it promises to give voice, the liberal language of rights that infuses the work of both trials and truth commissions may silence the complexities of lived experiences. Suffering is inherently difficult to narrate in a verbal, linear form and this is even more the case when storytelling is constrained by the demands of institutions that expect experiences to be recounted according to a particular 'script'. Criminal tribunals, for instance, function according to strict rules that circumscribe the avenues for survivors' participation and storytelling, and constrain possibilities for the recognition of their unique experiences and grievances.[14] And despite their broader mandates, and their purportedly 'victim-centred' nature, truth commissions also contain their own silences, as they shape individuals' stories to conform to narratives of nation-building, reconciliation and national unity (and in the process, tend to occlude stories of unfinished business, retribution and revenge).[15] A range of recent critiques bring these silences to the fore, underscoring that human rights discourse is not 'neutral' or 'universal' and raising important questions about the ways in which stories of violence are listened to, recognised, represented and disseminated.[16]

Some of the most fresh and illuminating insights on silence are emerging from social science and ethnographic scholarship that seeks to go beyond an analysis of normative institutional responses to conflict and focus on the 'everyday' strategies that people utilise to reconstruct their lives.[17] While there are many different definitions

---

[11] See, for example, Stanley Elizabeth *Torture, Truth and Justice: The Case of Timor Leste* Routledge New York & London 2009 p 117; Kent Lia *The Dynamics of Transitional Justice: International Models and Local Realities in East Timor* Routledge New York & London 2012 p 101. The CAVR itself acknowledged that many women victims of sexual violence did not report these cases to the Commission because of the fear of social or family humiliation or rejection. See CAVR above note 4 at Part 7.7 p 109.

[12] Guthrey Holly 'How Does the Truth Heal? An Exploration of *Voice* and Pathways toward Victim Healing in Solomon Islands and Timor-Leste' Unpublished PhD Thesis University of Otago New Zealand 2013 p 62 and 121; Kent above note 11 at 152.

[13] Ross above note 9 at 79.

[14] Franke Katherine M 'Gendered Subjects of Transitional Justice' (2006) 15(3) *Columbia Journal of Gender and Law* 813.

[15] Rawski Frederick 'Truth-Seeking and Local Histories in East Timor' (2002) 3(1) *Asia Pacific Journal on Human Rights and the Law* 77.

[16] See, for example, Nesiah Vasuki 'Missionary Zeal for a Secular Mission: Bringing Gender to Transitional Justice and Redemption to Feminism' in Kouvo Sari and Pearson Zoe (eds) *Feminist Perspectives on Contemporary International Law: Between Resistance and Compliance?* Hart Publishing Oxford & Portland 2011 p 151. See Ross above note 9 at 84.

[17] See, for example, Eastmond and Selimovic above note 6; Uvin Peter and Nee Ann 'Silence and Dialogue: Burundians' Alternatives to Transitional Justice' in Shaw Rosalind and Waldorf Lars (eds)

of the everyday, at its heart the concept revolves around a concern for people's 'routines, repetitions, routes and habits of daily living', including those adopted by individuals and communities attempting to make sense of conflict.[18]

The value of the concept of the everyday lies in its ability to bring about a reorientation of the analytical lens away from formal transitional justice institutions towards what Veena Das terms the 'small stories'.[19] These small stories illuminate the myriad ways in which people 'pursue mundane activities and practices to restore the basic fabrics of meaningful social relations, negotiate or recreate protective mechanisms and provide some sense of continuity in their lives and sense of self in relation to other'.[20] Explorations of the everyday start from the perspective that people seek to recreate meaning and rebuild the social order after conflict in multiple ways and often through routes other than public, individual, expressions of harm. They acknowledge, too, that this process is primarily a *social* rather than an individual one that is often grounded in the realm of the family and community. Implicit in many studies of the everyday is an understanding that, for those whose lives have been severely disrupted by conflict, and where 'normal' social and political interactions cannot be taken for granted, the resumption of everyday activities and interactions is no small task. In other words, the recreation of the everyday represents a significant achievement that is, over time, critical to rebuilding social worlds.[21]

An orientation towards the everyday is evident in a small but growing number of studies of post-conflict social repair and reconciliation in Timor-Leste.[22] Common to these studies is an emphasis on how, through their participation in ritual and social

---

Localizing Transitional Justice: Interventions and Priorities after Mass Violence Stanford University Press Stanford California 2010 at 157; Argeti-Pillen Alex *Masking Terror: How Women Contain Violence in Southern Sri Lanka* University of Pennsylvania Press Philadelphia 2013; Baines Erin 'Spirits and Social Reconstruction after Mass Violence: Rethinking Transitional Justice' (2010) 109(436) *African Affairs* 409; Baines Erin and Gauvin Lara Rosenoff 'Motherhood and Social Repair after War and Displacement in Northern Uganda' (2014) *Journal of Refugee Studies* 282; Igreja Victor 'Multiple Temporalities in Indigenous Justice and Healing Practices in Mozambique' (2012) 6(3) *International Journal of Transitional Justice* 1; Alcala Pilar Riano and Baines Erin 'Editorial Note' (2012) 6 *International Journal of Transitional Justice* 385; Grunebaum Heidi *Memorializing the Past: Everyday Life in South Africa after the Truth and Reconciliation Commission* Transaction Publishers New York & London 2011; Gready Paul 'Reconciliation, Relationships and the Everyday' in Gready Paul *The Era of Transitional Justice: The Aftermath of the Truth and Reconciliation Commission in South Africa and Beyond* Routledge New York & London 2011 p 195.

18 Grunebaum above note 17 at 117. See also Alcala and Baines above note 17.

19 Das Veena 'Trauma and Testimony: Implications for Political Community' (2003) 3 (3) *Anthropological Theory* 293 at 300.

20 Alcala and Baines above note 17 at 386.

21 Das Veena and Kleinman Arthur 'Introduction' in Das Veena Kleinman Arthur Lock Margaret Ramphele Mamphela and Reynolds Pamela (eds) *Remaking a World: Testimony, Trauma and Social Suffering* University of California Press Berkeley California & London 2001 p 1–2.

22 See, for example, Field Annette 'Places of Suffering and Pathways to Healing: Post-Conflict Life in Bidau, East Timor' Unpublished PhD thesis James Cook University 2004; Robins Simon *Families of the Missing: A Test for Contemporary Approaches to Transitional Justice* Routledge New York & London 2013; Bovensiepen Judith *The Land of Gold: Post-Conflict Recovery and Cultural Revival in Independent Timor-Leste* Cornell University Southeast Asia Program Publications (SEAP) Ithaca 2015; McWilliam Andrew 'Fataluku Healing and Cultural Resilience in East Timor' (2008) 73(2) *Ethnos: Journal of Anthropology* 217.

activities, people are slowly remaking social connections between kinship groups, household groups, friends and neighbours. Some studies highlight the significance of seemingly mundane activities such as rebuilding houses, and attending church services and sporting events.[23] Others focus on rituals such as wedding celebrations, mortuary rites and the rebuilding of *uma luliks* (sacred houses), and highlight how people are working to reinvigorate ancestral practices that seek to re-establish a mythical, primordial unity with the land.[24]

Approached through the lens of the everyday, it becomes clear that silence should not necessarily be dismissed as a marker of absence, lack, pathology or continuing repression.[25] The apparent absence of verbal discussion about the past conflict might indicate that individuals and communities are acknowledging its legacy in other ways, for instance, by participating in ritual or community life. The lens of the everyday may also reveal that silence is a pragmatic tactic that enables a focus on the here and now[26] or a degree of control over personal security.[27] Silence might also at times be a condition that allows relationships to be re-established and long-term peace fostered.[28]

The 'pragmatic' dimensions of silence have been brought to the fore by recent studies by Eastmond and Selimovic and Uvin and Nee.[29] Eastmond and Selimovic's study of post-war relations amongst three generations of Serbs and Bosniaks in Foca and Sarajevo highlights that silence in that context might be understood, at least in part, as a tactic for rebuilding lives and focusing on the present and the future. They observe that in a context where much of the population live in difficult circumstances and are preoccupied with livelihood concerns, people appear to gravitate towards 'putting aside the conflicting narratives of the war' in order to 'focus on managing the present, rather than scrutinising the past'.[30] Uvin and Nee's study of citizens' attitudes to justice in Burundi similarly found that people preferred not to talk about the past because, in that context, it was felt that speaking publicly would lead to increased conflict.[31] The preference for silence was sharpened by the realities of life in a society where there is no access to formal justice systems and faith in the rule of law is limited. Amid these constraints, people have developed pragmatic survival strategies in response to their profound vulnerability: they 'need to maintain relations at all costs, for apart from their bodies, the little bit of social capital they have is the only thing that may make the difference between total destruction and simple poverty'.[32]

---

[23] Field above note 22.
[24] See, for example, Bovensiepen above note 22; McWilliam above note 22.
[25] See, for example, Kidron Carol 'Toward an Ethnography of Silence: The Lived Presence of the Past among Holocaust Trauma Descendants in Israel' (2009) 50(1) *Current Anthropology* 7.
[26] Eastmond and Selimovic above note 6.
[27] See, for example, Guthrey above note 12.
[28] Eastmond and Selimovic above note 6 at 515.
[29] As above; Uvin and Nee above note 17.
[30] Eastmond and Selimovic above note 6 at 522.
[31] Uvin and Nee above note 17 at 166.
[32] As above at 173.

Eastmond and Selimovic's study also identifies that silence is not only a pragmatic choice but might at times be an instrument that 'fosters relationships and opens up common ground'.[33] They suggest that the citizens of Foca and Sarajevo seek, through their silence, to express 'good neighbourliness' and respect for others, a condition that allows for functional social relations to resume. This indicates that their silence might be read, in part, as a silence of 'civility' that might enable tentative forms of trust to emerge.[34] This, in turn, might also offer hope for peace.

To recognise that silence may be associated with the possibility of resuming everyday life is not to valorise it. Although it is a source of meaning, security and belonging, the everyday is also, as Alcala and Baines suggest, 'the site of violence, not just as it is imposed but as it is embraced and reproduced'.[35] Silence can be associated with 'repression, shame and humiliation',[36] which is a reflection of the silencing power of 'structures, practices, traditions and discourses' that prevent certain voices from reaching the public sphere.[37] These silences often play out in gender-discriminatory ways and are exacerbated by the constrictions of poverty, social exclusion and isolation.[38] To acknowledge and unpack these constrictions, however, does not necessarily mean they can be easily overcome through a straightforward process of speaking out (especially within the constrained possibilities of a criminal trial or truth commission). In other words, transitional justice is not a 'silver bullet' that enables the structural barriers and forms of vulnerability that persist in many conflict-affected societies to be cast aside. For those deeply enmeshed within these constrained circumstances, as well as webs of sociality that are critical to their survival, individual, public truth-telling 'may not always be the most functional means of addressing [the pain of the past]'.[39] It may also be the case that, where silence is productive to the rebuilding of relationships, transitional justice mechanisms focused on 'speaking out' will unintentionally complicate existing coping strategies by undermining the social ties that underpin them.[40]

The following sections examine several case studies from Timor-Leste through the lens of the everyday. These cases bring to the fore the 'civil' and 'pragmatic' dimensions of silence while also underscoring the significance of relational and embodied forms of communication in the Timor-Leste context. In essence these sections bring

---

33 Eastmond and Selimovic above note 6 at 515.

34 As above at 514; see also Beck Teresa Koloma 'Forgetting the Embodied Past: Body Memory in Transitional Justice' in Buckley-Zistel Susanne Beck Teresa Koloma Braun Christian and Mieth Friederike (eds) *Transitional Justice Theories* Routledge Oxon & New York 2014 p 196.

35 Alcala and Baines above note 17 at 388.

36 Connerton Paul 'Seven Types of Forgetting' (2008) 1 *Memory Studies* 59. See also Beck above note 34.

37 Hansen Lene 'The Little Mermaid's Silent Security Dilemma and the Absence of Gender in the Copenhagen School' (2000) 29 *Millenium: Journal of International Studies* 285.

38 See Obrdovic-Wochnik Jelena 'The "Silent Dilemma" of Transitional Justice: Silencing and Coming to Terms with the Past in Serbia' (2011) 7 *The International Journal of Transitional Justice* 336.

39 Eastmond and Selimovic above note 6 at 503.

40 Uvin and Nee above note 17 at 174; Beck above note 34 at 196; see also Buckley-Zistel Susanne 'Remembering to Forget: Chosen Amnesia as a Strategy for Local Coexistence in Post-Genocide Rwanda' (2005) 76 *Africa* 131.

together two different strands of analysis: scholarship on post-conflict silences and the everyday, which has given limited attention to the body and relationships as sites of communication, and scholarship on relationality and embodiment which, while prominent within the anthropological literature, has paid scant attention to processes of post-conflict recovery and reconciliation. Weaving these strands together helps to deepen understandings of how communities in Timor-Leste are rebuilding social life after the conflict while also enriching existing scholarship on silence and the everyday.

3.0 The Silences of East Timorese Military 'Wives'

During the 24-year Indonesian occupation of Timor-Leste, from 1974–1999, an unknown number of women were coerced into long-term sexual relationships with members of the Indonesian military. The CAVR had made a special effort to highlight these experiences of harm in its final report, noting that, of the hundreds of cases of sexual violence it had been able document, 26% were instances of what it referred to as 'sexual slavery'.[41] It found that women — often young teenagers — were coerced into a number of different kinds of relationships. In some cases, a military officer lived with a woman and her family, or the woman was held in a house rented by the military. In other cases, women were detained in military installations, where they often became the sexual property of a number of men. Others were not physically detained but were summoned regularly to military installations for sexual purposes. The CAVR highlighted how many of these coercive relationships lasted for several years and, in some cases, women endured consecutive relationships as 'ownership' of them was passed from one military battalion to its replacement.[42] For some women, these abusive relationships did not end until the Indonesian military departed Timor-Leste in 1999.

In 2011 I had the opportunity to interview 19 women who had endured sexual relationships such as these. The interviews, which sought to learn more about the women's present-day lives and circumstances, were conducted as part of a collaborative research project coordinated by the Timor-Leste office of the International Center of Transitional Justice (ICTJ).[43] The research team included four experienced East Timorese women researchers and, given the sensitivity of the topic, potential interviewees were approached through the ICTJ's existing networks.[44] A member of the team initially approached each woman via telephone or in person, and took time to ensure that they had an understanding of the project's aims and were aware that they could decline to participate, or withdraw from the project, at any time. The project was also conducted on the basis that it would inform the ICTJ's pre-existing work with women survivors of violence, and that, following the interviews, the women would be linked in to a support network and, where possible, also connected to government support services.[45]

---

[41] CAVR above note 4 at Part 7.7.

[42] As above at Part 7.7 p 2.

[43] For a more detailed discussion of the project see Kent Lia 'Narratives of Suffering and Endurance: Coercive Sexual Relationships, Truth Commissions and Possibilities for Gender Justice in Timor-Leste' (2014) 8(2) *International Journal of Transitional Justice* 289.

[44] These researchers were based at the ICTJ and the Alola Foundation.

[45] All interviews were conducted in Tetum and organised in a flexible manner to enable the women to tell their own stories in their own way. Interviews were recorded and later transcribed and translated

While some women approached by the research team declined to be interviewed, somewhat surprisingly, many agreed to participate. This was the case even though many explained that they had not spoken of their past experiences publicly to the CAVR (or any other institutional body), nor had they talked to their children, or, in cases where women had remarried, their East Timorese husbands. While women's motivations for deciding to participate were undoubtedly diverse, it may be that some perceived a difference between telling their stories at a public forum and recounting them in the context of a small, intimate, interview encounter. It may also have been the case that the women were keen to talk to researchers with an interest in their *present* lives and circumstances (rather than their past experiences of harm) and were attracted by the possibility of future support.[46]

All the women interviewed were based in rural areas of Timor-Leste, in the districts of Baucau, Los Palos and Ainaro. Despite their diverse locations, the women shared a number of common characteristics. Most were engaged in subsistence agriculture and had had little formal education. Several had borne children as a result of their unions with the military and most, although not all, remained unmarried. A number of common themes also emerged from the women's narratives of their lives, including the theme of marginalisation and stigmatisation. This theme was evident in women's descriptions of being labelled as '*lonte*' (whore) by their families and communities, the extent to which they believed themselves to be 'gossiped about' and their explanations of not wishing to remarry because they felt '*moe*' (shy/ashamed). Some also spoke of how, because of this stigmatisation, they were reluctant to go to church or participate in other activities that are integral to social and community life, explaining that they preferred to lead a quiet life at home. Even though most had not spoken to their children or family members about their past experiences, this did not mean their family members did not know about them — in a sense, they might be understood as what Taussig refers to as 'public secrets': knowledge that is widely known but cannot be publicly acknowledged or talked about.[47]

That many of these women opt to remain silent about some aspects of their past is, on one reading, not surprising. Their silence might be understood as a reflection of the limited social capital these women possess in a context in which survival — both social and economic — is fundamentally dependent on the maintenance of reciprocal familial and kinship relations. On the one hand, the principles of exchange and social alliance that continue to order East Timorese society remain fundamental to the reproduction of community and provide a powerful sense of meaning, belonging and security to many people.[48] It is through these ordering principles that women

into English. Interviews were also conducted on the basis that women's names would be changed in any public documents.

[46] As in all researcher encounters, there were inevitably power relations between researcher and participants. These relations of power may have had an influence on the information women chose to reveal or not reveal and the ways they chose to tell their stories.

[47] The term 'public secret' refers to the knowledge of what not to know. See Taussig Michael *Defacement: Public Secrecy and the Labor of the Negative* Stanford University Press Palo Alto 1999 p 2.

[48] McWilliam Andrew and Traube Elizabeth 'Land and Life in Timor-Leste' in McWilliam Andrew and Traube Elizabeth (eds) *Land and Life in Timor-Leste: Ethnographic Essays* ANU E Press Canberra 2011 p 3.

derive their status, a status that is linked to their roles within the sphere of the home, including the care of children.[49] On the other hand, these reflect the influence of a conservative Catholicism that places a high value on women's chastity and purity.[50] Amid these constrictions, former military wives are often perceived (and perceive themselves) as soiled and as violating the proper roles of Timorese womanhood. This has a profound effect on their social relations and marriage prospects, and makes it difficult for them to improve their social status and that of their children. On this reading, the women's silences might be understood, then, as a reflection of social structures which, while providing a sense of security and belonging to many Timorese, also have a *silencing* power that plays out in corrosive ways for those who do not conform to the gendered social roles expected of them.

Nationalist narratives, which have become more pronounced since the CAVR completed its work, reinforce the silencing power of several structures, discourses and practices. Over the past decade, it has been increasingly apparent that the liberal human rights narrative of the conflict produced by the CAVR has been overtaken by the political leadership's promotion of its own selective narrative of the conflict, which elevates the heroic acts of those involved in the resistance struggle. Servicing the leadership's own vision of 'transition' and its drive to build a unified national identity, the heroic narrative, invoked through commemorative events, museums, monuments and a veterans' valorisation scheme, tells a story of the East Timorese people as the *ema ki'ik* (little people) who through acts of perseverance, courage and national unity, eventually achieved their goal of independence.[51] By delineating who counts as a 'hero', this narrative embeds its own silences. It is, for instance, a deeply gendered narrative that celebrates the (mostly male) armed resistance struggle and ignores women's diverse contributions to the independence struggle. The extent to which women are celebrated for their maternal roles — as widows and mothers of the fallen — only serves to further marginalise those who do not conform to these roles. The heroic narrative thus commonly constructs military wives as dangerous, poisonous or as 'traitors'.

Just as the silences of former military wives reflect some degree of gendered subjugation, they also unsettle the therapeutic and emancipatory assumptions of truth-telling. They speak to the limits of truth commissions in shifting deeply entrenched patriarchal values (which are being asserted with renewed vigour in the interests of nation-building). These silences also underline how one-off opportunities for public storytelling can create new dangers for women who will remain intimately entangled with their communities and kinship networks long after their moment in the public spotlight. Indeed, the women's continuing experiences of stigmatisation suggest that the CAVR's attempts to recognise them collectively as 'victims of sexual slavery' did little to transform perceptions of them in East Timorese society or their local

[49] Niner Sara 'Barlake: An Exploration of Marriage Practices and Issues of Women's Status in Timor-Leste' (2012) 11 *Local Global* 140.

[50] Niner Sara 'Hakat Klot (Narrow Steps): Negotiating Gender in Post-Conflict Timor-Leste' (2011) 13(3) *International Feminist Journal of Politics* 140.

[51] For an overview of some of the factors that have informed this narrative see Kent Lia 'After the Truth Commission: Gender and Citizenship in Timor-Leste' (2016) 17(1) *Human Rights Review* 51.

communities. Given the Timorese leadership's tendency to portray rights discourse as a foreign imposition, such forms of recognition may even be counterproductive.[52]

To stop with these observations about the silencing nature of nationalist and transitional justice discourses, however, also leaves out other dimensions of these women's silences, in particular, the degree to which they embody a degree of (constrained) agency. While this agency should not be conflated with ideas of 'autonomy' and 'free choice', it can nonetheless be heard in the women's narratives. It can be heard, for instance, in the women's descriptions of their everyday preoccupations, which, for those with children, centre on their maternal obligations, and the need to create better lives for their descendants. In addition to growing rice and vegetables to feed their families, many of the women were engaged in economic efforts, making, for example, small *dosi* (sweets), coconut oil or *pisang goreng* (fried bananas) to sell in the marketplace, to help cover the costs of their children's education. They saw their efforts to feed and educate their children, and protect them from discriminatory attitudes (including, for many, not discussing the paternity of their children with them or others), as paramount. These labours, the women hoped, would help to ensure that future generations would not suffer as they had — that suffering and hardship would end with them. They might also be seen as attempts to reclaim social value as accepted members of society by performing the role of the 'good mother'.[53]

Within the limited space available to them to negotiate social acceptability, the women seek, through their silence, to protect their reputations and fulfil their maternal obligations by building better lives for their children and striving for material well-being and social acceptability. Their strategies embody a pragmatism that is not only oriented to the maintenance of everyday life in the present; it also seeks to provide for a better future.

The ways some women expressed a desire to protect the reputations of other women, particularly the small number of those who, through remarriage, have been able to regain a degree of social acceptability also contains echoes of Eastmond and Selimovic's idea of a 'civil silence'. The women's silence was at least partly informed by a shared recognition that speaking of the past would be counterproductive to the building of relationships and potentially dangerous to the women and others. To take just one example, Maria, an unmarried woman from Los Palos, when asked whether she talked about her past experiences with other women in her community who had similar experiences, explained simply that she did not, because 'some have married already and some have children already'.[54]

The need for a 'silence of civility' also speaks to the ways in which the conflict permeated everyday life and of how, in the coercive circumstances of the military occupation, many East Timorese men and women 'collaborated' with, or worked directly for, the Indonesian regime. These dynamics inevitably intersected with, and exacerbated, historical patterns of gendered relations and meant that, in the case of former military 'wives', family or community members were often complicit in their

[52] Smith Sarah 'When Gender Started: The United Nations in Post-Occupation Timor-Leste' (2015) 27(1) *Global Change, Peace and Security* 55.
[53] See Baines and Gauvin above note 17 at 12.
[54] See Kent above note 43 at 304.

abuse. To speak publicly about these 'intimate enemies'[55] — of those who sacrificed the women to the military in exchange for the collective security of the community or household, or of those East Timorese men who had raped them alongside the Indonesian military, or had 'kept watch' while they were abused inside their homes or in military detention centres — is profoundly dangerous. It undermines powerful national narratives of resistance and unity and the construction of men as the protectors of 'their' women during the conflict. More importantly, it has the potential to undermine close-knit kinship ties, perpetuate intergenerational rifts between families and disrupt possibilities for future marriage alliances. In this context, the women's silence might enable them to nurture and maintain the intimate social, political relationships with their extended kin that are essential to viable social life.

To be clear, this is not to suggest that these women's silences should necessarily be viewed only in a positive light. Rather, it is to acknowledge that they contain multiple meanings that are embedded in the 'rich textures of everyday life'.[56] Close attention to these women's silences shows that they have an acute understanding of their political, social and cultural constraints and of the extent to which, in a context of enduring stigma, poverty and marginalisation, there can be no straightforward rupture with the past. Given that they are intricately entwined with their families and communities that are at once a source of social support, belonging and meaning, and of stigmatisation, silence offers a strategy for re-establishing everyday life. Viewed through the lens of the everyday, that is, it is clear that the silence of former military wives is not only a silence of repression or pathology, but embodies a degree of agency.

4.0 Embodied and Relational Forms of Communication

This section turns now to two examples — illustrated through the narratives of Anna, Joao and Nuno — that highlight the value of the lens of the everyday for examining the ways in which East Timorese families and communities are remaking their social worlds through practices and rituals that foreground relational and embodied forms of communication, rather than public, verbal disclosure.

The first example concerns the efforts by East Timorese families to recover and rebury the bodies of those who died during the Indonesian occupation. Anthropologists and Timor-Leste scholars have observed that a revitalisation of customary practices has taken place since the end of the Indonesian occupation.[57] Reburial efforts are an important, and highly visible, part of this renewal process. Facilitated in part by the availability of funding through the government's veterans' schemes, these practices involve expeditions to remote parts of the country by family groups to recover the remains of loved ones whose bodies were often dumped or hastily buried in shallow

---

[55] Theidon Kimberly *Intimate Enemies: Violence and Reconciliation in Peru* University of Pennsylvania Press Philadelphia 2012.

[56] Gready above note 17 at 223.

[57] See, for example, McWilliam above note 22; Bovensiepen Judith 'Paying for the Dead: On the Politics of Death in Independent Timor-Leste' (2014) 15(12) *The Asia Pacific Journal of Anthropology* 103; Grenfell Damian 'Remembering the Dead from the Customary to the Modern in Timor-Leste' (2012) 11 *Local Global* 97.

bush graves. The families then rebury them. These expeditions and their associated rituals 'engage complex networks of exchange and obligation'[58] and involve an enormous amount of planning and expense (in a context in which many struggle to feed themselves on a day-to-day basis).[59]

The time, energy and resources invested by families in these mortuary rituals underscore the significance of the dead, of the ancestors and, more generally, the presence of *lulik* ('sacred' or 'forbidden') in Timorese socio-political life.[60] Anthropologist Judith Bovensiepen, writing of the sub-district of Laclubar, describes *lulik* 'as an active agent that can create and destroy life', a 'vital energy force that resides in ancestral houses and objects, as well as animating the environment'.[61] Associated with specific places such as rock, rivers and hilltops and having the potential to appear in the shape of human or non-human spiritual beings, '*lulik* is a potency specifically connected with the ancestral realm' and can communicate important messages from the ancestors.[62] It has the power to bestow good fortune upon the living as well as to cause 'illness, death, confusion and madness' if matters *lulik* are transgressed.[63] Because *lulik* has an ongoing, affective presence in the lives of the living, and a power to directly influence the course of current affairs, it is a force that must be constantly negotiated, and has the power to inspire both 'reverence and awe' as well as 'intense fear and anxiety'. [64]

Given the power and agency possessed by the ancestors, there is a particular urgency about the need to conduct mortuary rituals, particularly in cases where people are thought to have died 'bad' deaths — i.e. deaths due to sudden and violent circumstances — where it is often suggested that the dead will continue to 'wander' as ghosts, and torment the lives of their descendants as well as those responsible for the death.[65] Rituals are required to release the spirit of the deceased from the pain and suffering they experienced, render them spiritually harmless and restore the balance between the worlds of the living and the dead.[66]

For those able to recover the remains of their loved ones, secondary burial rituals are enacted which involve both Catholic and customary elements. Families then make frequent visits back to the gravesite to conduct vigils that involve placing flowers or lighting candles to give sustenance to the spirit. Initial vigils are sometimes described as 'guarding the bitter flowers', later vigils as 'guarding the sweet flowers';[67] the former represent 'the heaviness (*todan*) of the loss, the latter as a time to celebrate

[58] McWilliam above note 22 at 225.
[59] As above; see also Grenfell above note 57.
[60] Bovensiepen above note 57 at 105; McWilliam Andrew, Palmer Lisa and Shepherd Christopher 'Lulik Encounters and Cultural Frictions in East Timor: Past and Present' (2014) 25(3) *The Australian Journal of Anthropology* 304.
[61] Bovensiepen above note 57 at 122.
[62] As above.
[63] As above; McWilliam Palmer and Shepherd above note 60 at 305.
[64] Bovensiepen above note 57 at 122.
[65] As above at 166.
[66] McWilliam above note 22 at 225; Sakti Victoria Kumala 'Thinking Too Much: Tracing Local Patterns of Emotional Distress after Mass Violence in Timor-Leste' (2013) 14(5) *The Asia Pacific Journal of Anthropology* 438.
[67] Bovensiepen above note 57 at 108.

the transformation of the person as a living being to that of an ancestor'.[68] For many families, however, the whereabouts of bodies is unknown: some are thought to have been burnt or dumped in the sea or in unmarked graves. Witnesses are also scarce and forensic evidence has often deteriorated after years in the tropical conditions. In these cases, the place of the deceased is sometimes said to appear to a descendent in a dream.[69] In cases where remains cannot be found, rituals sometimes incorporate stones or animal remains taken from the site where the body was thought to be located.[70]

In some cases, witnesses have approached families of the missing to reveal the location of bodies and the circumstances of deaths. This experience was described by 'Anna', a young educated government employee in Dili whose father, a member of the FALINTIL armed resistance, went missing during the conflict.[71] Anna's family had been living in uncertainty for over 30 years until, in 2009, they received a visit from a man — the cousin of a family acquaintance — who identified himself as a witness to her father's death and sought to explain to the family the circumstances of his death and the location of his remains.

Anna explained that hearing confirmation of her father's death gave rise to conflicting emotions. While she and her family were relieved that the appropriate rituals could finally be conducted to put his spirit to rest (and protect the family from future misfortune), this relief was tinged with a sense of bitterness because, during the conflict, Anna's mother had continued to contribute funds to the FALINTIL forces, and to send letters of support to her father via those who described themselves as *estafeda* (messengers) for the resistance. These self-described '*estafeda*' had visited the family from time to time, and had persuaded them that Anna's father was still alive in order to collect funds. Anna now feels that she and her family had been 'tricked', yet the realisation that the resistance movement may not always have been 'pure' in its motivations must remain a public secret that cannot be spoken of.

The man who identified himself as a witness explained that Anna's father had been killed along with nine other members of FALINTIL in a remote area of Timor-Leste. Anna's family invited the families of all nine men together for a meeting and to make a plan for looking for the bodies. They decided not to involve the police because of the lack of forensic testing available in Timor-Leste and the fact that it would take too long to go through official channels. They organised a week-long expedition to the site, involving 30 people from the nine families. Several four-wheel drive vehicles were hired at a great deal of expense. When they arrived at the local area, a local witness, a man who had been a member of the Indonesia military, showed them the place where the men were reported to have been shot. Given it had been 30 years since the deaths, it was clear, Anna said, that a river had washed the bodies away.

---

[68] Grenfell Damian 'Of Time and History: The Dead of War, Memory and the National Imaginary in Timor-Leste' (2015) 48(3) *Communication, Politics and Culture* 16 at 24.

[69] McWilliam above note 22 at 225.

[70] Robins Simon *An Assessment of the Needs of Families of the Missing in Timor-Leste* Report for the Post War Reconstruction and Development Unit (2010) 12 University of York York.

[71] FALINTIL (*Forces Armadas de Libertacao Nacional de Timor-Leste*/Armed Forces for the National Liberation of East Timor).

Anna explained that while they didn't find the bodies, the families took some stones and soil from the site, as well as some bones and teeth which were most likely animal bones. With monetary assistance from the Minister for Social Solidarity, they purchased a coffin, and took the substances they had retrieved to the 'Garden of Heroes' veterans' cemetery, in Metinaro. Because the men had all held high positions within FALINTIL, the families were given a place in the cemetery. With the agreement of all nine families, the stones, dirt, bones and teeth were placed together in one coffin, and the names of each man inscribed on the outside of the coffin.

As Anna's story suggests, the recovery of her father's remains (or objects that might substitute for it) involved a degree of disclosure by witnesses to the death, and discussion amongst other families of the dead. Yet, this communication occurred in the specific context of the family and involved a very different form of speaking than the individual, confessional kind of storytelling prescribed by transitional justice discourse. Establishing 'facts' such as whether the bones recovered were human or animal, which bones belonged to which family and the identity of the perpetrator of the deaths seems to have been less urgent than the need to complete the ritual and restore good relations with the dead. Moreover, communication occurred not only between living persons but, critically, between the living and the dead. The collective journey to the site by the 30 representatives of the nine families, and the efforts to recover the remains and conduct appropriate death rituals, were themselves powerful embodied and relational forms of communication, signalling both to the dead, and to the extended family, that right relations had been restored with the spirit world.

The second example which highlights how people are working with the legacies of the conflict outside formal institutional contexts and in ways that do not elevate verbal communication, concerns the efforts by East Timorese to return to their families and communities from Indonesian West Timor. Around 400,000 East Timorese people are thought to have been displaced from Timor-Leste into neighbouring West Timor after the 1999 referendum for self-determination, many at the behest of pro-Indonesian East Timorese militia groups. These groups, which had been armed and trained by the Indonesian military, wreaked a trail of destruction after the referendum, looting and burning houses, and killing over 1000. While it is difficult to obtain firm figures, some suggest that the population of East Timorese in West Timor currently sits at around 100,000 people.[72] Damaledo refers to members of this group as those who are 'guilty by association' because, while they are not members of militias, the Indonesian police force or the military, they are comprised of family members and relatives of militias and the Indonesian security forces, and thus are vulnerable to incrimination.[73]

During the period of United Nations administration of East Timor, a formal repatriation programme was initiated by UNTAET, in coordination with UNHCR and IOM, and refugee returns peaked just prior to Timor-Leste gaining formal

[72] International Crisis Group 'Timor-Leste: Reconciliation and Return from Indonesia' *Asia Briefing No 122* Crisis Group Dili/Brussels 18 April 2011 p 3.

[73] Damaledo Andrey *From Refugee to Citizen: An Examination of the Identity of the Ex-East Timorese Refugees in Indonesia* Unpublished Masters thesis University of Queensland 2009 p 24.

independence in May 2002.[74] Since then, numbers of returnees have dwindled and those remaining in West Timor have been designated (*warga baru*) 'new citizens' of Indonesia.[75] Nonetheless, a 'small but steady stream' of East Timorese continue informally and voluntarily to return to their homes, with little or no assistance from the state.[76] Some return with the assistance of local NGOs, while others return illegally, offering bribes to border patrol officers or taking risky paths along *jalan tikus* (goat tracks) to avoid the attention of the authorities.[77]

Given their extended absence from their communities, perceptions of their dubious pro-Indonesian associations and the significant financial, social and political implications[78] that are entailed in uprooting lives once again, it is common for potential returnees to make multiple visits to their communities over a period of years before definitively returning. During these visits, people participate in family rituals such as weddings and funerals, and investigate the status of their land and their prospects for economic survival. Their embodied presence in their communities acts as a form of communication in itself — a sign that they have not cut links with their homeland — and as a 'testing of the waters' as to whether their return would be welcomed.

Writing of the process of displacement in Uganda, Baines and Gauvin observe that displacement not only entails the physical removal of people from their homes, but also radically undercuts their sense of social belonging by fracturing 'the family, the home and communities'.[79] It is because of this social splintering that 'social reconstruction' is a critical part of the process of return and resettlement.[80] Processes of return might be understood, they suggest, as struggles to 'reclaim and regenerate one's relational, place-based existence'.[81]

These observations seem apt for describing the ways in which, following families' returns to Timor-Leste, they engage in a range of negotiations and informal practices that seek to reassert ties to kin, land and ancestors. One such practice was described by Nuno who, together with his family of 11, had returned from West Timor to his village in the district of Los Palos in 2013. Nuno detailed the process of rebuilding the family house that had been burned during the 1999 referendum. He explained how, before rebuilding commenced, he was required to make the land '*malirin*' (cool) by overseeing a series of rituals involving all the members of the kinship group. This involved the slaughtering of goats and pigs, and the mixing of their blood with coconut water, which was then sprinkled on the land. Following the rebuilding of the house, which took a week to complete and involved all able members of the extended family, the

74 Thu Pyone Myat 'Displacement and Repatriation in a Rural Timorese Village' in Ingram Sue, Kent Lia and McWilliam Andrew (eds) *A New Era? Timor-Leste after the UN* ANU Press Canberra 2015 p 255.
75 Damaledo above note 73.
76 Thu above note 74 at 255.
77 As above at 256.
78 For instance, returnees must relinquish their Indonesian citizenship upon returning to Timor-Leste.
79 Baines and Gauvin above note 17 at 2.
80 As above.
81 As above at 14 citing Corntassel 'Re-Visioning Resurgence: Indigenous Pathways to Decolonization and Sustainable Self-Determination' (2012) 1(1) *Decolonization: Indigeneity, Education and Society* 86 at 88.

new house also had to be 'cooled' (*halo malirin*). This required the killing of another pig, and goat, and the reading of their entrails to see if the signs were good. The extended family and all those who participated in the house-rebuilding process then shared a meal together.

Joao, who had returned to his village in Manatuto in 2012 with his wife and two young children, along with four other families, described taking part in a similar set of practices. In this case, the practices centred on the family's *uma lulik* (sacred house), which had deteriorated due to years of neglect during the Indonesian occupation. Not long after his return, Joao and his extended family engaged in a process of rebuilding and repairing the *uma lulik*. Following this, they held a one-day ritual, during which all of the members of his extended family visited the *uma lulik* and offered prayers to the ancestors. Pigs, chickens and goats were slaughtered and the family shared a meal together. According to Joao, this ritual served as an important form of communication to the ancestors that Joao had returned, that the family was united again and that it would no longer be divided.

The practices described by Nuno and Joao might be understood as efforts at social renewal that work against the deeply splintering effects of Portuguese colonisation and Indonesian occupation. These practices underscore the centrality of social ties, ties to ancestral land and nationalist conceptions of *Rai Timor* (the motherland) to notions of belonging, identity and social and economic well-being.[82] By engaging in these practices, returnees and their extended family networks seek to re-establish webs of connection amongst kinship groups, repair frayed family networks and 'remake their ties to land', which is associated with the ancestors and 'the life-giving resources on which all families depend'.[83]

Collectively, the practices described by Anna, Joao and Nuno also underscore the degree to which knowledge in Timor-Leste is both 'embodied' and 'relational'. Writing of water politics and spiritual ecology in Timor-Leste, anthropologist Lisa Palmer observes that knowledge is 'never something external to the body'; it relies on 'the co-being and constant 'participation' of particular bodies which connect the dead to the living (and the not yet born)'.[84] The centrality of relatedness as a way of being, knowing and communicating has also been noted in the broader Melanesian context. Joel Robbins goes so far as to argue that social relatedness is something Melanesians take to be 'innate' — it is 'something that is always there from birth for all persons and thus a fundamental aspect of life that needs to be attended to'.[85]

The centrality of relatedness is apparent in each of these practices described above. This is a relatedness that encompasses connections with the extended family in the present, with the physical world including the ancestral land and with the ancestors. In each case, the successful completion of rituals and practices depends upon the

---

[82] McWilliam and Traube above note 48 at 15.

[83] As above at 2.

[84] Palmer Lisa *Water Politics and Spiritual Ecology: Custom, Environmental Governance and Development* Routledge Oxon & New York 2015 p 148.

[85] Robbins Joel 'Recognition, Reciprocity and Justice: Melanesian Reflections on the Rights of Relationships' in Clarke Kamari Maxine and Goodale Mark (eds) *Mirrors of Justice: Law and Power in the Post-Cold War Era* Cambridge University Press Cambridge 2009 p 175.

'working together and interdependence between persons, collectives and the living and the dead'.[86] The centrality of the *body* — which acts as a key mechanism of communication and of transmission of knowledge — is also evident. As Anna's story suggests, rituals to recover and rebury the dead communicate through the body (or its substitute) that the descendants of the dead have not forgotten their responsibilities to them. In the case of Nuno and Joao, it is their returning bodies that communicate to the ancestors, to their kinship network and to the broader community, signalling fidelity to the homeland, and a reassertion of bonds of kin, land and origin.

5.0 Rethinking The Dichotomy of Speech versus Silence

What emerges from the preceding discussion is that, while East Timorese may not always verbally articulate their experiences of violence in the public sphere, they are actively negotiating the legacies of the conflict in an attempt to restore social life, and seek some form of repair and resolution, following years of conflict, distrust and dislocation.[87] The examples above illuminate that 'silence' reveals a great deal about the desire of many to maintain critical relationships, and to achieve a better life for their children, in a context of continuing violence, poverty and stigmatisation. They also speak to the significance of relational and embodied ways of knowing, communicating and responding to violence and of the agency and power of the ancestors. Although the practices and strategies in which people are engaged are not always successful, what is clear is that an enormous amount of *work* is taking place in the form of listening, delicacy, negotiation, the demonstration of commitment to family, kin, ancestors and land and discernment as to when to speak and when to stay silent. What emerges, in other words, is that the apparent absence of verbal communication about the conflict does not equate to forgetting or absence.

Collectively, the case studies discussed above reaffirm the importance of attending to the realm of the 'everyday'. Specifically, they highlight that everyday practices and strategies of social repair need to be taken seriously as they are often critical to the reconstruction of meaning, belonging, security and identity, even for those at the margins of society. What is at stake for East Timorese, as for many conflict-affected societies, 'is the reconstruction of social relationships, moral communities, cultural forms, economic networks and the reinvention of ritual life' which might enable people to make sense of suffering.[88] Many of these concerns, and the complex obligations people have to the living and the dead, necessarily fall outside the parameters of institutional transitional justice responses. The discussion above also enriches the existing literature on post-conflict social repair in at least two ways. First, it highlights that explorations of post-conflict silences and the everyday would do well to take greater account of the significance of non-verbal, relational and embodied, forms of communication. Second, it brings to the fore the extent of the daily *work* and fine calibration that underpins and informs many everyday strategies of social repair.

[86] Sakti above note 66 at 449.
[87] See McWilliam above note 22 at 218.
[88] Theidon above note 55 at 35.

Attending to the everyday disrupts the juxtaposition of speech versus silence, as it becomes clear that multiple ways of negotiating the legacies of violent conflict are possible, and that these may involve forms of communication that do not conform to the individualised, confessional model of healing prescribed by transitional justice mechanisms. Challenged, too, is the narrative of 'rupture' that is closely linked to ideas of therapeutic truth-telling. Indeed, what emerges from attention to everyday strategies of social repair in Timor-Leste is that these efforts are *ongoing*. While tentative forms of 'closure' and resolution may be possible, individuals, families and communities remain engaged in a dialogue with the past, rather than making a complete break with it. This dialogue is inherently built upon relationships; it requires the '"participation" of particular bodies which connect the dead to the living (and the not yet born)'.[89] That the dead play a central role in this ongoing dialogue — communicating through the dreams of their descendants, or in response to prayers at their gravesites — also draws attention to the existence of multiple temporalities, which destabilise the idea of rupture in a more radical sense.[90] The immediate, embodied presence of the spirit world in the here and now confounds a linear notion of time and highlights the degree to which 'the present is folded back into an always existing origin' that does not dissipate but is 'carried through the earth, the water, and the trees and the rocks' and forms part of a community 'comprised of kind and kind both living and deceased'.[91]

To attend to the multiple ways in which people seek to re-establish everyday life (and the place of silence within this) does not imply that the focus on speech by transitional justice scholars and practitioners should be abandoned. Of course it is valuable that, in Timor-Leste, as elsewhere, efforts are made to provide opportunities for people to speak about their experiences of harm and to construct a public, historical record of past conflict. The continual efforts by transitional justice practitioners to develop more sensitive ways of collecting and reporting survivors' testimonies are also needed to ensure that the experience of storytelling at a public truth-commission hearing, or of giving testimony is, at the very least, not harmful. It is certainly also the case that the limitations of truth-telling are increasingly recognised by transitional justice advocates, and that alternative forms of truth-telling are being explored, for example, through the arts, drama, public exhibitions and memorials. These forms of truth-telling are important because they might enable the public recognition of collective truths that cannot be spoken about.[92]

The point I wish to make is simply that the over-investment of speech with therapeutic and emancipatory power for individuals and the nation is problematic. This not only obscures the silences of transitional justice itself — the terms upon which coming to terms with the past are prescribed — but also makes it difficult to attend to the circumstances that mean, for some, speaking publicly is not possible or desirable. The privileging of speech, moreover, 'blinds us' to other forms of non-verbal expression or

89 Palmer above note 84 at 148.
90 See Igreja above note 17.
91 Grenfell above note 68 at 25.
92 I am grateful to an anonymous reviewer for this insight.

communication.[93] All of this suggests that rather than approaching silence with predetermined assumptions — viewing it as a 'problem' that needs to be fixed through new and better ways of collecting stories — transitional justice scholars and practitioners might pay more attention to its diverse meanings, and to the rich realm of everyday life in which they are embedded.

Disclosure Statement

No potential conflict of interest was reported by the author.

[93] Kidron above note 25 at 19.

Women Lawyers and the Struggle for Change in Conflict and Transition

Anna Bryson and Kieran McEvoy*

Abstract. This article examines the particular experiences of female 'cause-lawyers' in conflicted and transitional societies. Drawn from an ongoing comparative project which involved fieldwork in Cambodia, Chile, Israel, Palestine, Tunisia and South Africa, the paper looks at opportunities, obstacles and the obduracy required from such lawyers to 'make a difference' in these challenging contexts. Drawing upon the theoretical literature on the sociology of the legal profession, cause-lawyers, gender and transitional justice, and the structure/agency nexus, the article considers in turn the conflict/cause-lawyering intersection and the work of cause-lawyers in transitional contexts. It concludes by arguing that the case study of cause-lawyers offers a rebuttal to the charge that transitional justice is just like 'ordinary justice'. It also contends that, notwithstanding the durability of patriarchal power in transitional contexts, law remains a site of struggle, not acquiescence, and many of these cause-lawyers have and continue to exercise both agency and responsibility in 'taking on' that power.

1.0 Introduction

[I]t was tough. I think it was tough for men and women because, you know, we were fighting a system where the prosecutors or the presiding officers, everybody was hostile. ... It was a hard long fight right through. But being a woman obviously makes it even more difficult, you know.[1]

---

*The authors would like to acknowledge the Economic and Social Research Council (ESRC) which funded this research (Grant Reference ES/J009849/1), the anonymous reviewers and our colleagues on the project, Professor Louise Mallinder and Marny Requa. In addition, we would also like to thank those who gave useful feedback on previous versions of this paper presented at the Socio-Legal Studies Association inWarwick and the Law and Society Conference in Seattle in 2015.

[1] Personal interview with veteran struggle lawyer, Cape Town, South Africa, 12 August 2014.

> *There aren't a lot of women in, you know, in high ranking positions in the Bar Association ... And of course there's the organisational culture that comes with that — what is important, how you measure success, who is influential and how you become influential ... from the very beginning it's very masculine, it's a very masculine profession.*[2]

The study of transitional justice is already replete with analysis of the legal work and effect of various international and domestic courts and tribunals, amnesties, truth commissions and rule of law programmes.[3] The 'rule of law' is widely accepted as perhaps the key material and symbolic marker that denotes the break with the past in transitional societies.[4] While there is a significant literature on judicial appointments, independence and decision-making in transitional contexts,[5] the role of lawyers as social, political and moral actors outside the courts, or indeed as the 'real people at work in the system'[6] is much less developed. It is true that anthropologically influenced work on legal pluralism, postcolonial lawyering and transitional justice 'from below' does explore contests over the ownership of justice and the dominance of lawyers.[7] Indeed interdisciplinary critiques of excessive legalism are becoming increasingly common in the field.[8] While some scholars have examined the challenges of lawyering in conflicted and transitional societies,[9] such studies usually

---

[2] Personal interview with human rights lawyer and activist, Tel Aviv, Israel, 14 May 2014.

[3] Schabas William A and Bernaz Nadia *Routledge Handbook of International Criminal Law* Routledge Abingdon 2011; Mallinder Louise *Amnesty, Human Rights and Political Transitions: Bridging the Peace and Justice Divide* Hart Publishing Oxford 2008; Chapman Audrey R and Van der Merwe Hugo (eds) *Truth and Reconciliation in South Africa: Did the TRC Deliver?* University of Pennsylvania Press Philadelphia 2009.

[4] Teitel Ruti *Transitional Justice* Oxford University Press Oxford 2000; Czarnota Adam, Krygier Martin and Sadurski Wojciech (eds) *Rethinking the Rule of Law After Communism* Central European University Press Budapest 2006; Couso Javier, Huneeus Alexandra and Sieder Raches (eds) *Cultures of Legality: Judicialization and Political Activism in Latin America* Cambridge University Press Cambridge 2010.

[5] See, for example, Morison John, McEvoy Kieran and Anthony Gordon (eds) *Judges, Transition and Human Rights* Oxford University Press Oxford 2007; Hilbrink Lisa *Judges Beyond Politics in Democracy and Dictatorship: Lessons from Chile* Cambridge University Press Cambridge 2007.

[6] Friedman Lawrence *The Legal System: A Social Science Perspective* Russell Sage New York 1975 p 155.

[7] Engle Merry Sally *Human Rights and Gender Violence: Translating International Law into Local Justice* University of Chicago Press Chicago 2005; Sharafi Mitra 'A New History of Colonial Lawyering: Lihowski and Legal Identities' (2007) 32(4) *Law and Social Inquiry* 1059; McEvoy Kieran 'Beyond Legalism: Towards a Thicker Understanding of Transitional Justice' (2007) 34(4) *Journal of Law and Society* 411.

[8] See, for example, McEvoy Kieran and McGregor Lorna (eds) *Transitional Justice from Below: Grassroots Activism and the Struggle for Social Change* Hart Publishing Oxford 2008; Clark Phil *The Gacaca Courts, Post-Genocide Justice and Reconciliation in Rwanda* Cambridge University Press Cambridge 2010; Palmer Nicola *Courts in Conflict: Interpreting the Layers of Justice in Post-Genocide Rwanda* Oxford University Press Oxford 2015.

[9] Abel Richard L *Politics By Other Means: Law and the Struggle Against Apartheid in South Africa 1980–1994* Routledge London 1995; Caiger Andrew *Cause Lawyering in South Africa: The Process of Empowering a Rights Based Legal Culture and its Socio-Political Impact* Austin & Winfield San Francisco 2005; Dezalay Yves and Garth Bryant G *The Internationalization of Palace Wars: Lawyers, Economists and the Contest to Transform Latin American States* University of Chicago Press Chicago 2002; Hajjar Lisa *Courting Conflict: The Israeli Military Court System in the West*

focus on one case study, and correspondingly few examine the particular role of female lawyers in such contexts.

This article is drawn from a large comparative study of lawyers in six jurisdictions, namely Cambodia, Chile, Israel, Palestine, Tunisia and South Africa.[10] In 2014 we conducted a total of 40 semi-structured interviews with women lawyers and activists (from a total of over 120 interviews spread across the jurisdictions). Although our questions on gender were addressed to both male and female interviewees the quotes cited in this article are exclusively drawn from interviews with women.[11] The jurisdictions were chosen in order that we might do 'structured, focused comparisons'[12] drawing on semi-structured interviews with key actors in order to provide a balance that allows for a nuanced grasp of the local and the potential for cautious 'mid-range theorising'.[13] The case studies were specifically chosen to capture different dynamics which interested us: (a) countries with a history of violence and/or oppression at different stages of transition; (b) jurisdictions from the principal 'legal families'[14] (i.e. the Common Law tradition, the Civil Law Tradition, Islamic tradition, as well as Asian and African legal tradition); and (c) jurisdictions which variously had experience of cause- or struggle-lawyering, international justice and past focused transitional justice. As evidenced by the quotes above, the focus of the interviews was both on the material areas of struggle in which the interviewees were engaged and also their experiences as women lawyers working in what were often viewed as patriarchal legal cultures.

For the current paper, we seek to explore issues which illuminate the struggles of women lawyers in such settings while still acknowledging the very real distinctions both between the lawyers themselves and between case studies at varying stages of conflict and transition. As Meintjies, Pillay and Turshen have argued, 'women who

---

Bank and Gaza University of California Press Santa Monica 2005; Collins Cath *Post-Transitional Justice: Human Rights Trials in Chile and El Salvador* Pennsylvania State University Press University Park 2010.

[10] As noted above, this major international comparative research project is funded by the Economic and Social Research Council (ES/J009849/1). See www.lawyersconflictandtransition.org (last visited 8 January 2016).

[11] In Cambodia due to ongoing concerns regarding both personal safety and professional life, each of the three women we interviewed asked to be referred to simply as 'an international lawyer'. In Chile we spoke to a government lawyer, the director of a human rights organisation, a legal academic and human rights activist, a lawyer in private practice and a civil society activist. Our cohort in Israel included three legal academics and human rights activists, a politician and lawyer, three lawyers working in human rights NGOs and two lawyers working in private practice. In Palestine the women we interviewed included three female lawyers employed by human rights NGOs, a lawyer in private practice and a civil society activist. In Tunisia female interviewees included one of Ben Ali's former lawyers and allies, two Europeans working for Tunisian-based NGOs, three 'cause-lawyers' working in private practice and two lawyers working for human rights NGOs. Finally, in South Africa we interviewed two celebrated female cause-lawyers, a legal academic and activist and a former ANC activist.

[12] Zartman I William 'Comparative Case Studies' (2005) 10 *International Negotiation* 3 at 7.

[13] Merton Robert *On Theoretical Sociology* Free Press New York 1968.

[14] Glenn H Patrick 'Comparative Legal Families and Comparative Legal Traditions' in Reimann Mathias and Zimmermann Reinhard (eds) *The Oxford Handbook of Comparative Law* Oxford University Press Oxford 2006 p 421–440.

live through war and conflict do not fall into a single group'.[15] To seek to present the experiences of women lawyers as 'the same' in one jurisdiction, never mind six, would fall into the well-identified trap of essentialising the lives of women in transitional justice while getting on with the 'serious business' of discussing the lives of men in all of their intricacies and complexities.[16] As is discussed below, there are important ways in which gender intersects with variables such as race, class and religion, and of course the local context in which these women lawyers work directly impacts upon their professional and personal lives. With regard to the latter, each jurisdiction has its own unique historical, cultural, religious and political variables, as well as different legal cultures. For example, in Chile, one cannot but acknowledge the very specific influence of the Catholic Church in shaping both approaches to dealing with the past and related issues concerning the cause of female equality. In South Africa, the particular prominence of some women in the struggle (with many straddling the ranks of struggle-lawyers and the women's movement) is sometimes evidenced to eulogise the advances in women's civil and political rights in transition — an assumption which we question.[17] In a somewhat analogous fashion, the experiences of women cause-lawyers in Israel and Palestine must be framed within the broader reality of the ongoing occupation and associated conflict. Central to our approach to comparative research is to 'make sense of difference'.[18] While foregrounding important distinctions between the lawyers we interviewed and the local variables across all of the case studies, we seek to draw out key themes which allow us the opportunity to develop what Popper referred to as 'contingent empirical generalisations', that is to say contingent because they apply usually under certain (specified) conditions, and empirical because they are derived from close analyses of a range of historical cases.[19]

It might be useful at this stage to offer a brief overview of some of the key concepts which inform the discussions in this paper. In particular, we draw on some of the most relevant literature on cause-lawyers, gender and the legal profession, gender in transitional justice and the structure agency nexus.

In all of the societies we have been researching law has been used as a tool of repression by the state and, to varying degrees, as one source of resistance by those engaged in political and social struggles for change. Inevitably in such contexts, the role of lawyers becomes crucial, whether as detached professionals 'delivering a service' to their clients or as self-conscious *political* actors who use 'legal skills to pursue ends and ideals that transcend client service' within and beyond the court as part of such

---

[15] Meintjies Sheila, Pillay Anu and Turshen Meredeth (eds) *The Aftermath: Women in Post-Conflict Transformation* Zed Books London 2001 p 16.

[16] Alam Mayesha *Women and Transitional Justice* Palgrave London 2004 p 3.

[17] Hassim notes, for example, that '[t]he transition to democracy in South Africa ushered in a formal institutional framework and a government that has been held up as a model of serious commitment to the ideal of gender equality'. Hassim Shireen 'The Gender Pact and Democratic Consolidation: Institutionalizing Gender Equality in the South African State' (2003) *Feminist Studies* 29(3) 505 at 505. See further Waylen Georgina *Engendering Transitions: Women's Mobilizations, Institutions and Gender Outcomes* Oxford University Press Oxford 2007 p 199–202.

[18] Nelken David *Comparative Criminal Justice: Making Sense of Difference* Sage Publications London 2010.

[19] Popper Karl *The Logic of Scientific Discovery* Routledge London 1959.

broader struggles.[20] 'Cause-lawyering' is the genre of scholarship most associated with analysing such lawyers. Sarat and Scheingold have edited a number of important US-based and international collections detailing the ways in which cause-lawyers contest prevailing political, social, moral or legal power. While there are multiple definitions, at its core cause-lawyering is a form of 'moral activism' which transcends the boundaries between the legal and the political, wherein committed lawyers 'do more' than simply deploy their technical services on behalf of their client.[21] Such lawyers may engage in both pro bono and paid work, strategic litigation, develop networks and relationships, or indeed become part of broader social or political movements and view their responsibilities as going well beyond the court room or lawyers' office to argue and mobilise publicly for the 'cause'.[22] Cause-lawyers are essentially much more comfortable than conventional lawyers with the view that the law and lawyering is quintessentially political.

Within the broader sociology of the legal profession from which the cause-lawyering literature emerges, there is not surprisingly a significant focus on gender. A range of scholar-activists have captured well the close interrelationship between feminist law reform and the gendered structure of the legal profession.[23] For example, Menkel-Meadow has argued that the 'story' of women's entry to the legal profession is, for most nations, an 'easy one to tell': university education expanded exponentially in the 1970s, many of the most significant formal barriers to women entering the profession were lifted and, in tandem with wider cultural developments and changing societal attitudes towards women's roles in family and professional life, women did make advances in the legal profession.[24] However, despite women now constituting over half of law school entrants in many settled democracies, numerous analyses have charted that informal barriers to advancement (as reflected in earnings, career progression and status), still persist. Further markers of inequality include the concentration of women in silos of 'gendered legal work' (for example, over-representation in government, public interest and family law) and significantly higher attrition rates

[20] Sarat Austin and Scheingold Stuart A *Something to Believe In: Politics, Professionalism and Cause-Lawyering* Stanford University Press Palo Alto 2004 p 3–4.

[21] Boukalas Christos 'Politics as Legal Action / Lawyers as Political Actors: Towards a Reconceptualisation of Cause Lawyering' (2013) 22(3) *Social & Legal Studies* 395.

[22] Devyani Prabhat 'After 9/11: Guantánamo and the Mobilization of Lawyers' (2011) 54 *Studies in Law, Politics, and Society* 213; Garcia Melanie 'The Lawyer as Gatekeeper: Ethical Guidelines for Representing a Client with a Social Change Agenda' (2011) 24 *Georgetown Journal of Legal Ethics* 551.

[23] Prominent scholar-activists include Catharine MacKinnon, Ruth Bader Ginsburg, Martha Fineman, Mari Matsuda and Frances Webber. See Grant Bowman Cynthia and Schneider Elizabeth M 'Feminist Legal Theory, Feminist Lawmaking, and the Legal Profession' (1998) 67(2) *Fordham Law Review* 249; Scales Ann *Legal Feminism: Activism, Lawyering, and Legal Theory* New York University Press New York 2006.

[24] Menkel-Meadow Carrie 'The Comparative Sociology of Women Lawyers: The "Feminization" of the Legal Profession' (1986) 24(4) *Osgoode Hall Law Journal* 897 at 897. Not surprisingly many of these key developments reflected (and informed) evolving feminist legal theories. For an analysis of the competing sway of difference and dominance theories see, for example, MacKinnon Catharine *Feminism Unmodified: Discourses on Life and Law* Harvard University Press Cambridge 1987 p 32–45.

amongst female lawyers in many areas of the profession.[25] Some of the richest discussions on these material realities explore whether patriarchal legal cultures are changed by the increased numbers of women or whether women 'adapt' to essentially male working practices and norms;[26] whether women perform law differently to men;[27] whether women define success in the legal profession differently to men;[28] and how gender intersects with race, ethnicity and other variables in the legal profession.[29] Notwithstanding the 'exceptional' circumstances of the conflicted and transitional societies in which we conducted our research (discussed below), many of these debates were very familiar to the women lawyers we interviewed.

Our views in this paper are also of course influenced by the rich literature on gender and transitional justice. That literature is discussed in detail elsewhere in this issue, but for our purposes a number of themes are particularly relevant. Firstly, we note the tendency in transitional justice to frame the experiences of women in binary terms as either passive victims (for example, in court proceedings, before truth commissions, applying for reparations) or as agents (for example, as politicians,

[25] See, for example, Larson Magali S *The Rise of Professionalism: A Sociological Analysis* University of California Press Berkeley 1977; Curran Barbara A *The Lawyer Statistical Report: A Statistical Profile of the US Legal Profession in the 1980s* American Bar Foundation Chicago 1985; Hagan John 'The Gender Stratification of Income Inequality Among Lawyers' (1990) 68(3) *Social Forces* 835; Bolton Sharon C and Muzio Daniel 'Can't Live With 'Em; Can't Live Without 'Em: Gendered Segmentation in the Legal Profession (2007) 41(1) *Sociology* 47; Payne-Pikus Monique, Hagan John and Nelson Robert L 'Experiencing Discrimination: Race and Retention in America's Largest Law Firms' (2010) 44(3) *Law and Society* 553. For the relevant Australian data see 'Beyond the Statistical Gap: 2009 Court Appearance Strategy for Advancing Appearances by Female Advocates in Australian Courts' Law Council of Australia 2009 p 10–11, 15–16; 'National Attrition and Re-engagement Study (NARS) Report' Law Council of Australia 2012 p 9.

[26] Menkel-Meadow Carrie above note 24 at 897. Schultz and Shaw's authoritative overview of women in the legal profession addresses this fundamental question in the context of fifteen civil and common law jurisdictions. Schultz Ulrike and Shaw Gisela (eds) *Women in the World's Legal Professions* Oxford University Press Oxford 2003.

[27] Butler's *Gender Trouble* attacks what she considers to be an underlying assumption of feminist theory, namely that there is a gendered identity that requires representation in discourse and politics. It advances from the notion that gender is essentially 'performative' and that the associated 'acts' constitute — rather than express — the illusion of a stable gender identity. Butler Judith *Gender Trouble: Feminism and the Subversion of Identity* Routledge London 1990.

[28] See, for example, Menkel-Meadow Carrie 'Portia in a Different Voice: Speculations on a Women's Lawyering Process' (1985) 1 *Berkeley Women's Law Journal* 39; Menkel-Meadow Carrie 'Exploring a Research Agenda of the Feminization of the Legal Profession: Theories of Gender and Social Change' (1989) 14(2) *Law and Social Inquiry* 289; Menkel-Meadow Carrie 'Portia Redux: Another Look at Gender, Feminism and Legal Ethics' in Parker Stephen and Sampford Charles (eds) *Legal Ethics and Legal Practice: Contemporary Issues* Clarendon Press Oxford 1995 p 25.

[29] Tomlinson Jennifer, Muzio Daniel, Sommerlad Hilary, Webley Lisa and Duff Liz 'Structure, Agency and Career Strategies of White Women and Black and Minority Ethnic Individuals in the Legal Profession' (2013) 66(2) *Human Relations* 245 at 246; Hanlon Gerard 'Institutional Forms and Organizational Structures: Homology, Trust and Reputational Capital in Professional Service Firms' (2004) 11(2) *Organization* 186; Sommerlad Hilary 'The "Social Magic" of Merit: Diversity, Equity, and Inclusion in the English and Welsh Legal Profession' (2015) 83 *Fordham Law Review* 2330; Pearce Russell G, Wald Eli and Ballakrishnen Swethaa 'Difference Blindness vs Bias Awareness: Why Law Firms With the Best of Intentions Have Failed to Create Diverse Partnerships' (2015) 83 *Fordham Law Review* 2407.

NGO activists, negotiators, judges and lawyers).[30] Secondly, efforts to ensure that gender-based harms form part of the legal architecture of transitional justice and that women are involved in all stages of a peace process have been key features of transitional justice praxis and scholarship since at least the 1990s.[31] But in spite of this formal and institutional attention to gendered harms and the participatory rights of women, it is clear that the inclusion of women (whether as victims or agents) has offered no guarantee of substantive and material gains.[32] Moreover there are familiar challenges which relate directly to the work of women cause-lawyers. From some commentators, the inherent limitations of legalism for women in particular[33] channels precious resources and energies into legal strategies, thus distracting from other potentially more successful tactics, camouflaging root problems and issues and providing a veneer of legitimacy for fundamentally flawed institutions and procedures.[34] In addition, in

---

[30] Waylen above note 17; Ní Aoláin Fionnuala 'Advancing Feminist Positioning in the Field of Transitional Justice' (2012) 6(2) *International Journal of Transitional Justice* 1 at 5. For a fascinating account of the struggle to ensure that women were included in the constitutional negotiations to create a Democratic South Africa see Albertyn Catherine 'Women and the Transition to Democracy in South Africa' in Kaganas Felicity and Murray Christina (eds) *Gender and the New South African Legal Order* Juta Cape Town 1994 p 54.

[31] See, for example, Mayesha above note 16; Bedont Barbara and Hail-Martinez Katherine 'Ending Impunity for Gender Crimes Under the International Criminal Court' (1999) 6 *Journal of World Affairs* 65; Campbell Kirsten 'The Gender of Transitional Justice: Law, Sexual Violence and the International Criminal Tribunal for the Former Yugoslavia' (2007) 3 *International Journal of Transitional Justice* 411. UN Security Council Resolution 1325 (2000) emphasised the need for increased participation of women at all stages of peace processes. In October 2015, the UN Security Council unanimously adopted Resolution 2242 to improve implementation of that agenda. Speaking at the launch of the report Phumzile Mlambo-Ngcuka, Executive Director of the UN Entity for Gender Equality and the Empowerment of Women, stated that 'a growing body of evidence had shown that perhaps the greatest but most under-used tool for building peace was the meaningful inclusion of women'. Full text available at <www.un.org/press/en/2015/sc12076.doc.htm> Accessed 19 January 2016.

[32] For an analysis of the extent to which the gender perspective of UN Security Council Resolution 1325 was reflected in peace agreements signed between January 1990 and January 2010 see Bell Christine and O'Rourke Catherine 'Peace Agreements or Pieces of Paper? The Impact of UNSC Resolution 1325 on Peace Processes and their Agreements' (2010) 59(4) *International and Comparative Law Quarterly* 941. For a criticism of the resolution as an apt example of 'gender mainstreaming' see Ní Aoláin Fionnuala, Haynes Francesca and Cahn Naomi *On the Frontlines: Gender, War, and the Post-Conflict Process* Oxford University Press Oxford 2011 p 11, 16–18. See also Mertus Julie 'Shouting from the Bottom of a Well: The Impact of International Trials for Wartime Rape on Women's Agency' (2004) 6 *International Feminist Journal of Politics* 110 and O'Rourke Catherine *Gender Politics in Transitional Justice* Routledge London 2013 p 63–82.

[33] The result for women may be, as suggested by Harris Rimmer, new curtains, cut from the same cloth. Harris Rimmer Susan 'Sexing the Subject of Transitional Justice' (2014) 32(1) *Australian Feminist Law Journal* 136 at 123. See further Chinkin Christine, Charlesworth Hilary and Wright Shelley 'Feminist Approaches to International Law: Reflections from Another Century' in Buss Doris and Maji Ambreena (eds) *International Law: Modern Feminist Approaches* Hart Publishing Oxford and Portland Oregon 2005 p 17–47.

[34] Bell and O'Rourke suggested in a seminal essay in 2007 that transitional justice mechanisms should be assessed strategically, in terms of the likely substantive and material gains for women. Bell Christine and O'Rourke Catherine 'Does Feminism Need a Theory of Transitional Justice? An Introductory Essay' (2007) 1 *International Journal of Transitional Justice* 23. Similarly Ní Aoláin notes that 'an uncritical and narrowly liberal conception of gender equality directs our gaze away from the cultural, material and geopolitical sites in which transitional justice practices have emerged'. Ní Aoláin

many transitional contexts there are almost always complex intersections between gender and the larger big 'P' political struggles. We note in particular that 'opportunities for progress' may in hindsight be viewed as moments of retrenchment, as patriarchal cultures and practices often prove highly resistant to transitional energies once political change is embedded.[35] Again all of these themes were reflected in the experiences of the women lawyers we interviewed.

Finally, the paper is informed by some of the most relevant academic discussions on the intersection between structure and agency. That literature is notoriously complex.[36] At base level, the study of the structure agency nexus concerns the extent to which human behaviour or actions (agency) is shaped by forces which are beyond their control. As Marx famously observed, 'men [sic] make their own history but they do not make it just as they please, they do not make it under circumstances chosen by themselves, but under circumstances directly encountered, given and transmitted from the past'.[37] The structural context, or what Durkheim has termed 'social facts' of the social, political, cultural, legal and of course gendered realties of sites such as Pinochet's Chile, Apartheid South Africa, contemporary Palestine or the other contexts discussed herein inevitably influenced the work of the cause-lawyers we interviewed.[38] However, as we discuss further in the conclusion, the energetic and inventive approach to activism which many of these lawyers brought and bring to their work, provides a useful corrective to an overly deterministic and at worse disempowering reading of the power of structural variables to control human action. Structures are not 'immutable constraints'.[39] Notwithstanding the durability of some such structural constraints, the agency exercised by women cause-lawyers

above note 30 at 2. See further Yarwood Lisa (ed.) *Women and Transitional Justice: The Experience of Women as Participants* London Routledge 2013.

35 Ní Aoláin and Hamilton suggest, for example, that 'the moment' of transition can, from a feminist perspective, be one of 'retrenchment'. Such retrenchment, they suggest, is arguably located in the core private/public division that accompanies the rule of law in theory and practice. Ní Aoláin Fionnuala and Hamilton Michael 'Gender and the Rule of Law in Transitional Societies' 11 March 2009 Minnesota Legal Studies Research Paper No 09–12 p 102. Citing the specific example of the work of truth commissions, Ní Aoláin and Turner further suggest that the construction of narratives of former conflict often translates into a 'retrenchment of patriarchal family norms and the reassignment of highly circumscribed gender roles for women'. Ní Aoláin Fionnuala and Turner Catherine 'Gender, Truth and Transition' (2007) 16 *UCLA Women's Law Journal* 229 at 273.

36 For an overview see Bourdieu Pierre *Outline of a Theory of Practice* trans Nice Richard Cambridge University Press Cambridge 1997; Giddens Anthony *The Constitution of Society: Outline of the Theory of Structuration* Polity Press Oxford 1984; Elder-Vas David *The Causal Power of Social Structures: Emergence, Structure and Agency* Cambridge University Press Cambridge 2010; Archer Margaret *Structure, Agency and the Internal Conversation* Cambridge University Press Cambridge 2003.

37 Marx Karl 'The Eighteenth Brumaire of Louis Bonaparte' in Feuer Lewis (ed.) *Marx and Engels: Basic Writings on Politics and Philosophy* Doubleday New York 1959 p 320.

38 Durkheim Emile *The Rules of Sociological Method* Free Press republished Free Press New York 2014, especially Chapters One and Two.

39 Ewick Patricia and Silbey Susan *The Common Place of Law: Stories from Everyday Life* University of Chicago Press Chicago 1998 p 41.

in even the most difficult of circumstances underlines the fact that in Sarat and Scheingold's terms, they are there to be 'taken on'.[40]

2.0 Cause-Lawyers and 'The Struggle'

> *Q: Do you see yourself as a political lawyer?*
>
> *A: Yes.*
>
> *Q: Let's define that, tell me what is a political or a cause-lawyer?*
>
> *A: A political lawyer I would say is a person who does not act for the money but he sees his work as part of the struggle, as the aiding part, as the backbone of the struggle and uses the limited possibilities available through the law to improve the general good.*[41]

It is something of a truism that political conflict and struggles against authoritarian regimes may offer somewhat paradoxical opportunities for women's empowerment.[42] On the one hand the gendered realities of sexual abuse, poverty and what True has called the 'political economy' of violence against women, which is so often synonymous with conflict, has been well documented.[43] On the other hand, the involvement of men in conflict, whether in the context of involvement in armed organisations, imprisonment or even being killed or injured, may offer the chance for women to become what Meintjies, Pillay and Turshen have referred to as 'agents of change'.[44] Such agency is not restricted to the familial sphere and may be reflected in community, political or professional life.[45] Recalling her experience of the first intifada, one Palestinian lawyer in the West Bank told us:

> *The mum became a huge kind of 'responsibility-taker' in a way that wasn't [the case] in the past. In addition women were entering the political sphere and not just the political sphere, but the activist sphere ... many of the men actually were imprisoned and what does that mean*

[40] Sarat Austin and Scheingold Stuart 'The Dynamics of Cause Lawyering' in Sarat Austin and Scheingold Stuart (eds) *The Worlds Cause Lawyers Make: Structure and Agency in Legal Practice* Stanford University Press California 2005 p 7.

[41] Personal interview with human rights lawyer, Ramallah, Palestine, 20 May 2014. As in other contexts, female interviewees sometimes employed the male pronoun to refer to women and men.

[42] Meintjies Sheila, Pillay Anu and Turshen Meredeth 'There is No Aftermath for Women' in Meintjies Pillay and Turshen above note 15 at 7.

[43] Giles Wenona and Hyndman Jennifer (eds) *Sites of Violence: Gender and Conflict Zones* University of California Press Berkeley 2004; Buvinic Mayra, Das Gupta Monica, Casabonne Ursula and Verwimp Philip 'Violent Conflict and Gender Inequality: An Overview' (2013) 28(1) *World Bank Research Observer* 110; True Jacqui *The Political Economy of Violence Against Women* Oxford University Press Oxford 2012.

[44] Meintjies Pillay and Turshen above note 15 at 16. Of course some women also become directly involved in armed struggle themselves. See, for example, Ibanez Ana Cristina 'El Salvador: War and Untold Stories, Women Guerrillas' in Mosner Caroline O N and Clark Fiona C (eds) *Victims, Perpetrators or Actors: Gender, Armed Conflict and Political Violence* Zed Books London 2001 p 117; Yarwood above note 34.

[45] Bell and O'Rourke above note 32 at 41. See further Ní Aoláin Fionnuala, Hayes Francesca and Cahn Naomi *On the Frontlines: Gender, War and the Post-Conflict Process* Oxford University Press Oxford 2011 p 6; O'Rourke above note 32 at 4–5.

> *for the woman that has to stay home and become the breadwinner and take care of the family and do all the traditional [male] roles? ... I think all of that kind of spurred more of an understanding of what their rights could be or should be.*[46]

In the legal profession, the sheer volume of arrests, trials and human rights violations associated with periods of protracted violence and conflict not surprisingly creates opportunities for lawyers — both male and female — who are willing to take on such 'political' cases. As noted above, across the six jurisdictions we interviewed a total of 40 women human rights activists and lawyers. In some instances, these women have become what Hansford has described as 'legendary' lawyers.[47] Certainly figures such as Leah Tsemel, Gaby Lasky, Carmen Hertz, Radhia Nassaoui, Yasmin Sooka, Priscilla Jana and others interviewed for this project have all received national or international accolades as well as criticism and harassment for their work as 'cause-lawyers'. For some of these women, their work on gender-related issues intersected with cause-lawyering on other broader political struggles:

> *I was involved in women's organisations from the very beginning and thought that was the direction I was going ... when I came back after having that time outside of Israel and getting some new perspective, I realised that what I think is really the most urgent and most important thing to deal with is Palestinian rights.*[48]

> *I was involved first as an activist in student politics, protesting against the regime ... when I became a lawyer I was involved in defending students and human rights activists ... I was also a member of a feminist association and we worked on what we saw as political issues as well, including delicate and sensitive cases such as rape or sexual harassment or any kind of assault that is directed against a girl or a woman. I worked on a case about an old lady seventy years old, [name] who was harassed on all levels economically, sexually, socially all levels and it took two years, campaign of two years in order to get her justice. Many other cases such as representing a 12 year [old] child who was the victim of rape or sexual harassment where the judge and prosecutor wish to dismiss the case because of her age ... such cases are 'feminist' on the surface but of course behind such cases there are many political waves.*[49]

Other women cause-lawyers viewed themselves primarily as political activists engaged in the broader political struggle and their work was seen as an expression of their commitment to the political struggle as a whole. In effect for some such lawyers, there appears little difference between law and politics, as they set about 'fabricating political action with legal tools and legal action that responds to political necessity'.[50] Indeed for some, the status of lawyer was one that allowed an expression of their

[46] Personal interview with international human rights lawyer, Ramallah, Palestine, 22 May 2014.
[47] Hansford Justin 'The Legal Ethics of Nelson Mandela' forthcoming *New York Law Review*, available at: www.ssrn.com abstract no 2556320.
[48] Personal interview with international human rights lawyer, Tel Aviv, Israel, 14 May 2014.
[49] Personal interview with cause lawyer, Tunis, Tunisia, 16 June 2014.
[50] See Sarat and Scheingold above note 40 at 9; Boukalas Christos 'Politics as Legal Action/Lawyers as Political Actors: Towards a Reconceptualisation of Cause Lawyering (2013) 22(3) *Social and Legal Studies* 395; Michalowski Raymond 'All or Nothing: An Inquiry into the (Im)Possibility of Cause Lawyering Under Cuban Socialism' in Sarat Austin and Scheingold Stuart A *Cause Lawyering: Political Commitments and Professional Responsibilities* Oxford University Press Oxford 1998.

activism, a space to work on what Sarat and Scheingold term 'a transformative agenda' that is often not available in other walks of life in repressive regimes.[51]

> *I myself was an activist, a political activist before becoming a lawyer you know. I was always of course a supporter of the ANC ... in my student days I became a very active person in the Black Consciousness movement ... And then I qualified as a lawyer ... I was also an activist; then I had become a very active member, underground member of the ANC and part of an ANC cell. But that's beside the point. The point is that to become a human rights lawyer in any conflict situation I think you cannot separate your moral duties and your political duties from your legal duties. I think it's all one.*[52]

> *I've been a lawyer since 1985 so as with many students I was a university activist and then when I started being a lawyer I started defending political detainees, political prisoners arrested for freedom of expression issues and so on ... I like the profession. Being a lawyer has been the only perhaps the only area of national life that Ben Ali could not co-opt.*[53]

> *I went into exile after the coup because my husband was killed so I left the country with my son and I was away for three years. And when I came back I went immediately and started to work at the Vicaría de la Solidaridad — as a full time lawyer there at the Vicaría. And that was at the beginning of '77. I went there because of my political convictions. I went there to defend the people who were being persecuted and to denounce the crimes that were happening. It was the first real space of resistance that opened in Chile. And that was the role that we played. We were a generation that they tried to eliminate, that they tried to persecute, we were that 60s generation. That's the reason I became a human rights lawyer.*[54]

Needless to say that for many such lawyers there were (and in some cases still are) significant personal consequences for engagement in such work. In extremis, in Cambodia the systematic murder of lawyers, judges and professors was part of the genocidal strategy of the Khmer Rouge to eradicate the educated, the bourgeoisie and all others deemed a threat to the regime.[55] In Chile, while some lawyers who were deemed to be affiliated to leftist or communist organisations were murdered, disappeared or

[51] Sarat and Scheingold above note 20 at 20.

[52] Personal interview with international human rights lawyer, Cape Town, South Africa, 12 August 2014.

[53] Personal interview with cause-lawyer and prisoner rights activist, Tunis, Tunisia, 20 June 2014. Zine al-Abidine Ben Ali was the authoritarian President of Tunisia for 23 years. In January 2011 he was forced to resign and flee to Saudi Arabia; he was subsequently sentenced in absentia for embezzlement and corruption.

[54] Personal interview with international human rights lawyer, Santiago, Chile, 28 April 2014. The Vicariate of Solidarity was an agency of the Chilean Catholic Church under the Archdiocese of Santiago which became one of Chile's most high-profile NGOs litigating on behalf of political prisoners and others abducted and tortured by the Pinochet regime. Its effectiveness and ability to operate was widely attributed to the protection of the Church.

[55] It is estimated that the Khmer Rouge regime murdered all but 6–12 of the country's 400–600 lawyers. See Donovan Dolores A 'Cambodia: Building a Legal System from Scratch' (1993) 27(2) *The International Lawyer* 445. One of our Cambodian interviewees stated: 'In Cambodia they killed not just lawyers, they killed everybody — they killed a whole generation. Today you'll hardly find people of my generation aged between 50 and 60 ... those that are the foundation of a country, those that are educated — teachers, lawyers, doctors, psychiatrists, engineers, they all were gone ... lawyers, particularly lawyers, you know, I think only a few survived'. Personal interview with NGO lawyer, Phnom Penh, Cambodia, 10 March 2014.

expelled, lawyers did enjoy some degree of protection because of their professional, international or local affiliations. Even so, the violence and intimidation was often directed at others associated with cause-lawyers.[56]

> *The protection of the Church gave us some kind of immunity, some level for various reasons ... the Cardinal had a permanent interlocutor with the military he could talk to them. Almost all of our activities were public they weren't clandestine. We were the main interlocutor with the UN we would go to Geneva but there were exceptions ... In my case they killed the little woman who worked in my house who helped me with cleaning my house so she's one of the people officially recognised as victim of human rights violations. They killed her to intimidate me.*[57]

In other contexts, pressure came in the form of threats, harassment (often sexualised) and intimidation by the police, military or even opposing lawyers. An Israeli lawyer highlighted the particular danger of sexual violence — whether actual or implied — when she was identified as a human rights activist.

> *One of them was an incident I had where I was verbally attacked for the work I did and for being a woman. In Tel Aviv while sitting in a bar. This was a bar we used to come after work with the office so he recognised [named cause-lawyer, head of the firm] of course and then me by association. The next week while I was there not surrounded by colleagues and male colleagues and kind of unprotected he just started saying horrible things. And what was worse for me about that experience was that I didn't respond the way that I wanted to, I was just so shocked. He said 'If I see you in a dark alley you should be raped.' And the management in the place did nothing. I ended up leaving. It took me a while to realise how much it influenced me because I found myself sitting at home and saying oh, I should have said this, I should have did that and this is very typical for kind of victims of sexual harassment ... So I think this incident kind of left a stamp on me. Later on when the threats and the derogatory speech were more general, you know, directed at all people doing human rights, being a fifth wheel and traitors etc., stuff that even politicians here say, I think it kind of always brought me back to that incident.*[58]

Another human rights activist in Israel recounted similar instances of being threatened with both physical and sexual violence in custody, including being shackled in a cell with other female detainees and tortured with a taser gun.[59] In the case of Tunisia, such direct intimidation was also over-layered with gendered efforts to diminish the reputation of the women lawyers.

> *It was difficult for us because they would beat us sometimes, but they would beat us less than they do the men. I was actually kicked by one of the policemen wearing those big heavy boots and my leg was swollen for a while. But they would more often say we were women with a bad*

[56] See Snyder Edward C 'Dirty Legal War: Human Rights and the Rule of Law in Chile 1973–1995' (1994) 2 *Tulsa Journal of Comparative and International Law* 253.
[57] Personal interview with international human rights lawyer, Santiago, Chile, 28 April 2014.
[58] From a personal point of view she also noted that dealing with the military courts and witnessing the suffering that was inflicted on young people especially, day after day, eventually took a toll. Personal interview with legal academic and human rights activist, Tel Aviv, Israel, 14 May 2014.
[59] Personal interview with human rights activist, Ramallah, Palestine, 22 May 2014.

reputation ... they would always accuse us of being informants, of cooperating with foreigners, as 'sell-outs' as it were, as well as being women of bad reputation.[60]

Interviewees also talked to us about the personal, familial and relationship toll of involvement in cause-lawyering in such contexts. In some instances, this appeared a more extreme version of the 'total commitment' and long working hours complaints associated with commercial legal firms.[61] A well-known Israeli cause lawyer noted:

There used to be a time when I read the newspaper in the morning and I knew that in the evening I would represent the person who planted the bomb ... It was difficult for my family — very much, oh very much. To be hated, you know, and it was sheer hatred but I didn't care so much, for me it was okay.[62]

Speaking to the South African context, a former ANC activist noted that being a 'struggle-lawyer' like other forms of intense political activism during the conflict and transition was not compatible with 'normal' family life:

I think being a struggle-lawyer is — it's not nine to five, firstly. It can be at any time and normally all the arrests were only ever happening from night onwards — so you couldn't have a nine to five. So there's the time that you have to put in, but there's also the kind of danger you were in.[63]

As in other contexts, the familial consequences of such work and activism were often most acutely felt once the 'adrenalin' of conflict began to subside — in the case of South Africa after the 1994 elections which saw the ANC come to power and Nelson Mandela elected President. She continued:

I don't think there was a single, well maybe a handful of activists that still have their original partners that they had when they started out. For the rest, no, divorce rate is very high ... I think the amount you had to put in, you know, and it wasn't just time. You had to put yourself in and the implications of that on family and that were quite high ... there was also the gender issue. So the female activists, you know, we're also not sitting in our slippers anymore, you know, we can do things for ourselves. And we have opinions and for those who became activists it meant they fought a bitter battle at home as well for their voices to be heard ... and after the elections where things started settling down and now we all

[60] Personal interview with cause-lawyer, Tunis, Tunisia, 20 June 2014.

[61] For those who accept the 'double-burden' as a given, the reform of working practices — in particular the demands for long and unsociable working hours and the corresponding celebration of the 'ideal employee' as one who works full time, overtime and with no career interruptions — is an absolute priority. See Cha Youngjoo 'Overwork and the Persistence of Gender Segregation in Occupations' (2013) 27(2) *Gender and Society* 158; Williams Joan C *Unbending Gender: Why Family and Work Conflict and What to do About it* Oxford University Press New York 2000; Korzec Rebecca 'Working on the "Mommy-Track": Motherhood and Women Lawyers' (1997) 8 *Hastings Women's Law Journal* 117.

[62] Personal interview with human rights lawyer, Ramallah, Palestine, 20 May 2014.

[63] Personal interview with former ANC and human rights activist, Johannesburg, South Africa, 15 August 2014.

> *have to find ways of getting into a normal life. What is a normal life? You know, you've lived on this adrenaline for so long.*[64]

In sum, many of the issues raised by the women cause-lawyers we interviewed resonated with the experiences of male cause-lawyers elsewhere. The explicit politicisation of lawyering and the conception of legal settings as a site of struggle are very familiar themes in the cause-lawyering and sociology of lawyers literature. In the context of women lawyers, their experience of struggle also intersects in complex ways with gender — both in terms of the areas in which they work (for example, whether they are focused explicitly on gender equality or other aspects of political and social struggle) and in the ways in which they are treated by state officials, legal adversaries and others. Moreover, both during periods of conflict and transition (which we discuss in more detail below) the price paid for doing such work on a personal, professional and familial level can be high indeed.

3.0 Cause-Lawyers and the Transition

As discussed above, there is now a significant literature on gender, activism and transitional justice. One of the successes for feminists over the last two to three decades has been the increased recognition of gender-based harms and violations as a key focus of transitional justice.[65] There is a sense, as O'Rourke has noted, that 'the doctrine and institutions of international law have never been more supportive of delivering positive human rights outcomes for women from domestic processes of transitional justice'.[66] Specifically numbered among the 'gains' in this area are the inclusion of crimes of sexual violence as a 'grave breach' of the Geneva conventions;[67] the establishment of rape as a crime against humanity in the Rome statute;[68] and what Franke refers to as 'paradigm-shifting' indictments and convictions at the International Criminal Tribunal for Rwanda (ICTR) and the International Criminal Tribunal for the Former Yugoslavia (ICTY) — variously recognising sexual violence as an element of genocide, torture and inhumane treatment.[69]

---

[64] As above.

[65] See, for example, Campbell above note 31 at 411.

[66] O'Rourke above note 32 at 7.

[67] Copelon Rhonda 'Surfacing Gender: Re-Engraving Crimes Against Women in Humanitarian Law' (1994) 5 *Hastings Women's Law Journal* 243; Copelon Rhonda 'Gender Crimes as War Crimes: Integrating Crimes Against Women into International Criminal Law' (2000) 46 *McGill Law Journal* 217.

[68] Oosterveld Valerie 'The Definition of "Gender" in the Rome Statute of the International Criminal Court: A Step Forward or Back for International Criminal Justice?' (2005) 18 *Harvard Human Rights Journal* 55.

[69] Franke Katherine M 'Gendered Subjects of Transitional Justice' (2006) 15(3) *Columbia Journal of Gender and Law* 813 at 816–817. The Inter-American Commission of Human Rights also accepted in *Gladys Carol Espinoza Gonzáles v the Republic of Peru* Case 11.157, Inter-American Commission of Human Rights Report No 67/11, 31 March 2011 that rape constituted torture. See further Green Jennifer, Copelon Rhonda, Cotter Patrick and Stephens Beth 'Affecting the Rules for the Prosecution of Rape and Other Gender-Based Violence Before the International Criminal Tribunal for the Former Yugoslavia: A Feminist Proposal and Critique' (1994) 5 *Hastings Women's Law Journal* 171; Askin

For the non-retributive variants of transitional justice, such as truth recovery or reparations, there has also been incremental but important progress. The early Latin American truth commissions were rightly berated for failing to recognise gender as a key dimension of truth seeking.[70] This was at least partially corrected in the Guatemalan, South African and Peruvian commissions in which sexual violence was addressed under the banner of torture and ill-treatment.[71] Concerns have nonetheless persisted about the issue of under-reportage of instances of sexual violence[72] and the aforementioned dangers of confining the frame of reference for gender-based harms to a narrow conception of sexual violence.[73] Ross meanwhile has produced a probing analysis of women's relationship to testimony and in particular the types of violence and suffering about which they choose (or feel pressured) to remain silent.[74] From a practical point of view others have suggested that well-designed truth commissions that yield valuable information about the patterns and themes of gender-based harms are of limited value if they do not help to yield substantive and material gains for women designed to repair as much as possible the damage done by such harms.[75] With regard to reparations, there has been significant work done to try to broaden the gaze of reparations (for example, to recognise forced 'marital' unions, domestic labour or property loss)[76] and indeed to advocate for a transformative version of gender reparations which can 'subvert existing patriarchal structures' rather than simply restore a flawed status quo ante.[77]

Kelly D 'A Decade of the Development of Gender Crimes in International Courts and Tribunals: 1993 to 2003' (2004) 11(3) *Human Rights Brief* 1; Bactrach Michael 'The Protection and Rights of Victims Under International Criminal Law' (2000) 34(1) *The International Lawyer* 7.

[70] Nesiah Vasuki et al 'Truth Commissions and Gender: Principles, Policies, and Procedures' (July 2006) International Center for Transitional Justice p 7.

[71] See Bell and O'Rourke above note 34 at 28.

[72] For example, just over 300 instances of sexual violence were reported to the UN-sponsored El Salvador Commission (1993). This is widely held to be a mere fraction of the real figure with under-reportage variously attributed to the social stigma attached to sexual violence, fears of ostracisation or retaliation and the failure of the commission to proactively solicit information on the theme. See Hoover Amelia 'Conflict and Gender: Data Overview' (November 2009) Benetech Human Rights Data Analysis Group Yale University p 2. Full text available at <www.preventgbvafrica.org/wp-content/uploads/2013/10/Conflict_and_Gender_Data_Overview.pdf> Accessed 18 April 2016.

[73] Ní Aoláin further cautions that the processes that 'construct' truth, in particular the privileging of certain kinds of memory (associated with 'public' allocations of power and territory), may have 'a consistent patriarchal under-current'. Ní Aoláin and Turner above note 35 at 273.

[74] Ross Fiona C *Bearing Witness: Women and the Truth and Reconciliation Process in South Africa* Pluto Press London 2003. See further Millar Hayli 'Facilitating Women's Voices in Truth Recovery: An Assessment of Women's Participation and the Integration of a Gender Perspective in Truth Commissions' in Durham Helen and Gurd Tracey (eds) *Listening to the Silences: Women and War* Martinus Nijhoff Boston Leiden 2005 p 171–222.

[75] See Bell and O'Rourke above note 34.

[76] Rubio Marin Ruth 'The Gender of Reparations: Setting the Agenda' in Rubio Marin Ruth (ed.) *What Happened to the Women: Gender and Reparations for Human Rights Violations* Social Science Research Council New York 2006 p 31.

[77] Urban Walker Margaret 'Transformative Reparations? A Critical Look at a Current Trend in Thinking About Gender-Just Reparations' (2015) *International Journal of Transitional Justice* 1. Walker uses the useful illustration of the Moroccan Reconciliation Commission which apportioned

Unsurprisingly, in our interviews and discussions with female cause-lawyers across the relevant jurisdictions we found the same variety of experiences with regard to the areas in which people worked during the transition as during the conflict or 'struggle' phase. For example, some lawyers were engaged in struggles to ensure that gender-related issues were included in the transitional justice mechanisms operating in their particular jurisdiction while others applied themselves to specific aspects of dealing with the past work such as prosecution of past human rights abuses or filing civil actions on behalf of victims — or a combination of the two. We were also interested in exploring the ways in which their cause-lawyering was done, the networks in which they worked and their relations with civil society. At a conceptual level, we also sought to examine the ways in which activism and gender related struggles were *imagined* as part of the broader process of constructing and reproducing both the transition itself and the previous years of struggle.

In the same way as conflict and struggle provided some opportunities for female cause-lawyers, a strong theme permeating our interviews was the notion of transition as a 'window of opportunity'.[78] For example one lawyer and a founding member of the Women's National Coalition in South Africa told us:

> *People always said to us, you know, the first five or ten years is a great window of opportunity in every way — all the other African countries told us because they'd been down our road before — and although we thought that South Africa was the exception, it absolutely wasn't. So they were just saying 'use that space because it all really closes down' and of course it does close down. Institutions slowed down, bureaucracies become embedded — that kind of idea that 'we're going to change the state and it's going to be open and participative and efficient' disappears very quickly.*[79]

As O'Rourke, Keck and Sikkink and others have argued,[80] the potential for feminist lawyers and civil society organisations to seize such opportunities often requires a combination of using international human rights standards, transnational mobilisation with international partners, as well as strategic litigation and mobilisation in the domestic context. In addition, in some transitional jurisdictions (including Northern Ireland where we live and work), heightened awareness of past rights abuses has seen increased legal, political and civil society attention focused on creating a more human rights aware culture as a buttress against such atrocities happening again.[81] Even in contexts where such favourable conditions existed, cause-lawyers working

benefits among family members of deceased victims in ways that departed from Morocco's gender-biased inheritance law, resisting the established gender hierarchy.

[78] Gready Paul *The Era of Transitional Justice* Routledge London 2011; Root Rebecca 'Through the Window of Opportunity: The Transitional Justice Network in Peru' (2009) 31(2) *Human Rights Quarterly* 473.

[79] Personal interview with legal academic and human rights activist, Johannesburg, South Africa, 13 August 2014.

[80] Keck Margaret and Kathryn Sikkink *Activists Beyond Borders: Advocacy Networks in International Politics* Cornell University Press New York 1998; O'Rourke above note 32.

[81] Roht-Arriaza Naomi and Mariezcurrena Javier (eds) *Transitional Justice in the Twenty-First Century: Beyond Truth Versus Justice* Cambridge University Press Cambridge 2006; Harvey Colin 'Bringing Humanity Home: A Transformative Human Rights Culture in Northern Ireland' in

on gender-related issues were sometimes struggling to make progress in practice. As one self-identified cause-lawyer prosecutor in Chile told us:

> *Even though in 2005 we passed a major domestic violence legislation even now the criminal courts don't want to hear these cases. They don't often convict maybe because there's this understanding, a basic understanding that women's issues are not human rights issues, they are family issues. In the cases of sexual violence and torture in the dictatorship, it has also been extremely difficult. I have spent over a year arguing for the cases to be heard by members of the Appellate court, just like all the other cases of the former dictatorship ... We are trying to get them to understand that the violence suffered by women was a violence that was different from that of men but that it was also a kind of torture.*[82]

In the case of Chile, this disconnect between the crimes of the past and receptiveness to gender-based arguments in the transition speaks to the durability of a conservative and patriarchal political and legal culture.[83] In a similar vein in Cambodia, despite the fact that rape, sexual exploitation, sexual slavery and 'forced marriages' were all features of the Khmer Rouge regime, the Extraordinary Chamber in the Courts of Cambodia has only managed (after persistent lobbying by activists) to add 'forced marriages' to the charge sheet in one case — Case 002.[84] A number of the cause-lawyers we spoke to argued that such past abuses underpinned the culture of impunity regarding sexual violence in contemporary Cambodia. As one international lawyer told us:

> *A UN report came out in June 2013 on violence against women and it shows that incidents of rape in Cambodia is even higher than other countries in the region. So it's really a big issue and domestic violence is occurring a lot ... Men can buy women whenever they want, they can marry them whenever they want and they can beat them whenever they want and rape them so there are very little consequences because they are above the women ... the legal system doesn't work so when a woman is raped and she goes to the police and the police will try to settle the dispute by negotiating a price with the perpetrator. The police will get maybe 25% and then the rest goes to the family and everybody shuts up and it's justice. And for me, it's fine that they do this but they cannot drop the criminal prosecution, it's fine that he pays compensation and they agree on it but he has to be prosecuted as well.*[85]

McAlinden Anne Marie and Dwyer Clare (eds) *Criminal Justice in Transition* Hart Publishing Oxford 2015 p 47–67.

[82] Personal interview with Chilean human rights lawyer, Santiago, Chile, 28 April 2014.

[83] Macias Teresa '"Tortured Women and Hungry Widows": Patriarchal Neoliberalism and the Logic of Compensational Justice in Chile' (2013) 28(2) *Affilia* 126.

[84] Killean Rachel 'An Incomplete Narrative: Prosecuting Sexual Violence Crimes at the Extraordinary Chambers in the Courts of Cambodia' (2015) 13 *Journal of International Criminal Justice* 331. See also Elander Maria 'Prosecuting the Khmer Rouge Marriages' (2016) 42(1) *Australian Feminist Law Journal* 163. In April 2014, the ECCC Co-Prosecutor made two announcements that the Prosecution were 'requesting the investigation of sexual or gender-based violence' as an element of the broader charges in two further cases (003 and 004). The Cambodian government is opposed to these cases going ahead, arguing that the prosecutions in cases 001 and 002 should suffice, and that further prosecutions will 'lead the country into instability'. See further Brinkley Joel 'Justice Squandered: Cambodia's Khmer Rouge Tribunal' (2013) *World Affairs Journal*. Available at <www.worldaffairsjournal.org/article/justice-squandered-cambodia%E2%80%99s-khmer-rouge-tribunal> Accessed 10 May 2016.

[85] Personal interview with international human rights lawyer, Phnom Penh, Cambodia, 10 March 2014. The report cited is Fulu Emma et al 'Why Do Some Men Use Violence Against Women and

In other contexts, where there has been a much more dramatic political and legal transformation, the obstacles and cultural silences on gender-related issues facing cause-lawyers can be all the more insidious. For example, in his first State of the Nation address to Parliament, former President Nelson Mandela said 'freedom cannot be achieved unless women have been emancipated from all forms of oppression'.[86] Evidence of the importance of gender equality and women's rights are replete in the new South African Bill of Rights which is rightly acknowledged as one of the most progressive in the world.[87] Indeed for some commentators, gender became a 'moral touchstone' by which to judge the transition in South Africa.[88] Notwithstanding the undoubtedly important political and legal advances that have been made, rape and sexual violence against women remains an endemic problem.[89] Even within the cause-lawyer community, gendered silences remain — not least because of the veneration of cause-lawyers themselves who for many are a symbol of all that was good about the South African struggle. For example, one cause-lawyer related the story of a fellow activist who had been abused by her husband (himself a cause-lawyer):

> *She's probably one of the famous women and she came to me and she revealed the subject of domestic abuse. And I said to her, okay, we're going to help you and we're going to take your case out. And inside the movement there was such a powerful silence that she should not break, but even though we were willing to help her take the risk, she just didn't have the guts to do it because no one wanted her to speak about it. And I mean I keep saying to the women that, you see, we will never deal with domestic violence in our country unless that story of abuse is told in our country, and that's the story of the struggle that's not told.*[90]

For this interviewee, such a cover-up within the ranks of 'struggle-lawyers' reflected more broadly on the legal profession:

> *It's not a profession that took care of people and, you know ... nobody wanted to touch another lawyer and I found that like the legal hypocrisy really incredible ... I kind of thought this is a terrible profession, there is no sense of solidarity, caring or solidarity.*[91]

As noted above, a key element to the advancement of gender-based issues for cause-lawyers in all of the jurisdictions studied has been the development of relationships with civil society organisations, NGOs and other activists both locally and

How Can We Prevent It? Quantitative Findings from the United Nations Multi-Country Study of Men and Violence in Asia and the Pacific' (2013) UNDP, UNFPA, UN Women and UNV Asia-Pacific Regional Joint Programme for Gender-Based Violence Prevention.

[86] Cited in Cowan Ruth B 'Women's Representation on the Courts in the Republic of South Africa' (2006) 6(2) *University of Maryland Law Journal of Race, Religion, Gender & Class* 292.

[87] As above at 291.

[88] Albertyn Catherine 'Defending and Securing Rights Through Law: Feminism, Law and the Courts in South Africa' (2005) 32(2) *Politikon: South African Journal of Political Studies* 217.

[89] Jewkes Rachel and Naeema Abrahams 'The Epidemiology of Rape and Sexual Coercion in South Africa: An Overview' (2002) 55(7) *Social Science & Medicine* 1231.

[90] Personal interview with international human rights lawyer, Johannesburg, South Africa, 16 August 2014.

[91] As above.

internationally. For many such organisations networks of 'organized women' are the driving force for gender-related struggles in transitional societies.[92] Such relations between lawyers and civil society organisations have been a rich source of analysis for a number of years in the cause-lawyering literature more generally. For some, there are risks that if lawyers assume too much prominence in such social movements, strategies may become overly legalistic and thus divert scarce resources from other potentially more transformative methods of political and social struggle.[93] Other accounts suggest that a range of variables including the local legal and political context in which lawyers and social movements are operating, the capacity of the movement, the professional and personal imperatives of the lawyers themselves (as above, some of whom may have been 'activists first') and other factors may contribute to a more fluid and dynamic relationship wherein the capacity for lawyers and legal strategy to dominate is reduced.[94] The latter variant of the relationship was, broadly speaking, the most common in our research on women cause-lawyers. As one prominent lawyer in South Africa responded in relation to the question of whether lawyers tended to dominate in the social movements in which she was involved:

> *Not in the women's movement, no, because you were held to account. I mean in fact they changed me in many ways ... because I did go in as a bit of a lawyer; you do learn to be the person who says how it is, right, 'cause that's what we do as lawyers; we pronounce on certainty, even though we know it's uncertainty. You know, and they were having none of that. So it was a wonderful experience for me because I was really challenged and questioned ... I had a valid voice but then so did other people ... I mean I remember just learning, having to learn very quickly, that, you know, that was my place and that I had validity and I had things to say but, you know, I was not the oracle.*[95]

We have noted that 'the moment' of transition can, from a feminist perspective, be viewed as one of 'retrenchment'.[96] Ní Aoláin develops this argument by suggesting that, whilst transition can create new 'opportunities, ideas and sites of intervention', that newness can equally hide 'deep pitfalls of structural and entrenched gender discrimination'.[97] Certainly in some contexts, the political negotiations and compromises

---

[92] Waylen above note 17.

[93] Scheingold Stuart A *The Politics of Rights: Lawyers, Public Policy and Political Change* 2nd ed University of Michigan Press Ann Arbor 2004; Jones Lynn C 'The Haves Come Out Ahead: How Cause Lawyers Frame the Legal System for Movements' in Sarat Austin and Scheingold Stuart A (eds) *Cause Lawyers and Social Movements* Stanford University Press Stanford 2006 p 182–196.

[94] McCann Michael (ed.) *Law and Social Movements* Ashgate Aldershot 2006; Boutcher Steven 'Mobilizing in the Shadow of the Law: Lesbian and Gay Rights in the Aftermath of Bowers v Hardwick' (2011) 31 *Research in Social Movements, Conflict and Change* 175.

[95] Personal interview with legal academic and human rights activist, Johannesburg, South Africa, 13 August 2014.

[96] See Ní Aoláin and Turner above note 35 at 273. In the case of South Africa, Albertyn similarly cautions that constitutionalism and rights can introduce a dangerous sense of apathy: 'One of the tasks for women in South Africa is to ensure that the interim Constitution, with its rights framework, is not used in a way which restricts rather than furthers the goal of gender equality ... all of this needs to take place within a vision of social reconstruction that addresses the material bases of women's inequality'. Albertyn above note 30 at p 62–63.

[97] Ní Aoláin above note 30 at 3.

required to build broad fronts in civil society during a transition appeared to require 'sacrificing' gendered issues in order to sustain important alliances. In South Africa, for example, leaders in the women's movement told us that they 'really had to fight the men' to prevent the customary law provisions in the constitution being used to undermine the rights of rural women because of the ANC's desire to placate tribal leaders.[98] Similarly, in Chile as one veteran lawyer and civil society leader told us:

> *Violence against women was a product of the international agenda — in Latin America and more particularly here in Chile. On the other hand, our demands, the women's movement demands, have been hijacked by the Catholic Church. The Catholic Church was hugely important during the dictatorship and one of the issues on the table at the beginning of the transition period was that of women's rights. But this was an issue that was negotiated with the Catholic Church, and I can say this because I was one of the participants of that process. I was one of the few who insisted that the issue of abortion, for example, had to be tackled straight on, but the political leaders of the opposition would tell us: 'Those issues cannot be touched'. It was only two years ago that we had divorce in Chile!*[99]

Finally, as is evidenced across the jurisdictions we have been researching, there is a complex relationship between material and symbolic advances for women and the ways in which these societies imagine their own transition and in some instances the cause-lawyers who have been seeking to advance such struggles. Inevitably, such processes are shaped by the previous era of conflict or authoritarianism. The temporal nature of 'transitional' justice arguably creates false dichotomies between the exotic and terrible violence of the past and the assumed improvements of any new dispensation.[100] For example, as one interviewee told us in Tunis, '*amongst the biggest lies of the former regime is that Tunisia was the land of women's freedom and equal rights*'.[101] Similarly, in Israel, a state which is still very much in conflict and which is certainly demonstrating increased authoritarian tendencies, several cause-lawyers and activists critiqued the efforts of the Israeli government to 'pinkwash' the occupation and associated abuses of Palestinians by constantly referring international audiences to the country's comparatively 'progressive legislation and policies on gender and LGBT rights'.[102]

These contests regarding the ways in which both past and present are constructed and reproduced are also part of the struggle of cause-lawyers. It is all too easy for neat narratives to dominate and for what Mazzei describes as 'the voices in the cracks' to be silenced.[103] In South Africa, for example, the veneration of struggle-lawyers can produce narratives where both women and black lawyers are 'written out' of the ways in which the struggle and transition are remembered. Cause lawyers are not just litigators but rather, as Sarat and Scheingold have argued, they are involved in

[98] Personal interview with legal academic and human rights activist, Johannesburg, South Africa, 13 August 2014.
[99] Personal interview with Chilean human rights lawyer, Santiago, Chile, 30 April 2014.
[100] See Ní Aoláin and Turner above note 35 at 264.
[101] Personal interview with cause-lawyer, Tunis, Tunisia, 20 June 2014.
[102] Personal interview with legal academic and human rights activist, Tel Aviv, Israel, 14 May 2014.
[103] Mazzei Lisa A 'An Impossibly Full Voice' in Jackson Alecia Y and Mazzei Lisa A (eds) *Voice in Qualitative Inquiry: Challenging Conventional, Interpretive, and Critical Conceptions in Qualitative Research* Routledge London and New York 2009 p 45 at 47–48.

a 'mutually constitutive relationship' with the social, political and legal worlds in which they operate and which they help to create.[104]

4.0 Conclusion

> *Women's rights are seen as human rights, and that's again largely because there have been so many women who have been working in this field who've done a good job of pushing and making sure that it's not an issue that we wait to address when the occupation is over, but that you continually address it while the occupation is ongoing.*[105]

Just over a decade ago Posner and Vermeule offered a strong critique of the 'exceptionalist' strain in transitional justice. They argued that much transitional justice scholarship had 'gone wrong' by failing to grasp the connections between ordinary justice and ordinary politics in consolidated democracies and the challenges faced in transitional contexts.[106] In the context of female cause-lawyers, that critique provokes at least two interrelated questions: what if anything is unique or different about the contexts of conflict and transition in terms of shaping the experience of women lawyers? When the 'dust settles' what substantive difference has the contribution of female cause-lawyers made (directly or indirectly) to gender equality issues?

We have argued above that what is different about the experience of women lawyers in contexts of conflict and transition is evident in terms of opportunities, the politicisation of lawyering, the intersection of conflict and gender and the very real personal consequences for engagement in such work. As will be clear from our use of the cause-lawyering and sociology of lawyers literature, we share the view that those of us who work in transitional justice should remain open to theoretical and practical insights from non-transitional settings. We nonetheless contend that the particular scale, intensity and human consequences of the issues faced by cause-lawyers in authoritarian and conflicted contexts such as Cambodia, Chile, Tunisia, South Africa, Israel and Palestine are an obvious and compelling reason for a discrete focus on transitional justice. Moreover, as we know only too well from our own work in Northern Ireland, in contexts where transitions are so often marked by the scars of *our* particular past, being able to draw on themes and experiences from other transitional contexts offers a useful bulwark against parochialism and what Ignatieff (borrowing from Freud) has termed the 'narcissism of minor differences'[107] — factors which inevitably mitigate against successful conflict transformation. Indeed, in this research we have sought to avoid what Ní Aoláin has termed the dangers of reifying the 'gender agenda'.[108]

[104] Sarat Austin and Scheingold Stuart A 'The Dynamics of Cause Lawyering: Constraints and Opportunities' in Sarat and Scheingold above note 40 at 2.

[105] Personal interview with Palestinian human rights activist and legal academic, Jerusalem, Israel, 19 May 2014.

[106] Posner Eric A and Vermeule Adrian 'Transitional Justice as Ordinary Justice' (2004) 117 *Harvard Law Review* 761. See further Ohlin Jens David 'On the Very Idea of Transitional Justice' (2007) 8(1) *Whitehead Journal of Diplomacy and International Relations* 51.

[107] Ignatieff Michael *The Warrior's Honor: Ethnic War and the Modern Conscience* Henry Holt & Co New York 1998.

[108] Ní Aoláin Fionnuala above note 30 at 4.

We have thus acknowledged the very different historical, cultural, religious and political structures and contexts within which the cause-lawyers we interviewed live and work and sought to capture some of the range and complexity of that agency.

With regard to the issue of 'making a difference' to gender equality issues we have noted that the 'opportunities' arising for individual female lawyers during both conflict and transition do not automatically translate into wider material gains for women in the legal profession — or indeed wider society. Certainly in the contexts in which we have been researching, themes such as glass ceilings in the legal profession, silos of legal practice, patriarchal legal and political cultures and the strains on personal and familial relations are familiar to women lawyers anywhere. This inevitably raises the spectre of patriarchal state-building in the guise of transitional justice.[109] The related argument that feminists may have channelled precious energy and resources into resolutely patriarchal legal and political transitional processes was most forcefully made in South Africa. Here, as we have noted, the fact that more than 20 years out from the ending of apartheid deep gender inequalities persist inevitably gave rise to disillusionment. Reflecting on what she considered to be 'missed opportunities' for women in South Africa, a former ANC activist stated:

> *I think that golden age has gone ... I think we lost a lot of opportunities, we lost a lot of ground and we lost a lot of women ... Some of them have become diplomats, others went into the party hierarchy, into government ... you get into the structure and well the structure swallows you. And then that voice is no more, you know, it's not possible to put a foot out again and enter the other platform. So now we don't have those public spaces ... organisations we knew during the apartheid era no longer exist. Local structures are not there anymore and if you're out to mobilise people you need a vehicle to do it, you need a mechanism, and we don't have those mediating mechanisms anymore. So yeah, I think we've lost the momentum on that really.*[110]

The suggestion that the 'structure' swallows you up resonates with the arguments developed by Gready and colleagues in relation to the inability of transitional justice to withstand the impact of neoliberal economics.[111] It also lends weight to the argument made by Ní Aoláin and others that apparent 'gains' for women can sometimes be viewed in hindsight as 'a wily form of gendered window dressing'.[112] In the case of our field

---

[109] Ní Aoláin and Turner above note 35 at 229; Snyder Jack and Vinjamuri Leslie 'Advocacy and Scholarship in the Study of International War Crime Tribunals and Transitional Justice' (2004) 7 *Annual Review of Political Science* 354.

[110] Personal interview with former ANC and human rights activist, Johannesburg, South Africa, 15 August 2014.

[111] Gready Paul *The Era of Transitional Justice: The Aftermath of the Truth and Reconciliation Commission in South Africa and Beyond* Routledge London 2011 p 8. See further McAuliff Pádraig 'Structural Causes of Conflict and the Superficiality of Transition' in Corradetti Claudio Eisikovits Nir and Volperotondi Jack (eds) *Theorizing Transitional Justice* Routledge London 2016 p 93; Dave Whyte 'The Crimes of Neo-Liberal Rule in Occupied Iraq' (2007) 47(2) *British Journal of Criminology* 177.

[112] Ní Aoláin above note 30 at 11; Katherine M Franke contends that '[i]n different ways, and by different means, rebuilding post conflict societies is almost inevitably a process of re-masculinization. Left untended, this process can take the form, for instance, of reinstalling men as good citizens by and through the ideological redefinition of "women's place", or of formulating new political leadership in the form of a "national father"'. Franke above note 69 at 824.

research, this caused us to question whether female cause-lawyers have somehow been complicit in propping up and perpetuating deeply gendered processes, accommodations and structures.[113] A number of the women we interviewed certainly adopted a pragmatic 'work the system' approach and essentially 'matched' the contribution of their male counterparts.[114] Resonating with Scheingold's famous 'myth of rights' critique,[115] we were also conscious that what Bourdieu referred to as the 'force of law' and the social prominence of some 'celebrity' female cause-lawyers could arguably displace resources or attention from other 'grassroots' gender struggles.[116]

Mindful of all of these structural challenges, we have nonetheless been buoyed by the experience of interviewing women cause-lawyers for this study. As noted, research on conflict and transition is sometimes inclined to cast men as active agents and women as largely passive victims.[117] This study provides a useful corrective to such tendencies. The women that we interviewed had fought hard to assert their *agency*, whatever the difficult circumstances of their work. As Kirchheimer has argued, in highly politicised contexts, law and legal settings provide a space for contests over political power and, by invoking claims to justice, lawyers inevitably challenge those in power to justify and rationalise existing power relations.[118] The women we spoke to were and in many cases remain at the very heart of the social and political struggles of their respective societies. O'Rourke has previously argued that, compared to previous eras, women have secured unprecedented 'influence, clout and leverage' and thrown down a challenge to feminists to take responsibility and 'ownership of the consequences of our advocacy and participation in transitional justice processes'.[119] Many of the cause-lawyers we interviewed have done exactly that.

Disclosure Statement

No potential conflict of interest was reported by the authors.

[113] More than 25 years ago Carol Smart produced a groundbreaking critique of feminist engagements with law. Adopting a post-structural analysis, she argued that law as a discourse inevitably excludes women by failing to account for women's experience and knowledge. Smart Carol *Feminism and the Power of Law* Routledge London 2011.

[114] Ní Aoláin cautions against 'an emphasis on including women to match off the presence of men', arguing that this may fail to address 'the hierarchies of race, ethnicity, religious affiliation and social status that privilege elite women partly because their biographies look the most like those of the men present and included in transitional processes'. Ní Aoláin above note 30 at 16.

[115] Scheingold Stuart *The Politics of Rights: Lawyers, Public Policy, and Political Change* 2nd ed Yale University Press New Haven 2004.

[116] Pierre Bourdieu 'The Force of Law: Towards a Sociology of the Juridical Field' (1987) 38 *Hastings Law Journal* 805. Manji also argues that, in the African context, lawyers can be viewed as part of a postcolonial bourgeoisie whose intimate bond with the state 'determines the approach taken and means that endeavours to ameliorate the position of women remain within the magnetic field of state law and within the dominant paradigm of legal centralism'. Manji Ambreena S 'Imagining Women's "Legal World": Towards a Feminist Theory of Legal Pluralism in Africa' (1999) 8(4) *Social and Legal Studies* 440.

[117] See for example, Campbell above note 31 at 427.

[118] Kirchheimer Otto *Political Justice: The Use of Legal Procedure for Political Ends* Princeton University Press Princeton 1961 p 430–431. See also Habermas Jürgen *Between Facts and Norms: Contributions to a Discourse Theory of Law and Democracy* trans Rehg William Polity Press Oxford 1996.

[119] O'Rourke above note 32 at 248.

Justice Claims in Colonial Contexts: Commissions of Inquiry in Historical Perspective

*Jennifer Balint, Julie Evans and Nesam McMillan**

Abstract. This paper considers the ways in which commissions of inquiry, as historical antecedents to the contemporary transitional justice mechanism of the truth commission, have been employed by colonial and former colonial powers in the past and present. Engaging with three commissions of inquiry undertaken by colonial and former colonial authorities regarding the Morant Bay Rebellion (1865), Rwandan genocide (1997) and the Coranderrk Aboriginal Reserve (1881), we demonstrate how commissions of inquiry can function to limit legal and political recognition of the underlying inequality of colonial relations and the need for broader structural reform. Despite this, we indicate the possibilities that remain in the articulation of claims to commissions of inquiry, which can open up spaces for structural injustices to be openly brought to the fore and put on record.

The most straightforward reason to set up a truth commission is that of sanctioned fact finding: to establish an accurate record of a country's past, and thus help to provide a fair record of a country's history and its government's much-disputed acts. Leaving an honest account of the violence prevents history from being lost or re-written, and allows a society to learn from its past.[1]

---

*The authors would like to acknowledge and thank Charlotte Mertens and Cameron Louis for their excellent research assistance and the editors of this Special Edition and the anonymous reviewers for their valuable comments. This work was supported by the Australian Research Council [LP110200054].

[1] Hayner Priscilla B 'Fifteen Truth Commissions, 1974–1993: A Comparative Study' in Kritz Neil J (ed.) *Transitional Justice: How Emerging Democracies Reckon with Former Regimes* United States Institute of Peace Washington 1995 p 225 at 227.

1.0 Introduction

Truth commissions are often framed as a relatively recent institutional innovation, emerging on the global stage with transitional justice itself.[2] In their capacity to transcend some of the most problematic limits of traditional legal approaches to redressing harm, they are often promoted as a more flexible and effective mode of dealing with past atrocity.[3] Whilst trials, for example, have strict evidentiary rules that shape what testimony can be heard and are restrictively focused on determining the legal guilt or innocence of the individual defendant, truth commissions (and other commissions of inquiry) have more expansive terms of reference and procedural guidelines. Truth commissions are purportedly aimed at uncovering a fuller picture of what happened in the past for the benefit of victims and society as a whole in order to provide, in Hayner's words above, 'a fair record of a country's history and its government's much-disputed acts'.

In the context of this special issue, we draw attention to Hayner's observations not so much for their pertinence to truth commissions *per se*. Rather, our concern is to highlight the broader history of commissions of inquiry within which truth commissions, as mechanisms of transition and conflict resolution, can be placed and to point to some recurrent observations about their operations over time and place. In contrast to the frequent portrayal of truth commissions as a recent development, we understand them as a distinctive manifestation of a justice mechanism that has a much longer legal and political history as a tool for governments to deploy at points of crisis across domestic, imperial and colonial contexts. Drawing on examples from past and present commissions of inquiry, the following discussion therefore explores the limits and possibilities of such fact-finding processes.

In particular, we are concerned with the ability of such commissions to, first, acknowledge and, second, address structural and historical injustice. Writing as participants in a broader collaborative project focused on questions of structural injustice and structural justice in settler-colonial Australia and other colonial contexts,[4] our focus is on the structural injustices that are established by colonial actions and

---

[2] See, for example, Hayner Priscilla B *Unspeakable Truths: Transitional Justice and the Challenge of Truth Commissions* 2nd ed Taylor and Francis Hoboken 2011 which provides an overview of truth commissions, starting in the 1970s/late twentieth century at xi–xii.

[3] See, for example, Rotberg Robert I and Thompson Dennis (ed.) *Truth v. Justice: The Morality of Truth Commissions* Princeton University Press Princeton 2000.

[4] The 'Minutes of Evidence' project is a collaboration between Indigenous and non-Indigenous education experts, performance artists, academics and government and community organisations. It is funded by an Australian Research Council Linkage grant with substantial support from 13 partner organisations. See <http://minutesofevidence.com.au>. The project partners are: The University of Melbourne, Ilbijerri Theatre Company, La Mama Theatre, The Department of Education and Training (Victoria), VicHealth, Creative Victoria, The Koorie Heritage Trust, The Victorian Aboriginal Education Association, Regional Arts Victoria, The State Library of Victoria, Deakin University, The University of Sussex, Royal Holloway University of London. Through research, performance and education, the project seeks to promote new and collaborative ways of understanding Australia's past and engaging with historical injustice and envisaging a structural justice. It examines how notions of justice have been formulated, invoked and confronted over time and place, and how the enduring legacies of past injustices continue into the present — despite official responses designed to redress them — so as to foster new ways of thinking about structural justice in the present and future.

practices that have entailed the reorganisation of societies in a manner designed to systematically oppress certain groups.[5] The local and global effects of such structural interventions endure well beyond the formal end of colonial rule, while in situations of ongoing settler-colonialism the initial dispossession of native peoples not only originally constituted the nation state but also continues to shape the conditions of social, political and cultural life for Indigenous and non-Indigenous peoples in the present. In the Australian case, such structural injustices inhere in persistent social and political resistance to fully recognising the unlawfulness of the country's past and to engaging lawfully with Aboriginal and Torres Strait Islander sovereignty, nationhood and law in the present.

Our analysis explores some of the ways in which commissions of inquiry have been employed by colonial and former colonial powers in the past and present to actively manage and respond to social and political controversies situated in the context of the colonialism and its legacies.[6] We examine in particular the extent to which concerns about legitimating state authority and maintaining colonial interests limit the capacity of commissions of inquiry to acknowledge and redress the underlying inequality of colonial relations themselves. From this perspective, commissions of inquiry may indeed signify official acknowledgement of injustice and even be oriented towards the resolution of mass harms, yet they also shut down the kind of conversations and fundamental reforms that would more adequately address the broader ideological, institutional, structural and governmental context in which they take place.

In advancing such a critique, however, we are nevertheless also attentive to the possibilities for justice, and for law, that remain. We accordingly consider, too, the ways in which official public inquiries — despite the constraints of their terms of reference or outcomes — can represent an opportunity for historical and structural injustices to be brought to the fore and put on record, thus enhancing public and official appreciability of colonial harm. Moreover, although we highlight the need to recognise the harmful and injurious impact of the colonial past, we do not simply regard this past as something to be escaped from or transcended. Instead we emphasise the centrality of the past as containing not only a powerful record of injustice but also the possibility for governments and individuals in the present to work towards a shared and equitable future.

We begin by placing contemporary commissions of inquiry within a longer historical trajectory of official public inquiries — from parliamentary inquiries to royal commissions to truth commissions — and drawing out key themes in critical analyses of their purpose and operations. Section Two focuses on one of these key themes: the political potential of commissions of inquiry to function as mechanisms for legitimating

---

[5] Wolfe Patrick 'Nation and MiscegeNation: Discursive Continuity in the Post-Mabo Era' (1994) 34 *Social Analysis* 94; Wolfe Patrick 'Land, Labor, and Difference: Elementary Structures of Race' (2001) 106 *American Historical Review* 866.

[6] In doing so, this paper substantially expands on an earlier conference paper. See Evans Julie and McMillan Nesam *Moving On? An Interdisciplinary Analysis of Official Responses to Structural Injustice* paper presented at the Australian Political Studies Association Conference, Australian National University, Canberra, 26–28 September 2011.

state authority, as a means for governments to gain control over and in some way resolve social and political crises in a manner that leaves prevailing interests and broader structural inequities untouched. To this end, such inquiries might be regarded as tools of governance that enable the injustice and mass harm arising from colonialism to be rhetorically or procedurally detached from the historical conditions that produce them. Section Three draws out the ways in which more recent commissions can still fail to comprehensively acknowledge and address colonial injustice due to their reluctance to engage fulsomely with history and its enduring implications. Section Four then considers the potential for official inquiries to nevertheless enable justice claims to be formulated and articulated, thereby facilitating recognition of structural inequities and their potential redress. Throughout our discussion, we demonstrate our arguments through the use of historical vignettes, actual commissions of inquiry undertaken by colonial and former colonial authorities regarding the Morant Bay Rebellion (1865), the Rwandan genocide (1997) and the Coranderrk Aboriginal Reserve (1881). These cases are separated by time and geography and yet collectively shed light on the capacity of commissions of inquiry to both acknowledge and address the structural and historical harms of colonialism.

2.0 Commissions of Inquiry: Historical and Critical Perspectives

The practice of deploying officially commissioned inquiries to collect information as a basis for public policy has been traced back to William the Conqueror. In 1085 the sovereign instructed his travelling 'royal commissioners' to undertake a comprehensive survey of England's landed property and determine its taxable potential to fund the defence of the realm. The findings of this commission were published the following year and by the twelfth century had become known as the Domesday Book on the grounds that the empirical knowledge presented was understood as demonstrably complete and authoritative.[7]

In many ways, these basic features of commissions of inquiry as tools of governance — especially as they appear in the Commonwealth-related countries of UK, Australia, Canada and New Zealand — are still in evidence although their particular forms and practices have varied significantly over time and place.[8] There is a relatively large literature on the politico-legal basis and administrative procedures of

[7] Clokie Hugh McDowall and Robinson William J *Royal Commissions of Inquiry: The Significance of Investigations in British Politics* Stanford University Press Stanford 1937; Lauriat Barbara '"The Examination of Everything": Royal Commissions in British Legal History' (2010) 31(1) *Statute Law Review* 24.

[8] For differences in the use, type and powers of commissions, including recent UN and other global inquiries, see, for example, Gilligan George 'Royal Commissions of Inquiry' (2002) 35(3) *The Australian and New Zealand Journal of Criminology* 289; Moore WH 'Executive Commissions of Inquiry' (1913) 13 *Colombia Law Review* 500; Prasser Scott and Tracey Helen (eds) *Royal Commissions and Public Inquiries: Practice and Potential* Connor Court Publishing Ballarat 2014; Henderson Christian 'Commissions of Inquiry: Flexible Temporariness or Permanent Predictability?' (2014) 45 *Netherlands Yearbook of International Law* 287; Van den Herik Larissa J 'An Inquiry into the Role of Commissions of Inquiry in International Law: Navigating the Tensions between Fact-Finding and Application of International Law' (2014) 13(3) *Chinese Journal of International Law* 507.

commissions of inquiry,[9] and praise for their enduring capacity to 'probe allegations of wrongdoing and maladministration, provide independent advice of policy problems, promote public participation and broker agreements with diverse interest groups' when many other modern democratic institutions have fallen into disrepute.[10] Nevertheless, the overtly public and political orientation of commissions of inquiry as quasi-legal mechanisms has long rendered them susceptible to intense criticism even within positivist accounts of their nature and purpose. In 1849, for example, Joseph Toulmin Smith published *Government by Commissions Illegal and Pernicious* that questioned not only the British government's frequent use of commissions but also their legal standing, criticisms that are widely held and remain in force to this day.[11]

For current purposes, however, we draw particular attention to those aspects of the literature that are informed by critical scholarship on questions of legitimacy and knowledge production, including in relation to colonial governance and its continuing effects in the present. In this latter strand of the literature, the perceived relationship between the past and the present wields considerable power in enabling or constraining prospects for structural reform.

Some analysts of commissions of inquiry understand their operations as a means to legitimate the actions of governments in times of crisis and shore up their ongoing power and authority.[12] Burton and Carlen observe that the official discourse surrounding commissions leads to 'the systemization of modes of argument that proclaim the state's legal and administrative rationality ... a necessary requirement of political and ideological hegemony'.[13] Meanwhile, Ashforth identifies their symbolic and ritual

[9] See, for example, Gosnell Harold F 'British Royal Commissions of Inquiry' (1934) 49(1) *Political Science Quarterly* 84; Hodgetts J E 'The Role of Royal Commissions in Canadian Government' in Hodgetts J E and Corbett D C (eds) *Canadian Public Administration* MacMillan Co of Canada Toronto (1960) 471; Hallett Leonard Arthur *Royal Commissions and Boards of Inquiry: Some Legal and Procedural Aspects* Law Book Co Sydney 1982; Campbell Enid *Contempt of Royal Commissions* Monash University Clayton 1984; Prasser Scott *Royal Commissions and Public Inquiries in Australia* LexisNexis Chatswood 2006; Inwood Gregory J and Johns Carolyn M *Commissions of Inquiry and Policy Change: A Comparative Analysis* University of Toronto Press Toronto 2014.

[10] Prasser as above at 6. See also Prasser and Tracey above note 8 at viii.

[11] Smith Joshua Toulmin *Government by Commissions Illegal and Pernicious: The Nature and Effects of All Commissions of Inquiry and Other Crown-Appointed Commissions: The Constitutional Principles of Taxation and the Rights, Duties and Importance of Local Self-Government* S Sweet London 1849; See also Frankel Oz 'Blue Books and the Victorian Reader' (2004) 46(2) *Victorian Studies* 308 at 318; Lauriat above note 7 at 28; Moore above note 8; Campbell above note 9; Pross Paul A, Christie I M and Yogis John A (eds) *Commissions of Inquiry* Carswell Toronto 1990; Prasser above note 8; Prasser and Tracey above note 9.

[12] Burton Frank and Carlen Pat *Official Discourse: On Discourse Analysis, Government Publications, Ideology and the State* Routledge & Paul Kegan Boston 1979; Ashforth Adam 'Reckoning Schemes of Legitimation: On Commissions of Inquiry as Power/Knowledge Forms' (1990a) 3(1) *Journal of Historical Sociology*; Ashforth Adam *The Politics of Official Discourse in Twentieth-Century South Africa* Oxford University Press New York 1990b; Gilligan above note 8; Gilligan George and Pratt John (eds) *Crime, Truth and Justice: Official Inquiry, Discourse, Knowledge* Willan Publishing Devon 2004; Orford Anne 'Commissioning the Truth' (2006) 3 *Columbia Journal of Gender and Law* 851; Frankel Oz 'Hard Facts for Fun Times' (2010) 10(3) *Common-Place: The Interactive Journal of Early American Life* 9; Bevernage Berber 'Writing the Past Out of the Present: History and the Politics of Time in Transitional Justice' (2010) 69(1) *History Workshop Journal* 111.

[13] Burton and Carlen as above at 49.

function in the reproduction of state power, claiming that conventional understandings of commissions as policymaking instruments of governments fail to grasp the significance of their political form.[14] Commissions can be thought of, rather, as 'a theatre of power':

> It is a theatre in which a central received 'truth' of modern State power is ritually played out before a public audience. This truth is that the subjects of power can speak freely of their interests, and will be heard; that State power is a benign partner with Society in pursuit of the Common Good. Public Inquiries mediate between the State and Society. They listen to Society and speak to the State; they interrogate society on behalf of the State.[15]

While agreeing that commissions have a legitimating function, other scholars note the need to acknowledge their diversity and unpredictability. Some inquiries perform a straightforward legal and pragmatic function — fact-finding, investigatory, information collecting — while others might perform a legitimation role within a social justice oriented political or ideological realm.[16] Brown points to the New South Wales Wood Royal Commission and related inquiries as examples of transformative commissions that held governments to account and allowed for progressive policy reform,[17] while Gilligan and Pratt assert that official public inquiries can also operate 'as a form of social repair, a kind of healing process'.[18]

Informed by post-structuralist understandings of knowledge production, a related section of the literature understands commissions of inquiry as comprising official discourse that effectively reproduces state power and the inequities that underpin it. This function is particularly evident where social order relies on the overt subordination of particular groups. Stenning and LaPrairie observe, for example, that three influential Canadian inquiries worked to silence Aboriginal voices and knowledge through reiterating flawed 'truths' that had been presented in earlier inquiries, largely to the exclusion of any dissenting or competing explanations.[19] Similar studies of official silencing of minority voices include the Freedmen Inquiries in the nineteenth-century US,[20]

---

[14] Ashforth (1990a) above note 12 at 1.

[15] Ashforth (1990a) as above at 9.

[16] Gilligan and Pratt above note 12; Gilligan above note 8 at 289; Lauriat above note 7.

[17] Brown David 'Royal Commissions and Criminal Justice: Behind the Ideal' in Gilligan and Pratt above note 12; See New South Wales Royal Commission into the New South Wales Police Service *Wood Royal Commission Report* NSW Royal Commission into the New South Wales Police Service Sydney 1997; for the transformative effects of the Woodward Commission in relation to Aboriginal land rights see also Aboriginal Land Rights Commission *Woodward Report* Australian Government Publishing Service Canberra 1974.

[18] Gilligan and Pratt above note 12 at 6.

[19] Stenning Philip and LaPrairie Carol '"Politics by Other Means": The Role of Commissions of Inquiry in Establishing the "Truth" about "Aboriginal Justice" in Canada' in Gilligan and Pratt above note 12 at 150.

[20] Frankel Oz 'The Predicament of Racial Knowledge: Government Studies of the Freedmen during the US Civil War' (2003) 70(1) *Social Research* 45.

inquiries into Indigenous affairs in Australia and New Zealand[21] and in recent truth commissions.[22]

While comparative historian Oz Frankel acknowledges the importance of understanding commissions of inquiry as 'performative, self-legitimising, and subject-creating dimensions of power' he warns, too, that focusing too heavily on these conceptions risks creating 'schematic, ahistorical accounts' or simply presenting a 'new master narrative of the rise and ascendance of the omnipotent state'.[23] Like Brown and others, Frankel cites occasional examples where commissions 'facilitated a complex and somewhat open-ended exchange relationship between government and diverse groups on various rungs of society'.[24]

When considered in the context of colonialism and its legacies, commissions of inquiry are commonly seen as reinforcing rather than challenging historical and structural injustices. In the nineteenth-century British Empire, commissioned inquiries proliferated both across and within the colonies as metropolitan and local governments sought systematic ways to meet the complexities of administration and the range of crises and controversies that were unfolding.[25] The need to respond to and manage humanitarian concerns at home and abroad about the damages caused by empire was particularly urgent once it became empirically irrefutable that, despite abolition, ex-slaves in plantation colonies would not be treated as free sovereign individuals and that the dispossession of indigenous peoples in settler colonies was causing widespread death and suffering.[26]

Critical analyses of past and present inquiries into colonial harms identify two key themes that we elaborate in discussion below. The first concerns the ways in which the official discourses created through such commissions serve to produce and reproduce racialised identities that legitimise elite power and interests despite the apparently emancipatory frameworks that often surrounded them.[27] The second highlights the

---

[21] Marchetti Elena 'Critical Reflection upon Australia's Royal Commission into Aboriginal Deaths in Custody' (2005) 5 *Macquarie Law Journal* 103; Marchetti Elena 'The Deep Colonizing Practices of the Australian Royal Commission into Aboriginal Deaths in Custody' (2006) 3 *Journal of Law and Society* 451; Orford above note 12; Paterson Lachy 'The Kohimārama Conference of 1860: A Contextual Reading' (2011) 12 *Journal of New Zealand Studies* 851.

[22] Bevernage above note 12.

[23]Frankel Oz 'Scenes of Commission: Royal Commission of Inquiry and the Culture of Social Investigation in Early Victorian Britain' (1999) 4(6) *European Legacy* 20 at 20. Frankel provides critical historical accounts of royal commissions in Victorian Britain (see Frankel above note 11; Frankel above note 20 and note 12) as well as comparative study of both countries (see Frankel Oz *States of Inquiry: Social Investigations, Explorations, and Print Culture in 19th Century Britain and the United States* John Hopkins University Press Baltimore 2006).

[24] Frankel 1999 as above at 24.

[25] Laidlaw Zoe *Colonial Connections 1815–45: Patronage, the Information Revolution and Colonial Government* Manchester University Press Manchester 2005.

[26] Laidlaw Zoe 'Investigating Empire: Humanitarians, Reform and the Commission of Eastern Inquiry' (2012) 40(5) *The Journal of Imperial and Commonwealth History* 749.

[27] See, for example, O'Connell Anne 'The Pauper, Slave and Aboriginal Subject: British Parliamentary Investigations and the Promotion of Civilized Conduct' (2009) 2 *Canadian Social Work Review/ Revue Canadienne de Service Sociale* 171; Marchetti (2006) above note 21; Woenne Susan T '"The True State of Affairs": Commissions of Inquiry Concerning Western Australian Aborigines' in Berndt Roland M and Berndt Catherine H (eds) *Aborigines of the West: Their Past and Their*

extent to which the influence of the past is understood as significant in the present. Within this framework, commissions of inquiry — and recent truth commissions in particular — operate as a tool of governance that can at once acknowledge the violence of the past and relegate it to memory, thereby denying the need to address the ongoing nature of structural violence.[28] Berber Bevernage sees such understandings of the relation between past and present as common to truth commissions generally, remarking that they:

> aim at the restoration, or creation, of a modern consciousness of time, thereby confirming a characteristically modernist disjuncture between past and present; … these commissions turn to modern historical discourse precisely *because of* the latter's refusal of the idea of the 'presence' or 'persistence' of the past. This I see as the principal paradox which underwrites the contemporary phenomenon of state-organized truth commissions.[29]

We turn now to consider these themes in relation to specific examples of commissioned inquiries into harms occurring in the context of the colonial relation, past and present.

3.0 Commissions of Inquiry and the Legitimation of State Authority

It is not uncommon for governments to launch some form of official inquiry into the causes of widespread social unrest or into the role of the state in suppressing it. Whilst this can be read as a sign of governmental willingness to acknowledge and redress the injustices in issue, as noted above, scholars have also highlighted the way in which commissions can actually operate in practice as a means of legitimating state authority and reproducing colonial relations. This can be keenly seen in the historical use of commissions of inquiry during the formal period of colonialism and, in particular, in the Morant Bay Rebellion in Jamaica, Governor Eyre's declaration of martial law, the British government's decision to shift from supporting Eyre's administration to agreeing to a public inquiry into his actions and the three years of legal and political controversy that subsequently ensued in England. Not only were the conditions of structural injustice and the fragility of colonial authority startlingly clear in Jamaica but support for the actions of the British government itself was also placed in question.[30] The discussion begins with ex-slaves demonstrating against conditions of continuing repression despite having been notionally granted their freedom almost three decades earlier.

Present University of Western Australian Press Perth 1980 p 324; Andersen Chris and Denis Claude 'Urban Natives and the Nation: Before and After the Royal Commission on Aboriginal Peoples' (2003) 40(4) *Canadian Review of Sociology and Anthropology* 373; Paterson above note 21. See also Black Christine, McVeigh Shaun and Johnstone Richard 'Of the South' (2007) 16 (2) *Griffith Law Review* 299.

[28] Andersen and Denis as above; Rose Deborah Bird 'Land Rights and Deep Colonising: The Erasure of Women' (1996) 3(85) *Aboriginal Law Bulletin* 6; Marchetti 2006 above note 21.

[29] Bevernage above note 12 at 116.

[30] For fuller discussion see Evans Julie *Edward Eyre, Race and Colonial Governance* Otago University Press Dunedin 2005.

On the morning of 11 October 1865, Paul Bogle, freedman, political activist and small landholder led several hundred supporters towards the town of Morant Bay. They headed towards the courthouse where crowds had recently protested against years of badly overcrowded gaols and unjust treatment by the magistracy, grievances that were fuelled by continuing poverty and discrimination despite the formal emancipation of the mass of the population in 1838. Bogle and others had previously written to Governor Eyre seeking protection for those protesters who had been threatened with arrest and advising him that 'we would be compelled to put our shoulders to the wheel' if the conditions of the last 27 years continued.[31] There had already been evidence of a turn to violence when police issuing warrants were confronted with over 300 men 'armed with cutlasses, sticks and spikes' who told them they must 'join their colour' and 'cleave to the black'.[32]

The structural injustices underlying emancipated people's growing anger were undeniable. While the slave trade had been abolished in 1807 and slavery outlawed in 1834, 'freed slaves' still had to complete a four-year 'apprenticeship'. Although supposedly fully sovereign individuals from 1838, they soon learned that full social, economic and political rights would only be theirs when they openly abided by Christian beliefs and middle-class values, including living in respectable houses and working hard for wages. Freedpeople sought to establish an independent peasant economy on small plots of land to enable them to meet these conditions. Planters, however, intended to maintain a plantation economy by replacing slaves with itinerant waged labour and continually blocked reformers' efforts to release land or extend civil privileges.

Such structured injustices fostered growing discontent amongst freedpeople who were disillusioned with their prospects for freedom. As well as pressing their case locally, they also petitioned the Queen to provide the land the planters had denied them in order to 'put our hands and heart to work, and cultivate coffee, corn, canes, cotton and tobacco'.[33] At every sign of protest however, whether through refusal to pay taxes or rescuing people from courthouses, Governor Eyre insisted on asserting state authority rather than examining prospects for reform. He reintroduced the whip and the treadmill to punish those stealing food from plantations and vilified any Europeans, including certain Baptist missionaries, who openly supported the cause of the poor.

Far from grounding its legitimacy in consent, local authority in the colony increasingly relied on coercion as the interests and privileges of the elite once again appeared so openly at odds with those of the majority population. When Eyre decided to circulate 50,000 copies of the Queen's refusal to grant the petitioners' request, tensions increased dramatically and the colony was at boiling point, particularly in Morant

[31] Cited in Gorrie John *Illustrations of Martial Law in Jamaica: Compiled from the Report of the Royal Commissioners Jamaica* London 1867 p 1.
[32] *Jamaica: Report of the Jamaica Royal Commission* 1866 Part I – Report, Presented to Both Houses of Parliament by Command of Her Majesty George Edward Eyre and William Spottiswoode London 1866.
[33] 'The Humble Petition of the Poor People of Jamaica and Parish of St. Ann's' enclosed in *Eyre to Cardwell* no. 117 25/4/1865, CO 137/390 National Archives London 1865.

Bay. By the time Paul Bogle and other demonstrators arrived at the courthouse armed with weapons stolen from the police station, the militia was waiting. The Chief Magistrate read the *Riot Act* and ordered the militia to fire. The crowd set fire to the courthouse, where magistrates and vestrymen were sheltering, and released prisoners from the gaol. Eighteen people were killed and 31 wounded before the rioters dispersed.

Eyre declared martial law on 13 October. The repression was swift and comprehensive, resulting in over 400 deaths, 600 floggings of men and women and the burning of over 1000 homes. While not participating in events at the courthouse, Bogle's associate George William Gordon, an influential activist and outspoken critic of Eyre in the colony's Assembly, was transferred from Kingston to come within the jurisdiction of martial law. Together with Bogle and many others, he was court-martialled and hanged. In the terror of the aftermath and frightened by prospects of further rebellion, the planter-dominated Assembly agreed to its own abolition, voting in favour of a return to Crown Colony status and executive government, dashing freedpeople's hopes that structural injustices would be locally acknowledged and addressed.

In line with its previous support for Eyre's repressive administration, the British government initially praised Eyre's quashing of the rebellion and his actions in 'saving' the colony. However, once reports about the brutality and duration of martial law eventually reached England, the government had to bow to public pressure and appoint a Royal Commission. Sir Henry Storks's report found that the desire for land and disillusionment with the justice system were the major causes of the rebellion, noting, too, that personal political grievances had motivated some rebels and that 'not a few contemplated the attainment of their ends by the death or expulsion of the white inhabitants of the island'. It was agreed that there was an intention to overthrow constituted authority in a small portion of the island, which might well have spread 'had more than momentary success been obtained by the insurgents', resulting in even greater loss of life and property. Eyre was praised for the 'skill, promptitude, and vigor' in speedily terminating the rebellion but criticised for prolonging martial law: the punishments were considered excessive, the death penalty 'unnecessarily frequent', the floggings 'reckless' and, at times, 'barbarous' and the burning of 1000 houses was 'wanton and cruel'.[34]

Eyre was relieved of his position as governor but there was little meaningful reflection on the structural injustices that had framed the grievances and events at Morant Bay. While a new government in Jamaica oversaw certain improvements in judicial procedures, health and sanitation services and, over time, support was extended to developing a landed peasantry, the return to Crown Colony rule effectively maintained colonial relations. In England, meanwhile, the 'Governor Eyre controversy' preoccupied British governments, courts and leading intellectuals for more than three years, with political and legal debates centring on the legitimacy of using martial law to manage social unrest whether at home or abroad. With reaction divided over the wisdom, morality and legality of Eyre's resort to maximal repression, the focus was firmly fixed on Eyre's response to the rebellion rather than its causes, either locally on the ground in Jamaica, or in the coercive relations of colonialism more broadly.

[34] Above note 32.

A parliamentary debate failed to persuade the government to withdraw its support for martial law as a tool of governance in the colonies while powerful middle-class opinion, influenced by Fenian riots at home and wars and mutinies abroad, together with a hardening public racism, eventually marginalised the critics of outright coercion. Although never formally indicted, Eyre was abandoned by his government and retired in obscurity to Devon with a reputation both in Britain and the West Indies as 'the butcher of Jamaica'. The injustices suffered by the freedpeople of Jamaica, meanwhile, continued well into the twentieth century.

Discussion of these events draws attention to the use of commissions of inquiry in colonial contexts where they could be called upon to fulfil a variety of political ends. In this case, the British government acknowledged that its electorate's capacity to tolerate the use of violence in governing colonial populations had been exceeded on this occasion and sought to legitimate its continuing authority at home by appointing a royal commission. Moreover, while the commission report had identified certain structural injustices as provoking unrest in Jamaica, domestic concern focused on Eyre's use of an extraordinary form of law, namely martial law, and not on the widespread use of other forms of violence and coercion that systematically established and sustained inequalities and discrimination not only in Jamaica but throughout the British Empire.

4.0 Colonial Contexts, Contemporary Disavowals

This inability of commissions of inquiry to comprehensively acknowledge and address the structural injustice occasioned by colonial rule is enduring. Even contemporary commissions of inquiry undertaken by former colonial powers demonstrate an inability to adequately recognise the significance of colonial histories and their ongoing impact. Despite their liberation from the strictures of formal colonial rule, and the need for its constant legitimation, more recent commissions of inquiry too approach certain instances of harm as bounded and discrete events disconnected from a broader social, legal and political context of colonial injustice. This can be traced, for example, through the mandate and operation of a 1997 parliamentary commission of inquiry instituted by Belgium, focusing on its actions and inactions with respect to the 1994 genocide in its former colony, Rwanda.

This commission of inquiry was established three years after the Rwandan genocide in response to social and political controversies in Belgium regarding its involvement in this event. Belgium had been a key contributor to the United Nations peacekeeping force (UNAMIR) that was in Rwanda at the time of the genocide. However, shortly after the genocide began, 10 Belgian peacekeepers were strategically murdered, prompting the Belgian government to not only withdraw its own peacekeepers but also lobby other nation states to support the complete withdrawal of the United Nations (UN) mission.[35] Belgium's actions were so significant due to the

[35] Des Forges Alison *'Leave None to Tell the Story': Genocide in Rwanda* Human Rights Watch New York 1999; Power Samantha 'Bystanders to Genocide: Why the United States Let the Rwandan Tragedy Happen' (2001) 288(2) *Atlantic Monthly* 84.

status of the Belgian contingent in UNAMIR, namely its best resourced, trained and capable component.[36] In the aftermath of the genocide, these occurrences gave rise to societal and political debate, focused on the deaths of the peacekeepers (whether the government could have prevented them) and the impact and nature of the Belgian withdrawal (which had clear implications for the Rwandan Tutsis who were being systematically persecuted at the time).[37]

Before the inquiry was instituted, information had begun to surface in the Belgian public domain that indicated that there were sufficient warnings of or information about both the genocide and the related deaths of the Belgian peacekeepers.[38] In light of such information, several government ministers lobbied for a commission of inquiry, eventually with support from the families of the murdered peacekeepers and the broader Belgian public (whose support was evidenced through both a petition containing over 20,000 signatures and a public opinion survey).[39] In 1996, an ad hoc group, comprised of four members of parliament, was established, producing a report later that year.[40] The conclusions of this group, which affirmed that the Belgian government had more forewarning of the 1994 events than had been represented, led to the formation of a Special Commission on Rwanda.[41] However, this Commission was ultimately replaced by a parliamentary commission, which would have enhanced judicial powers, enabling it to summon, and compel, witnesses and have greater access to official government paperwork.[42]

This inquiry was designed to examine the policies and actions of the Belgian government, as well as other external actors such as the UN, during the 1993–1994 period of contemporary Belgian intervention in Rwanda.[43] In the course of its proceedings, the inquiry heard from 95 witnesses, reviewed several government and military documents and undertook a brief visit to Rwanda.[44] The eventual report found that there were 17 areas of failure during this time, from deficiencies regarding the preparation of the Belgian contingent for its service in UNAMIR, to errors of information processing and sharing during their deployment to failures regarding the way in which the

[36] Suhrke Astri 'Facing Genocide: The Record of the Belgian Battalion in Rwanda' (1998) 29 *Security Dialogue* 37 at 38.

[37] Borton John and John Eriksson J *Lessons from Rwanda — Lessons for Today: Assessment of the Impact and Influence of the Joint Evaluation of Emergency Assistance to Rwanda* Danish Ministry of Foreign Affairs Denmark 2004; Kerstens Paul '"Deliver Us from Original Sin": Belgian Apologies to Rwanda and the Congo' in Gibney Mark, Howard-Hassmann Rhoda E, Coicaud Jean-Marc and Steiner Niklaus (eds) *The Age of Apology: Facing Up to the Past* University of Pennsylvania Press Philadelphia 2008 p 187 at 192; van Brabant Koenraad 'Security and Protection in Peacekeeping: A Critical Reading of the Belgian Inquiry into Events in Rwanda in 1994' (1999) 6(1) *International Peacekeeping* 143 at 151.

[38] Borton and Eriksson as above note in Annex 3.

[39] As above.

[40] As above.

[41] Adelman Howard *The Role of Non-African States in the Rwandan Genocide* Centre for Refugee Studies York 2009 p 2; van Brabant above note 37 at 143–144.

[42] Borton and Eriksson above note 37; van Brabant above note 37 at 144.

[43] Belgian Senate *Parliamentary Commission of Inquiry Regarding the Events in Rwanda* Belgian Senate Belgium 1997 p 7; Kerstens above note 37 at 192.

[44] Borton and Eriksson above note 37.

families of the murdered Belgian peacekeepers were treated at the time.[45] Chapter Four of the report of the commission sets out each of these areas of error and assigns responsibility for them. Chapter Five then sets out 55 recommendations, broadly grouped according to these identified fields of error, which are designed to prevent similar events from occurring in the future (it should also be noted that Chapters Four and Five are the only chapters available in English and, as such, form the primary basis for the analysis in this paper). After a change of government in Belgium, the commission of inquiry also led to an apology on behalf of the Belgian government to the Rwandan government and people for its actions and errors during this time.[46]

While the Rwandan government has endorsed this acknowledgement and apology,[47] as with the Morant Bay commission, the Belgian inquiry ultimately focused on a discrete set of occurrences (and corresponding responsibilities) at the expense of a broader engagement with the structuring and enduring effect of the colonial relation that had bound Rwanda and Belgium together.[48] This is despite the fact that both the genocide and the commission of inquiry took place in the context of the colonial encounter. This is not to simplistically claim that Belgium bore direct responsibility for the genocide, through either its historical or more recent actions. Rather, it is to draw on Stoler's work that has decisively highlighted the power and impact of 'imperial formations', 'ruins' of empire, beyond the official conclusion of colonial rule.[49] These 'ruins' and 'formations' can be found in the complex and diverse ways in which colonialism — as a present and past 'force' — still resonates in people's bodies, social structures and physical geographies, shaping, informing, restricting and constituting the nature and experience of social, legal, political and cultural life in Rwanda and Belgium. Such ruins may be found, for example, in the use of ethnic identity cards — a legacy of Belgian colonial rule — during the genocide in Rwanda to identify Tutsi victims to be killed.[50] It was Belgian colonial authorities who established such a system and racialised and solidified the division between Rwandan Hutus and Rwandan Tutsis that informed the genocidal violence.[51] The remnants of the hierarchical colonial relation, premised upon the oppression of peoples as a civilising enterprise, can also be located in the prominent involvement of Belgium in the UNAMIR peacekeeping force, despite the UN's emphasis on

[45] Belgian Senate above note 43.
[46] Verhofstadt Guy *Discours du Monsieur le Premier Ministre Guy Verhofstadt à l'occasion de la commemoration du 6e anniversaire du début du Génocide rwandais* Kigali Rwanda 7 April 2000.
[47] BBC News *Excerpts: Kagame Marks Genocide* 7 April 2007 <http://news.bbc.co.uk/2/hi/africa/3609001.stm> Accessed 15 April 2016.
[48] de Lame Danielle '(Im)possible Belgian Mourning for Rwanda' (2005) 48 *African Studies Review* 33 at 35; Kerstens above note 37 at 188.
[49] Stoler Laura Ann 'Imperial Debris: Reflections on Ruins and Ruination' (2008) 23(2) *Cultural Anthropology* 191. Stoler's work was brought to our attention through the insightful scholarship of Mertens Charlotte *Gendered Violence in the Congo: Violent Representations, Colonial Traces and Present Reconfigurations* University of Melbourne forthcoming end 2016.
[50] See, for example, Stanton Gregory H 'Could the Rwandan Genocide have been Prevented?' (2004) 6 *Journal of Genocide Research* 211 at 213.
[51] Des Forges above note 35 at 38; Hintjens Helen M 'Explaining the 1994 Genocide in Rwanda' (1999) 37(2) *The Journal of Modern African Studies* 241 at 249–250.

neutrality. And it may also be traced through the opposition that the Belgian contingent faced in Rwanda from extremist Rwandan groups amongst others that significantly referenced Belgium's colonial and postcolonial interactions with Rwanda.[52]

Meanwhile, in Belgium itself, the colonial relation between Belgium and Rwanda formed the context for the commission and public and governmental understandings of the genocide. The commission took place at a time in which the Belgian public was more generally reflecting on its colonial history in Africa. The murder of the Belgian peacekeepers is said to have 'shocked' and 'shaken' the Belgian public, who previously believed they had a positive postcolonial relationship with the Rwandan nation and people.[53] Government reactions to this occurrence (a commission of inquiry and an apology) have thus been framed by commentators as a means for the Belgian government and community to face up to its colonial past.[54]

Yet, it is precisely this colonial past and its significance that fails to substantively appear within the commission's findings. Whilst Chapter Two discusses Belgian's colonial history in Rwanda, this history is not then fulsomely connected to the contemporary focus of the inquiry, namely the events occurring in 1993 and 1994. In general, through such explicit discussions and other awkward references to the colonial relation between Rwanda and Belgium, the significance of this colonial history is downplayed, placed in the past rather than the present. Thus, in certain sections of the report, there is a sense that Belgium feels betrayed by the Rwandan people, whom it saw — in these postcolonial times — as a 'friend'. It is in this vein that the commission seeks to emphasise that Belgian:

> soldiers were murdered inside a Rwandan army barrack, which is therefore a public edifice under the protection of the authorities of a 'friendly' country with which we enjoyed close co-operation in development and technical/military matters.[55]

This statement, emphasising the collegiality and co-operation underpinning the relationship between Belgium and Rwanda belies the hierarchical nature of both their colonial history and Belgium's postcolonial aid and assistance to its former colony.

At other times, the colonial relation figures more prominently, but is deployed in a way to downplay any ongoing obligations that may stem from it. That is, in the inquiry report, the Belgian government acknowledges the undesirability of former colonial powers contributing troops to peacekeeping forces in their previous colonies,[56] particularly in light of UN policies regarding the desired neutrality of troop contributing countries. However, this does not lead to a comprehensive engagement with the enduring implications and effects of Belgium's colonial history. Rather it leads to the

---

52 Belgian Senate above note 43 at 10; Des Forges above note 35 at 217 and also more generally 38–39 and 199–200; van Brabant above note 37 at 149.

53 de Lame above note 48 at 35 and 38.

54 As above at 39; Kerstens above note 37 at 187.

55 Belgian Senate above note 43 at para 4.11.

56 Belgian Senate above note 43 at 9–10.

conclusion that Belgium, due to its past intervention, should now refrain from interfering in its former colonies.[57] As such, in its final recommendations, the commission of inquiry proclaims that:

> there cannot be confusion for the participating countries ... between the UN mission and the past and present links that exist between the countries in question. This is why it would be desirable for Belgium to cease furnishing contingents to UN operations carried out in former Belgian colonies.[58]

In this recommendation, there is an attempt to separate and distinguish the past from the present, a distinction which is fiercely maintained instead of interrogated and unsettled through an acknowledgement of the ongoing effects and implications of the colonial injustices of the past.

In a similar vein, the report offers an implicit response to the now dominant assertion that Belgium bears some responsibility for the genocidal violence due to the structuring impact of its colonial policies. Chapter Four thus begins with an affirmation of Rwandan responsibility for the 1994 violence, stating that:

> The commission would like to begin by recalling that the murder of the 10 Belgian paratroopers and the genocide were committed by Rwandans. The commission believes that the genocide was prepared, initiated and orchestrated by Rwandan leaders belonging to a small circle gravitating around those in power.[59]

Maintaining its focus on the actual perpetration of the genocide and, more generally, Belgium's policies regarding this event, the commission of inquiry addresses first and foremost Belgian involvement in Rwanda in 1993 and 1994. This focus on the genocide also marks the political apology offered by the then Prime Minister Guy Verhofstadt when he attended the annual commemorations of the genocide in Rwanda in 2000.[60]

In this way, whilst the genocide and the commission of inquiry may have caused the Belgian government and people to reflect on their colonial past, this reflection has been limited. In the place of a full account of Belgian colonial history and its structuring and enduring effects on Rwandan and Belgian life is a more restrictive wave of regret and remorse regarding the role that Belgium played during the 1994 Rwandan genocide. Indeed, public commentators have observed how the genocide and the Belgian withdrawal from Rwanda during the genocide have prompted greater guilt and introspection in the Belgian populace than Belgium's colonial

---

[57] Kerstens above note 37 at 192.

[58] Belgian Senate above note 43 at para 5.5. This linkage between the colonial past and a need for a reduced responsibility in the region in the present can also be found in the pre-genocide decision of the Belgian government to send significantly fewer soldiers to Rwanda due to 'past and current' ties and UN policies regarding non-neutral countries participating in peacekeeping forces (Delcroix Leo in Belgian Senate above note 43 at para 3.2.2.1).

[59] Belgian Senate above note 43.

[60] For a more comprehensive discussion of this apology see McMillan Nesam 'Regret, Remorse and the Work of Remembrance' (2010) 19(1) *Social & Legal Studies* 85; Negash Girma *Apologia Politica: States & Their Apologies* Proxy Lexington Books Lanham 2006.

policies and practices.[61] Moreover, it has been claimed that Belgian engagement with the colonial past is primarily located in the social and media spheres, rather than at the level of governance.[62] In this respect, it is notable that Prime Minister Verhofstadt's predecessor, former Prime Minister Jean-Luc Dehaene, declined to apologise to the Rwandan people (apologising only to the families of the murdered Belgian soldiers) and stated on other occasions (in relation to Belgian's colonial history in the Congo) that 'the colonial past is completely past ... There is really no strong emotional link any more. It does not move the people. It's part of the past. It's history'.[63]

This failure to more substantively engage with the colonial relation, which inaugurated and informs the relationship between Rwanda and Belgium, is thus disavowed through the deployment of a particular 'politics of time'.[64] Within this framework, Belgium's colonial actions, but also importantly *their enduring manifestations and resonances*, are placed in the past, as over and complete, something which can be 'moved on' from. Pertinently, as noted earlier, Bevernage contends that it is such a 'politics of time' that more broadly characterises the operation of contemporary truth commissions, which may silence modes of relating to the past that do not accord with the commission's vision of societal progress and repair through reconciliation. Bevernage highlights the artificial, or particular, nature of such conceptualisations of time, which preference an 'antinomic' understanding of time that can only approach it as question of temporal succession. He argues instead for an understanding of time and history that enables a recognition of the 'radical noncontemporaneity' of the past, present and future.[65] On this latter view, the past, present and future can and do coexist, in the way that they shape what is and what can be. Indeed, postcolonial theorists have demonstrated that it is colonialism par excellence that underscores the complex relation between the past, present and future — the way in which the past continues to shape present material conditions, local and global practices and discursive structures.[66] Such a reconceptualisation of the past, present and future enables greater acknowledgement of the ongoing impact of colonial injustice on present-day conditions and relations and the need for social, legal and political initiatives which redress it. However, and importantly, it

---

[61] Braeckman Colette 'Rwanda Trial Opens Belgians' Eyes' *BBC News* 7 June 2001 <http://news.bbc.co.uk/2/hi/europe/1375603.stm> Accessed 15 April 2016.

[62] Vanoost Lode 'Interview met Ludo De Witte' *De Wereld Morgen* 24 November 2014. Although the commission of inquiry did spark significant political debate its focus was elsewhere, see Bevernage Berber 'Politieke Verontschuldigingen in Belgie. Enkele bedenkingen over een morele en politieke economie' (2014) 129(4) *Low Countries Historical Review* 80.

[63] Dehaene Jean-Luc cited in Bates Stephen 'The Hidden Holocaust', *The Guardian* 13 May 1999; Bevernage as above at 82 <http://www.theguardian.com/theguardian/1999/may/13/features11.g22> Accessed 15 April 2016.

[64] Bevernage Berber 'The Past is Evil/Evil is Past: On Retrospective Politics, Philosophy of History and Temporal Manichaeism' (2015) 53(3) *History and Theory* 333 at 352.

[65] Bevernage as above at 352.

[66] See Said Edward *Orientalism* Monthly Review Press New York 1989; Young Robert *White Mythologies: Writing History and the West* Routledge New York 1990. For critical review and analysis, see Wolfe Patrick 'History and Imperialism: A Century of Theory, from Marx to Postcolonialism' (1997) 102(2) *American Historical Review* 388; Kennedy Dane 'Imperial History and Post-Colonial Theory' (1996) 24(3) *Journal of Imperial and Commonwealth History* 345; Shohat Ella 'Notes on the "Postcolonial"' (1992) 31/32 *Social Text* 103.

also underscores the possibilities for the future that are in fact grounded in the enduring nature of the past. That is, as Mark McMillan has argued, it is the past that helps 'us' (both parties to the colonial relation) to know ourselves and understand what responsibilities we might have to each other now and in the future.[67]

Contemporary failures of commissions of inquiry, however, testify to the more generalised presentist nature of transitional justice approaches. Dedicated towards the predominantly legalised redress of recent harm, transitional justice theory and practice has too evinced a tendency towards restrictive and presentist mandates. As we and others have argued elsewhere, this compromises the ability of transitional justice initiatives, such as commissions of inquiry, to provide a comprehensive account of the past and subsequently pursue a form of structural and historical justice.[68] And yet, here too, there are still possibilities that remain. As the next section considers, these possibilities reside in the ability for those seeking justice to use such commissions in unexpected ways.

5.0 Claiming Law: Placing Structural Injustice on the Record

The commission of inquiry continues to be sought by those making claims. Despite the colonial structure which locates and shapes these commissions, individuals and communities still deliberately seek them out. It is through the claims made on law — the calls that are made to law — that they play a role in shaping these inquiries. Law, through the claims made on it, is used as a particular tool of resistance. This resistance shapes the record we now have, and attempts to create something within, and beyond, the inquiry itself. This can be observed through the operation and record of an 1881 parliamentary inquiry established by the Chief Secretary of the colony of Victoria to examine the conditions and management of the Aboriginal station, Coranderrk.

The 1881 Victorian Parliamentary Inquiry into the Aboriginal Reserve at Coranderrk was established in response to the petitioning of its residents. A deputation of Coranderrk residents had walked four times from Coranderrk to Melbourne to present their claims. Led by the *Ngurungaeta* (clanhead) of the Wurundjeri people William Barak, Coranderrk residents petitioned the Chief Secretary Graham Berry for a public inquiry into the conditions on the station. The Coranderrk station had been established in 1863, 50 years after British settler-colonialism in Victoria, by surviving members of different clans who had been violently displaced from their traditional lands. It was one of six reserves founded by the colony,[69] and became a

[67] McMillan Mark *Responsibility to Complexity in Structural Justice* Keynote Speech at Just Encounters: Bringing Together Education, Arts and Research State Library of Victoria, 15 August 2014 <http://www.minutesofevidence.com.au/justencounters/> Accessed 19 April 2016.

[68] Balint Jennifer, Evans Julie and McMillan Nesam 'Rethinking Transitional Justice, Redressing Indigenous Harm: A New Conceptual Approach' (2014) 8(2) *International Journal of Transitional Justice* 194 at 201.

[69] These were Framlingham and Lake Condah for the Gunditjmara and Kirraewurrung clans of the western district, Ebenezer mission at Lake Hindmarsh for the tribes of Wimmera and Lower Murray regions, Ramahyuk and Lake Tyers for the Kurnai tribes of Gippsland and Coranderrk for the Kulin clans of central Victoria: Barwick Diane E *Rebellion at Coranderrk Issue 5 of Aboriginal History* Monograph Aboriginal History Incorporated Canberra 1998 p 52.

highly successful station through the work of the residents and the manager John Green. By 1874, despite having no secure title, they had constructed 32 cottages and outbuildings, stretched seven km of fencing, cleared over 1200 hectares from bush to pasture, with 65 hectares for crops and 450 cattle being farmed and established a key cash crop of hops which 'demanded the highest prices on the Melbourne market'; by 1875 it was described as 'virtually self-supporting'.[70]

Yet the station was prized land and sought after by white settlers. The Board for the Protection of Aborigines began to consider breaking up the Coranderrk station, removing the Aboriginal residents and selling the land. John Green, who had been the first manager of Coranderrk, and who had established an excellent working relationship with the Aboriginal residents, was forced out by the Board who eventually installed the Reverend Strickland, an Anglican missionary, as manager, leading to further hardship. The petitioning by residents to protect what they had achieved became known as the 'Coranderrk rebellion'.[71] It resulted in two official inquiries: a royal commission in 1877 and a parliamentary board of inquiry into the management of Coranderrk in 1881.

The inquiry was held over two and half months in late 1881. It comprised of 10 hearings, three of which were held at Coranderrk station, 120 km from Melbourne, with nine appointed Commissioners, including the sole woman, Anne Fraser Bon, a white settler who had been an ongoing supporter and friend to the Coranderrk residents. Sixty-nine witnesses were heard, including, uniquely, 23 Aboriginal residents: 18 men, four women and one young boy gave evidence. This was both in person and by letters submitted to the Inquiry. They did this at great personal risk to themselves, with the knowledge that they could be moved away from their family to another station, and have their rations and supplies taken away from them for questioning the Board's actions and authority.[72]

When Martin Simpson declared to the Inquiry, 'We came to see that the blacks get justice'[73], it was a justice both centred on the dire conditions to which the residents were subject that saw children dying due to a failure by the Board to provide sufficient blankets, and men and women not being paid for the work they were employed to do. It was also a broader structural justice that was sought, as shown in the petition that preceded the inquiry:

> We want the Board and the Inspector, Captain Page, to be no longer over us. We want only one man here, and that is Mr John Green, and the station to be under the Chief Secretary; then we will show the country that the station could self-support itself.[74]

[70] Broome Richard *Aboriginal Australians: A History since 1788* Allen & Unwin Crow's Nest 2010 p 83–84.

[71] See further Barwick above note 69.

[72] See Nanni Giordano and James Andrea *Coranderrk: We Will Show the Country* Aboriginal Studies Press Canberra 2013 p 31.

[73] *Report of the Board Appointed to Enquire Into, and Report Upon, the Present Condition and Management of the Coranderrk Aboriginal Station, Together with the Minutes of Evidence* Victoria 1882 at 10.

[74] As above at 98.

The response from 'The Board Appointed to Enquire into, and Report upon, the Present Condition and Management of the Coranderrk Station' found for the residents. It concluded, 'We are of opinion that the station is not so well managed as could be desired'[75] and recommended changes to the administration of the station, including that 'An hospital, with proper medical attendance, should be provided, where the aged and the sick could be treated, instead of being sent to Melbourne, where they are never satisfied and but seldom cured'[76] and 'We recommend that a superintendent be engaged who thoroughly understands the management of a farm and stock, as well as the Aborigines, and under no consideration should the management be divided'.[77]

The Report found in favour of the concerns voiced by residents, yet it found no hearing in 1882 Victoria. The Inquiry was ultimately succeeded by further interventionist and destructive legal policies, through the enactment of the *Aborigines Protection Act 1886* (Vic) (also known as the 'Half-caste Act') and the *Crown Lands Reserves Act 1893* (Vic).[78] The 'Half-caste Act' was to give the Board complete control over Aboriginal peoples: in their 1884 report to the Parliament of the Colony of Victoria that preceded the new legislation, the Board stated that 'The Board for the Protection of the Aborigines are unanimously of opinion that all able-bodied half-castes capable of earning their living should be merged as soon as practicable in the general population of the colony'.[79] Proposals were made that those under the age of 35 would be required to seek work and settlement elsewhere, that rations, clothing and blankets be at the discretion of the Board, that at the age of 13 children would be apprenticed to trades, farmers or settlers for boys or as servants to 'good families' for girls and that orphans be transferred to the Orphanage or Industrial Schools.[80] The Board of Protection, who had lobbied for this new legislation, was to comment that the intention of this policy was to erase all traces of Aboriginal identity among the 'half-castes'.[81]

The mandate of the Coranderrk Inquiry was circumscribed; it was to examine the conditions and management of the station. Yet the claims made to the Inquiry, and its underlying need, demonstrate a more structural concern: the manner in which Aboriginal peoples had been dispossessed from their traditional lands and were subject now to colonial rule, with the grave consequences to life and livelihood that this entailed. While some of these structural conditions were evident at the Inquiry, through testimony given by settlers and members of the Board of Protection, this was not the focus of the Inquiry, nor was it intended to be. It was the determination of the

[75] As above at iii.

[76] As above at iii.

[77] As above at iv.

[78] *An Act to revoke in the whole or in part the Permanent Reservation under Orders in Council off certain Crown Lands and to enable such lands to be used Agricultural Village and Homestead Settlement* Parliamentary Papers of Victoria 1893 no 1347 at 153.

[79] Board for the Protection of the Aborigines *Twentieth Report of the Board for the Protection of the Aborigines in the Colony of Victoria* John Ferres Government Printer Melbourne 1884.

[80] As above at 5.

[81] As the Board noted in its 1884 report: 'from the earliest period of their recollection, they may be accustomed to regard themselves as members of the community at large, and may not be constrained to carry with them through life the impression of the indolent habits and manner of their original black friends' in Nanni and James above note 72 at 184.

Aboriginal witnesses and their supporters to speak more expansively about the broader injustices, as well as the evidence of European witnesses including members of the Board of Protection, that told a deeper story of structural injustice.

It is through the space of testimony that was claimed in the 1881 Inquiry that we can observe the shaping of the legal and historical record, despite the more modest intentions of the Inquiry. When Alice Grant told the Inquiry she no longer did the ironing for Mrs Strickland, the wife of the manager at Coranderrk, due to her not receiving any wages for doing it, and in response to the question 'You do not believe in working for nothing?', replied 'No', she clearly put on the record the inequity of the failure to pay wages for work done by Aboriginal people, which had been a decision by the Board of Protection.[82] Tommy Michie's statement, submitted in a letter to the Inquiry, 'I think they have done enough in this country to ruin the natives without taking it from us anymore', while testifying to the poor management of the station since John Green had been forced out, took the inquiry from being about conditions on the station to the heart of dispossession.[83] Caroline Morgan's powerful explication of the failure to provide adequate blankets by the Board, with the result that she 'Tore it into two — I have two beds', preceded by 'This is my evidence' showed the terrible lived realities of life under colonial protection.[84]

In response to the question 'Would you like the Government to give you all the food you want, and all the clothing, and no work?', William Barak responded:

> If they had everything right and the Government leave us here, give us this ground and let us manage here and get all the money. Why do not the people do it themselves – do what they like, and go on and do the work

making the inquiry about the central question of land ownership and sovereignty.[85] John Green's testimony, as former manager of the station, in showing the collaboration and respect between himself and the Aboriginal residents, demonstrated a way forward: 'If the Aboriginal is put into the question, he will strive to keep his own law. That is where I consider you have failed.'[86]

The commission of inquiry process provided a space for witnesses to contest the cruelties and rigid enforcement of colonial rule, challenge the Board's characterisations of Aboriginal residents as unwilling to work, child-like and lawless, and articulate different ways forward. The Inquiry effectively created what we may understand as a 'middle ground': establishing the potential for a meeting point between Aboriginal experiences and perspectives and colonial interests and mindsets, including those of settlers who contested dominant narratives.[87] While we can ask 'what remains of

[82] *Report of the Board* above note 72 at 68.
[83] As above at 9.
[84] As above at 67–68.
[85] As above at 9–10.
[86] As above at 135–136.
[87] The concept of middle ground promoting a capacity for equitable relations between different peoples was influentially explained by historian Richard White. See White Richard *The Middle Ground: Indians, Empires, and Republics in the Great Lakes Region, 1650–1815* Cambridge University Press New York 1991. See also Carter Paul 'Public Space: Its Mythopoetic Foundations and the Limits of the Law' (2007) 16(2) *Griffith Law Review* 430.

law?' in commission of inquiry processes that are deliberately ahistorical, that fail to deliver a justice that addresses the structural conditions of injustice, we can reply that what remains is that people come to law to lay claims and to provide their testimony of lived realities. In so doing, we suggest, they establish a space where injustice can be laid bare — and considerations of just alternatives can enter the legal record.

The residents and their supporters who testified at the Inquiry demonstrated a commitment to law and to justice. They used their testimony as an act of resistance and agency, deliberately carving out a space of justice in the face of the encompassing colonial structure. Their testimony reveals the process of negotiation and contestation within colonialism that postcolonial theorists have articulated, and the possibilities inherent within it.[88]

6.0 Conclusion

In seeking to promote public understanding and discussion of structural justice we hope to contribute to the growing body of work that is looking both within and beyond conventional mechanisms of reform. We can recognise commissions of inquiry as governance mechanisms tailored towards addressing socio-political controversies in order to 'move on'. We can acknowledge that they will have a limited remit in engendering structural change. But we can also recognise that these commissions may open up a space of appreciability through being seized by those who make claims on them.

A question that has motivated our work is why it is that in so many places, despite efforts at reform, oppression continues. This paper places itself as addressing this question through an analysis of the mechanism of the commission of inquiry in relation to colonial and former colonial powers. It has provided two central responses. Firstly, that these commissions play a political function and are used as a means of governance: through the apparent resolving of crises while deliberately not addressing the underlying structural conditions of the colonial exploitation that produce these harms. Secondly, commissions of inquiry can locate themselves in the present and as concerned with current harms: thus, again, failing to account for the broader colonial context in which they occur, which is both historically located and presently felt.

While commissions of inquiry may recognise the injustices reported to them, as discussed in the sections above their focus on discrete rather than broader structural harms and their longer historical trajectory means their impact can be limited. As mechanisms of governance, they function with necessarily curtailed mandates that allow for the recognition of harm without the need for broader structural change. What they may unexpectedly achieve, however, is an opening up of a space in which structural injustices can be openly brought to the fore and put on record. The process of the commission may enable this and open up 'new possibilities for

[88] See, for example, Bhabha Homi *The Location of Culture* Routledge New York 1994; McClintock Anne *Imperial Leather: Race, Gender, and Sexuality in the Colonial Contest* Routledge New York 1995; Cooper Frederick and Stoler Ann Laura *Tensions of Empire: Colonial Cultures in a Bourgeois World* California University Press Berkeley 1997.

dissent and contestations'.[89] Whether these are heard is dependent on the political and social frameworks in which they are situated — and without attention to these, as we have discussed, they function as means of securing governance not change. In situations of colonialism, where colonial patterns and frameworks continue, these commissions are unable to initiate the broader recognition necessary for structural change. The record of claims generated through the commission is left to be reactivated at a later stage. That we have this record, however, through the claims made on it, articulates a realm of possibility and change that would otherwise not be offered.

Disclosure Statement

No potential conflict of interest was reported by the authors.

[89] In the context of early nineteenth-century Victorian commissions of inquiry, Frankel has explored how 'even as these inquiries confirmed and strengthen social gradations as well as hierarchies of knowledge and expertise, they nevertheless allowed British lower classes' participation in official discourse as knowers, not just sufferers, and opened new possibilities for dissent and contestations'. Frankel Oz *Vulnerable Populations and Epistemic Justice in Early Victorian Britain* paper presented at International Institute for the Sociology of Law, Onati, 2–3 July 2015 at 4.

WHOSE REPARATION CLAIMS COUNT? GENDER, HISTORY AND (IN)JUSTICE

Natalia Gerodetti

Abstract. The recognition and compensation of historic injustices is part and parcel of a politics of recognition and of socio-legal attempts at reconciliation and redemption. The notion of 'restorative justice' has recently gained political salience by invoking national governments to face and deal with historical injustice and often judicial recourse is used as a means to redress, through legislation, the legacy of historical wrongs in which democratic nation states have been implicated. At least it would appear so when considering the proliferation of apologies and reparations issued in recent years on behalf of public bodies. Yet, despite a proliferation of apologies, memorials, commemorations and other means of dealing with past practices, some claims for reparation regarding historic wrongs remain unaddressed, unsuccessful or unheard. This article analyses discourses of eugenic legacies and restorative justice claims using a gender-sensitive perspective and examines reparation claims in relation to coerced sterilisations comparing Switzerland with Sweden and several states in the United States.

True reconciliation does not consist in merely forgetting the past.

Nelson Mandela, 7 January 1996

1.0 INTRODUCTION AND OVERVIEW

Contemporary democracies seem to be faced with political, juridical and ethical questions about their relations to the past and the resulting obligations, particularly with regard to the maintenance of meanings of a democratic future. Thus, the central role that reparations have played in recent transitions to democracy in South Africa, but also Latin America and elsewhere, can be taken as a signifier of that collective act of pausing, reflecting and accounting for past actions to then find ways of moving into the future. While these debates have often been framed in relation to transitional justice in post-conflict democracies, the historic wrongs that have occurred in countries with an established democratic tradition should be of equal interest, and subjected to a critical gender-sensitive inquiry. This article asks how eugenically motivated coerced sterilisations are the subject of contemporary reparation claims and whether feminist theories of transitional justice and reparations can be usefully brought to bear on interpreting these different historic injustice claims. The paper draws on theories of justice and reparations in order to query whether we find ourselves in new situations of 'abnormal justice'—concurrently dealing with redistribution, recognition and representation—not just at the *time of wrongdoing* but also in contemporary struggles around reparation, understood as a contested set of ideas about recognition, acknowledgement, apologies and financial redress for past injustices.[1]

There has been a proliferation of the 'memory industry', with apologies for historic wrongs constituting an important element in the production of historical memory.[2] Alexandra Stern's seminal work on American eugenics argues that apologies are central to the production of historical memory of eugenics in the United States, yet as mnemonic acts which position the past, present and future, they also 'necessarily privilege certain historical plotlines over others'.[3] Recognising historic injustice and allowing public discourses about possible forms of reparation have received significant public as well as academic interest in the past few years. Yet public discourses of past practices should not merely be seen in the context of corrective history, or in the realm of judicial discourses about corrective justice. Instead, the suggestion here is that compensation claims regarding involuntary sterilisation need to be contextualised as a powerful collision between history, politics, law and the media and thereby provide a platform for a socio-legal examination. Moreover, looking specifically at the (predominantly) gendered practice of coerced sterilisation, this article examines how established democracies[4] deal with reparation claims with what Rubio-Marín calls 'Sexual and Reproductive Violence' (SRV).[5]

The way in which contemporary societies deal with historical practices through contemporary claims for reparations has ramifications for the notion of biopolitics and its associated social, legal and political heritage. The old biopolitics, which eugenics is seen to be part of, may no longer be in the immediate arena of administration of public health in Western nations but it remains a public issue through various political struggles to redress historical injustices emanating from eugenic practices.

---

1 Fraser Nancy *Scales of Justice: Reimagining Political Space in a Globalized World* Columbia University Press New York 2009; see also Fraser Nancy and Honneth Axel *Redistribution or Recognition? A Political-Philosophical Exchange* Verso London 2003.

2 Marrus Michael 'Official Apologies and the Quest for Historical Justice' (2007) 6 *Journal of Human Rights* 75; See also Barkan Elazar and Karn Alexander *Taking Wrongs Seriously: Apologies and Reconciliation* Stanford University Press Stanford 2006; Karn Alexander *Amending the Past: Europe's Holocaust Commissions and the Right to History* Wisconsin University Press Wisconsin 2015.

3 Stern Alexandra Minna 'Eugenics and Historical Memory in America' (2005) 3 *History Compass* 1.

4 The term established democracies is used here to denote nation states which have a history of democracy reaching back to modernity and it is used in contrast to the idea of post-conflict democracies.

5 Rubio-Marín Ruth (ed.) *The Gender of Reparations: Unsettling Sexual Hierarchies while Redressing Human Rights Violations* Cambridge University Press Cambridge 2009. See also Rubio-Marín Ruth and de Greiff Pablo 'Women and Reparations' (2007) 1 *International Journal of Transitional Justice* 318.

Eugenics has been put forward as a primary example of biopolitics by Foucault with its disciplining of individual bodies and regulations of the body collective of the population.[6] Yet parallel to the uncovering of national eugenic histories during the twentieth century there has also been increasing interest in the role of redress and reconciliation in relation to historical injustices towards the end of the last millennium, indicating that biopolitics of the past bears socio-political relevance to our contemporary world. Ideas of redress and reparations have influenced renewed debates over reparations for slavery in the United States, or the official apology and the monetary awards extended by the United States government to Japanese Americans illegally interned during World War II. They have also shaped the success of reparation lawsuits against Swiss banks, European insurance companies and German corporations for harms inflicted in the Nazi past[7] and are being brought into discussions for compensation regarding eugenic practices such as coerced sterilisations, or the forced removal of children.[8] However, compensation and reparation are not synonymous and furthermore, reparation is perhaps best seen as a process rather than an event. The numerous forms of reparations are outlined in detail by the United Nations Human Rights Committee and include restitution, compensation, rehabilitation, satisfaction and guarantees of non-repetition.[9]

The paper begins by providing an overview of emerging reparation claims with regard to past practices of coerced sterilisation before mapping eugenic practices and thinking within the concept of biopolitics. After contextualising contemporary reparation claims with a 'genealogy of the present'[10] the next section offers theoretical approaches to justice and reparations. Finally, due to their concurrent developments, Sweden and Switzerland are compared in order to examine similarities and differences in relation to gendered reparation claims and reproductive justice.

2.0 Mediatisation of Historic Wrongs

Debates about reparations for eugenic practices, particularly in relation to compensation demands for involuntary sterilisations, have witnessed an upsurge since the millennium. Since 1997, a series of prominent media scandals concerning eugenic practices in some US states, Sweden and Switzerland have made national and international

---

[6] Foucault Michel *The Will to Knowledge: The History of Sexuality Vol I* trans R Hurley Penguin London 1978 [1976] p 139.

[7] McCarthy Thomas 'Coming to Terms with our Past: On the Morality and Politics of Reparations for Slavery' (2004) 32 *Political Theory* 750.

[8] Although sterilisations and the removal of children were qualitatively different in character, with one being a medical technology and the other not, they were both informed by eugenic thinking. Eugenics comprised both *negative* and *positive* eugenics, that is, both the thinking and the practices which aimed to prevent *unworthy* offspring through interventions as well as the thinking and measures which were directive or advisory in character and which aimed at educating the *worthy* sections of society into appropriate reproductive behaviour.

[9] Basic Principles and Guidelines on the Right to a Remedy and Reparations for Victims of Gross Violations of International Human Rights and Serious Violations of International Humanitarian Law, UN Human Rights Committee, 56th meeting, Ch XI, E/CN.4/2005.L.10/Add.11 [BPG].

[10] Visker Rudi *Michel Foucault: Genealogy as Critique* Verso London 1995.

headlines and prompted a socio-legal discussion about redress.[11] In the Swedish case, Maija Runcis's thesis (published in 1998) that examined sterilisation policies in Sweden generated considerable interest and concern throughout Europe's popular and scientific press in 1997.[12] Although social historians had been previously aware of this, the media and public alike were shocked to discover that part of Sweden's 'prophylactic social welfare policy' aimed at preventing social problems, rather than compensating for them, through practices such as eugenic sterilisation.[13]

Runcis highlighted that between 1934 and 1976 in Sweden over 60,000 people were sterilised—sometimes by force, but often by persuasion, and notably overwhelmingly women.[14] In Switzerland, a government report was published in 1998 on the notorious *Kinder der Landstrasse* ('Children of the Country Roads') programme. This officially confirmed earlier reported claims that had led to the closing down of the project and which eventually resulted in a formal apology by the government.[15] Described by the then President of the Confederation, Ruth Dreifuss, as 'one of the darkest chapters in Swiss modern history',[16] the programme of the agency *Pro Juventute* was partly government funded and removed over 600 *Jenisch* (or often referred to in English as Yenish or even Yeniche, the main group of nomadic people within Switzerland) children from their parents, to be raised in orphanages, foster families and psychiatric institutions between 1926 and 1973. It aimed at eliminating vagrancy, but also to eradicate Jenisch culture, as its explicit aims were, in the words of its founding father Alfred Siegfried, to prevent the Jenisch from 'reproducing without restraints and bringing new generations of degenerate and abnormal children into the world'.[17]

Swiss eugenic history was not new to social historians as a number of studies since the early 1990s attest.[18] But following the 'Nazi Gold' scandal, which revealed that

[11] 'Europe's Taboo, Sterilization, Out of the Shadows', *Chicago Tribunal* 28 August 1997 <http://articles.chicagotribune.com/1997-08-28/news/9708280294_1_sterilisations-handicapped-nazi-dictator-adolf-hitler> Accessed 12 April 2016.

[12] Weindling Paul 'International Eugenics: Swedish Sterilisation in Context' (1999) 24 *Scandinavian Journal of History* 179.

[13] Kulawik Teresa 'The Nordic Model of the Welfare State and the Trouble with a Critical Perspective' Keynote lecture presented at the International Conference in Nordic Studies Norden at the Crossroads Helsinki 2002.

[14] Runcis Maija 'Striden om historien' in Aronsson Peter (ed.) *Makten över minnet: historiekultur i förändring* Studentlitteratur Lund 2000; see also Tydén Mattias 'The Scandinavian States: Reformed Eugenics Applied' in Bashford Alison and Levine Philippa (eds) *The Oxford Handbook of the History of Eugenics* Oxford University Press Oxford 2010.

[15] Leimgruber Walter Meier Thomas and Sablonier Roger *Das Hilfswerk für die Kinder der Landstrasse. Historische Studie aufgrund der Akten der Stiftung Pro Juventute im Schweizerischen Bundesarchiv* Bundesarchiv Dossier 9 Bern 1998.

[16] As above at 1.

[17] As above.

[18] See, for instance, Heller Geneviève, Jeanmonod Gilles and Gasser Jacques *Rejetées, rebelles, mal adaptées: Débats sur l'eugénisme — Pratiques de la stérilisation non volontaire en Suisse romande au XXe siècle* Georg Editeur Geneva 2002; Huonker Thomas *Diagnose: 'Moralisch Defekt'. Kastration, Sterilisation und Rassenhygiene im Dienst der Schweizer Sozialpolitik und Psychiatrie 1890–1970* Orell Füssli Verlag Zurich 2003; Keller Christoph *Der Schädelvermesser. Otto Schlaginhaufen — Anthropologe und Rassenhygieniker. Eine biographische Reportage* Limmat Verlag Zürich 1995; Mottier Véronique 'Narratives of National Identity: Sexuality, Race, and the Swiss "Dream of Order"' (2000) 26

Swiss banks profiteered from Nazi crimes, it further shook the foundations of Swiss identity, in particular its (self-) image as a neutral nation driven by humanitarian aims and social justice. Furthermore, it exposed a nation, whose political institutions of direct democracy and federalism were devised to allow for the expression and protection of cultural 'differences' within its borders, as having behaved in a discriminatory and damaging manner towards particular groups, thereby contributing to their continuous marginalisation. Different reactions to national pasts, such as those of Sweden, which was quick to launch a process of compensation following apologies from the then Swedish government, suggest the necessity of considering issues of redress and reconciliation in relation to eugenic pasts. Switzerland, by contrast, decided not to adopt legislation for compensation in December 2004.[19] In the US, meanwhile, a 'discursive architecture of apologies'[20] has been mounted in relation to involuntary sterilisations, with state governors of Virginia, Oregon, North Carolina, South Carolina and California apologising for past practices since 2002. In the following section, I will outline briefly the context of eugenics and involuntary sterilisation before examining a number of reparation claims juxtaposing the Swedish and the Swiss case.

3.0 Eugenic Utopia and Biopolitics

Eugenics, in its many different forms, was hugely influential in modernising societies since the late nineteenth century, and is seen to have constituted a mainstream body of thinking across Western nations, which constituted themselves through a 'quest for order'.[21] Underpinned by science and reason, modernising nations sought to create and maintain social and political order, no longer seen as *natural*, through the design, engineering and management of existence. In that pursuit, eugenics offered not just a scientific analysis of existing social problems but also strategies to solve these problems; strategies that were presented in the name of rationality and that targeted the regulation of the population's reproductive sexuality.[22]

Within discourses about threats to the nation's health, sexuality and gender, in conjunction with particular ideas about physical and mental abilities, came to constitute an axis of intervention. On these premises, eugenics became an approach and a tool to rationalise the management of the population's health, especially through the governance of reproductive sexuality, particularly women's sexuality. Many of the discussions focus on the differences between *voluntary* and *forced* sterilisation and the legal basis

---

Swiss Journal of Sociology 533; Wecker Regina 'Eugenik — individueller Ausschluss und nationaler Konsens' in Guex Sebastien et al (eds) *Krisen und Stabilisierung: Die Schweiz in der Zwischenkriegszeit* Chronos Zürich 1998 p 165.

[19] <https://www.bj.admin.ch/bj/de/home/gesellschaft/gesetzgebung/archiv/sterilisation.html> Accessed 12 April 2016.

[20] Stern above note 3 at 3.

[21] Bauman Zygmunt *Modernity and the Holocaust* Polity Press Cambridge 1989; Mottier above note 18.

[22] Gilroy Paul *The Black Atlantic: Modernity and Double Consciousness* Harvard University Press Cambridge 1995; Kevles Daniel *In the Name of Eugenics* University of California Press Berkeley 1995.

for either or both, yet relatively little is said about the fact that these did not constitute two ends of a continuum.[23] Indeed, as both the Swiss and the Swedish cases show, volunteering or 'voluntariness' to consent was upheld as a principle even though actual practices point clearly to pressures and/or threats under which consent was given. In addition, a closer look at the contexts of sterilisations reveals that they were often embedded in a complex catalogue of interventions and built upon existing social and political inequalities and gender regimes.[24]

As for the legality of sterilisation, Sweden had two national laws (from 1934 and 1941)[25] whereas in Switzerland, only the regional jurisdiction (Vaud) had a law on sterilisation from 1928 until 1985, with Bern having a directive (in 1931).[26] The Vaudois law, however, served to effectively curtail eugenicists' efforts to apply the law more widely, and sterilisation practices have been more prevalent in localities where psychiatrists were left to their own devices.[27] Criminal Law provisions were highly contested among psychiatrists who mostly preferred making more use of civil law legislation, which ultimately proved more useful to psychiatrists in maintaining their role as *gatekeepers* of reproductive sexuality. However, the absence of a specific legal framework has particular ramifications for contemporary reparation claims, as I will show later.

Eugenic practices were directed at changing the trajectory of the perceived dysgenic future and creating instead a utopian future society. As such, the idea of prevention is crucial to eugenics while at the same time, the effects of eugenic thinking and practices were always firmly located in the future, that is, present-day society. Eugenics was thus always imbued with a temporal dimension, so that questions of time — the relationship between past, present and future — are by no means crossed for the first time by contemporary reparation claims. Foucault has compellingly shown

[23] Missa Jean-Noël '"L'individu n'est rien, l'espèce est tout": analyse historique de l'évolution de la question de l'eugénisme au XXe siècle' in Missa J-N (ed.) *De l'eugénisme d'Etat à l'eugénisme privé* de Boeck Bruxelles 1999 p 9; Porter Dorothy 'Eugenics and the Sterilisation Debate in Sweden before World War II' (1999) 24 *Scandinavian Journal of History* 145.

[24] Gerodetti Natalia 'From Science to Social Technology: Eugenics and Politics in the Twentieth Century' (2006) 13 *Social Politics: International Studies in Gender, State and Society* 59.

[25] Enligt lagen (1934: 171) and Enligt Lagen (1941: 282) <https://www.riksdagen.se/sv/dokument-lagar/dokument/svensk-forfattningssamling/lag-1999332-om-ersattning-till-steriliserade-i_sfs-1999-332> Accessed 12 April 2016. See also Broberg Gunnar and Tyden Mattias 'Eugenics in Sweden: Efficient Care' in Broberg Gunnar and Roll-Hansen Nils (eds) *Eugenics and the Welfare State: Sterilisation Policy in Denmark, Sweden, Norway, and Finland* Michigan State Press Michigan 1996 p 77.

[26] For Vaud, see <http://www.publidoc.vd.ch/guestDownload/direct/Texte%20adopté%20par%20CE.pdf?path=/Company%20Home/VD/CHANC/SIEL/antilope/objet/CEGC/Rapport%20du%20CE/2013/09/439671_269_Texte%20adopté%20par%20CE_20151210_1220528.pdf. For Bern, see http://www.amtsdruckschriften.bar.admin.ch/viewOrigDoc.do?id=10031259> Accessed 12 April 2016.

[27] Medical personnel were reportedly glad about the absence of a legislative framework as it allowed them to conduct interventions without formal applications to health boards and only with the consent of the person and/or guardian which they felt was easy enough to obtain. For a full discussion see Gerodetti Natalia '"Unter besonders günstigen Verhältnissen arbeiten" Eugenic Thinking and Practice in Switzerland' in Westermann Stephanie Kühl Richard and Gross Dominik (eds) *Medizin im Dienste der Erbgesundheit: Beiträge zur Geschichte der Eugenik und Rassenhygiene* Literatur Verlag Berlin 2009 p 79.

throughout his work that genealogy is important to our conceptualisation of the contemporary world when he made a general and conceptual argument about the role of history in the present.[28] The interest here is not in how eugenics' legacy is being reconfigured, continued and discontinued in contemporary genetic politics, but in examining how the history of eugenics is a history of the present for several reasons.[29] Thus, in addition to eugenics' own ideas about the future, various contemporary judicial institutions are dealing with claims relating to eugenics, which makes it a present sociopolitical dilemma. That is, eugenics does, by means of invoking calls for reparation and therefore law as a mechanism of regulatory power, impact on contemporary politics and thus has a complex temporal impact.

Thus, in calls for reparation, the utopias of history form a central temporal axis. Before examining the gender-specific historic injustices around coerced sterilisations, it is helpful to outline some of the work on reparation and transitional justice and deal with its principles and strategies for implementation.[30]

4.0 Justice and Reparations

Redressing past wrongs is seen as essential to establishing conditions of justice in societies scarred by the enduring and pervasive effects of those wrongs. This is particularly pertinent where perpetrators of those wrongs include continuing corporate agents in the broad sense of bodies recognised in law as incorporated, such as states, firms, and other public and private institutions, such as welfare agencies or psychiatric units, and when those affected are large groups of individuals who were harmed precisely as members of a specific group, such as *the mentally deficient* or *abnormals.* The ultimate aim is to involve national governments in redressing the legacy of injustice through legislation but also through court proceedings.

Based on the principles of corrective or rectificatory justice, and in as much as it is practically possible and morally permissible, the correction of a legacy of past injustices is thought to be a moral-political requirement for enduring *corporate agents*, such as states. The principle of collective responsibility emerges from ideas about collective citizenship in that each generation of citizens not only inherits *the rights of membership*, although critical theorists have long pointed to the fact that citizenship rights have not been bestowed equally upon members, but also that each generation inherits *the burdens of membership.* National debts, be they financial or cultural, accrue to the political community as a whole either because they were state sanctioned and implemented or because state members collectively benefited so that by the same logic they ought to share inherited liabilities.[31]

The aim of corrective justice is not to relegate dealings with past injustices to the realm of guilt but to see collective responsibility as an element of a more complex

---

[28] Visker above note 10.
[29] As above.
[30] See, for instance, Thompson Janna *Taking Responsibility for the Past: Reparation and Historical Injustice* Polity Cambridge 2002; Torpey John (ed.) *Politics and the Past: On Repairing Historical Injustices* Rowman and Littlefield Lanham 2003.
[31] McCarthy above note 7.

narrative within 'the history of a relationship'.[32] Embedded in that notion is the perception that material reparations are not the only or primary form of reparation and that symbolic measures can be equally effective, consisting of public acknowledgement and public apologies, times and places of official commemoration, museums and exhibitions, revised textbooks and curricula, a strengthening of civic trust and solidarity and so on. Discourses on reconciliation warn against perceiving restoration as the object of reparative justice, but are also wary of the tendency to devolve into 'justice as the demands of the victim'.[33] While the depths of the body of literature on reparative justice is beyond the purposes of this article, the elements upon which it does wish to dwell are the two forms of reparation alluded to above, that is, material and symbolic forms of reparation for past injustices in the context of eugenics.

Similarly, this article does not seek to undertake a comprehensive theorising or review of feminist transitional justice but, nevertheless, I want to draw out several important contributions. Transitional justice paradigms have been much enriched by a body of feminist theorising, which posits gender and feminist thinking within its analysis.[34] Within transitional justice, reparations are seen to be constituted by material and symbolic redress to victims of human rights violations in the aftermath of widespread political violence. The historic wrongs affecting women in the case studies considered here did not happen against the backdrop of widespread political violence and moreover they do not affect a group of women who have built a strong sense of community or solidarity in the aftermath of the experienced wrong doing.

Nevertheless, the experience of coerced sterilisations constitutes, in Rubio-Marín's terms, a form of SRV.[35] Rubio-Marín subsumes forced sterilisations under the catalogue of practices of SRV and although her work is more explicitly on reparations in transitional justice contexts of post-conflict nations, her categorisation is nevertheless a useful one here.[36] Coerced sterilisation is not only a violation of someone's bodily integrity at the point of intervention but, crucially, locates its effect in the future by depriving women of the possibility of motherhood. Given that motherhood is a strong component of normative expectations of femininity — and thus identity and belonging to society — I propose that even within a non-post-conflict country coerced sterilisation can be aptly contextualised as a form of SRV.

Furthermore, both Rubio-Marín and Margaret Urban Walker identify the impact that normative concepts of masculinity and femininity have on the nature of violence committed and the reparations process that follows. In distinguishing violence against women before, during and after conflict, Walker argues that before conflict — and thus also useful for non-conflict situations such as democratic societies — violence against

[32] As above at 760.
[33] Thompson above note 30.
[34] O'Rourke Catherine *Gender Politics in Transitional Justice* Routledge London 2013; Painter Genevieve Renard 'Thinking Past Rights: Towards Feminist Theories of Reparations' (2012) 30 *Windsor Yearbook of Access to Justice* 1.
[35] Rubio-Marín above note 5 at 4.
[36] Rubio-Marín Ruth 'Reparations for Conflict-Related Sexual and Reproductive Violence: A Decalogue' (2012) 69 *William & Mary Journal of Women & Law* at 19.

women is normative, accepted and ordered.[37] The idea of 'gendered harm' has thus been developed by O'Rourke to draw attention to the specificities that arise from violations that women experience.[38] O'Rourke also develops a notion of gendered harm which draws attention to the connection of (legally recognised) gendered harm and (non-legally recognised) gender regimes and normativities existing within societies. She uses the notion of a 'web of gender-based harms'[39] to point to the interconnection of both the harm experienced during conflict and the effects of gender regimes in pre- and post-conflict society while Rubio-Marín draws a similar connection by examining gender-based harm within the long transition from pre- to post-conflict society.[40]

What is important to draw out here is that the harms experienced by women — when they are sexual and reproductive harms — continue to have an impact on women's experiences by framing their perceptions and status within their communities as 'spoiled identity'.[41] Sexual and reproductive violence is typically accompanied by 'social and symbolic multipliers of harm',[42] in the form of stigma, ostracism and rejection by actual or potential partners and family members. Through these social effects the 'original violation is extended, ramified, and augmented in multiple ways that significantly alter the women's physical safety and well-being, social reintegration and status, economic survival, and eligibility for marriage'.[43]

Reproductive violations are therefore continuous violations with both primary reproductive violation as well as consequent reactions from surrounding people and communities.[44] Such reactions add to the negative experience and not only comprehensively render victims stained or spoiled but also devalued. Drawing on Goffman, stigmatisation works by comprehensively 'spoiling identities' which separates the stigmatised person from society and from herself through a process whereby the person is perceived as less than human, or not as worthy as others. Read against the backdrop of normative constructions of women and femininity through marriage and even more so motherhood,[45] the idea of *spoiled identity* has particular pertinence to women whose reproductive abilities have been curtailed resulting in various forms of stigma management for the person.[46]

---

[37] Rubio-Marín above note 5; Urban Walker Margaret 'Gender and Violence in Focus: A Background for Gender Justice in Reparations' in Rubio-Marín Ruth (ed.) *The Gender of Reparations: Unsettling Sexual Hierarchies while Redressing Human Rights Violations* Cambridge University Press Cambridge 2009 p 22.

[38] O'Rourke above note 34 at 37.

[39] As above.

[40] Rubio-Marín above note 36.

[41] Goffman Erving *Stigma: Notes on the Management of Spoiled Identity* Penguin Harmondsworth 1990 [1963] p 3.

[42] Rubio-Marín above note 5 at 28 and 29.

[43] Urban Walker Margaret 'Gender and Violence in Focus: A Background for Gender Justice in Reparations' in Rubio-Marín Ruth (ed.) *The Gender of Reparations: Unsettling Sexual Hierarchies while Redressing Human Rights Violations* Cambridge University Press Cambridge 2009 p 31.

[44] The reproductive violations involved in coerced sterilisations have been shown to have been linked to other practices such as granting abortions upon consenting to sterilisations, or the receipt of a marriage licence only upon agreeing to a sterilisation.

[45] See, for instance, Smart Carol *Regulating Womanhood: Historical Essays on Marriage, Motherhood and Sexuality* Routledge London 1992.

[46] See also Nussbaum Martha *Hiding from Humanity: Disgust, Shame and the Law* Princeton University Press Princeton 2004.

While for those affected by historic sterilisation practices this may lie in the past, it is important to acknowledge the enduring effects of both primary and secondary violations that have occurred.

5.0 Reconciliating Eugenic Pasts

Coming to terms with eugenic pasts has resulted in a number of politico-legal struggles, which have sought to reconcile coerced sterilisations. A number of US states, such as Virginia (2002), Oregon (2002), North Carolina (2002) and California (2003)[47] have produced apologies for their sterilisation practices which have been interpreted as the acceptance of some form of accountability for past eugenic policies and measures.[48] Redress in the form of financial compensation, however, arrived only a decade later in North Carolina (2013)[49] and Virginia (2015).[50] Sweden, equally, has undergone a public engagement with past coercive welfare practices and after a media scandal in 1997 Swedish Social Minister Margot Wallström, who only in 1996 rejected an individual application for damages for forced sterilisation, has officially apologised for the nation, saying 'what happened was nothing but barbaric'.[51]

The Swedish Report,[52] following the publication of a series of articles in the *Dagens Nyheter*[53] about the particularly gendered dimensions of eugenically-motivated, coercive sterilisation, also initiated international debate such as in the United States and in Switzerland. The Swedish government was swift in its response to public reaction and set up a state commission to atone for the perceived atrocities and established that those sterilised without their consent should receive reparations.[54] The report asserted that 31,000 people were estimated to have been voluntarily sterilised. 6000 sterilisations (c. 10%) happened with explicit force, and 15,000 people (c. 25%) had signed the application though many of these did so in order to be allowed an abortion or be released from an institution.[55] In a further 6000 cases (c. 10%)

[47] Stern above note 3 at 211. 'Virginia Apologises for Eugenics Policy' *BBC News* 3 May 2002; 'Apology for Oregon Forces Sterilizations' *Los Angeles Times* 3 December 2002; North Carolina: <https://www.uvm.edu/~lkaelber/eugenics/NC/NC.html> Accessed 12 April 2016; 'California: State Issues Apology for Policy of Sterilization' *Los Angeles Times* 12 March 2003.

[48] Although notably the apology was *received* by victims only in the first three states, not California.

[49] The appropriations bill can be found at <http://www.ncleg.net/sessions/2013/bills/senate/pdf/s402v7.pdf> Accessed 12 April 2016.

[50] <http://www.dbhds.virginia.gov/individuals-and-families/sterilisation-compensation> Accessed 12 April 2016.

[51] Population Research Institute <https://www.pop.org/content/the-knife-in-the-closet-127#sthash.Fnprbx8E.dpuf> Accessed 12 April 2016.

[52] Regeringens Skrivelse *Redogörelse för steriliseringsfrågan i Sverige åren 1935-1975 och regeringens åtgärder* 2000 01/73: 1–27.

[53] For a thorough analysis of his articles and the ensuing debate, see Kroon Åsa 'Debattens dynamik: hur budskap och betydelser förvandlas i mediedebatter' (2001) 227 *Linköping studies in arts and science Linköping Tema University* 0282–9800 133.

[54] Regeringens above note 52.

[55] Many were performed during abortions, as mandatory before release from prisons or psychiatric wards, to qualify for public assistance or to avoid losing custody of children (see Regeringens as above). Runcis argued that the original motivation to *cleanse* society of the *feebleminded* broadened into a willingness to sterilise for socially or morally offensive behaviour. Local committees, with

there were also signs of persuasion or pressure and the remaining 4000 cases (c. 7%) could not be determined.[56] Ninety-three per cent of them were women which thus pointed to gendered aspects of eugenic administration.[57]

Crucially, the report proposed that where women were 'probably' sterilised against their will, they should be awarded compensation and where the sterilisation was voluntary (since 1976) there was to be no compensation. By 2001, 2300 applications had been received and 1600 were successful, receiving an identical sum of 175,000 Swedish crowns (approximately $25,000).[58] As Leif Persson, the vice-chairman of the Swedish Sterilisation Compensation board, said:

> It is a symbolic gesture to make up for past wrongs. The laws between 1941 and 1975 said that sterilisations must be voluntary, but we know that many people were sterilised against their will.[59]

However, while the Swedish decision of 1999 to compensate those affected by past eugenic practices was productive of a discourse (both political and mass media) about the history of sterilisations elsewhere, Lene Koch has also argued that the motivation behind this was more a historiography of indignation rather than a historiography of eugenics. In other words, while Sweden's public sphere was almost unanimously agreed on the need to compensate, it saw less of a need to search for a thorough reconstruction of the past. An imperative to produce further historical studies on Sweden's past was not commissioned until 2005 and its purpose was to provide 'supportive documentation for a discussion concerning the values of the Society and State actions'.[60] In Koch's view, the media was instrumental in cajoling Swedish politicians to take action and was an expression of a politicising and moralising attitude towards the past to serve contemporary interests. Underpinning the Swedish discussions and subsequent strategy was a wish to atone quickly and move on from the uncomfortable history so hard to reconcile with the image of a caring welfare state.

When the Swedish inquiry faced its uncomfortable history and set up a compensation package the commission head Carl-Gustaf Andren argued that payment could not be regarded as true compensation for involuntary sterilisation but that it would provide 'concrete and visible evidence of personal redress, an expression of taking a stand against and regretting what took place'.[61] The report refrained from accusing

---

significant variations in implementation of the laws, sometimes chose to recommend or impose sterilisation of *gypsies*, women who could not provide for numerous children, or sexually promiscuous women; see Runcis Maja *Steriliseringar i folkshemmet* [Sterilisation in the Swedish Welfare State] Ordfront Stockholm 1998.

[56] Regeringens above note 52 at 13.

[57] Runcis above note 55; Regeringens above note 52.

[58] Johannson Karin '1600 tvångssteriliserade har fått skadestånd' *Sydsvenskan* April 2005 <http://www.sydsvenskan.se/sverige/1-600-tvangssteriliserade-har-fatt-skadestand/> Accessed 12 April 2016.

[59] 'Sweden Pays Sterilisation Victims' *Deseret News* 1 November 1999 p 6.

[60] Koch Lene 'On Ethics, Scientist, and Democracy: Writing the History of Eugenic Sterilisation' in Doel Ronald and Söderqvist Thomas (eds) *A Historiography of Contemporary Science, Technology and Medicine: Writing Recent Science* Routledge London 2006 p 81 at 84.

[61] 'Sterilization Victims Ought to be Paid: Panel' *The Daily Gazette* (New York) 27 January 1999 p 15.

individuals but held that passivity and silence of politicians and loose interpretations of sterilisation laws by medical authorities enabled the operations to be forced on people.

6.0 Eugenics and Different Politics of Redemption

Prompted by the Swedish case and emerging research into Swiss eugenic practices, the Swiss government was equally faced with a reparation claim for coerced sterilisation in 1999. First articulated as a postulate in Parliament in 1997, a formal parliamentary initiative was submitted in 1999, forcing political engagement.[62] The outcome of the lengthy democratic process was the decree of national legislation regulating sterilisation in future, and a rejection of the proposal for compensation in December 2004.[63] Despite an initial welcome, the Federal Council paved the way for the final rejection of compensation measures with its position paper in 2003.[64] It contained an acknowledgement of the need to critically question as well as recognise the perhaps 'darker sides of recent social history' (as the government did with the previous, eugenically related 'Children of the Country Road' programme). The position paper conceded that sterilisations were partly based on 'eugenic reasons, in conjunction with social-hygienic or socio-economic goals, and partly they were taken in the presumed interest of the person concerned'.[65] But the position paper was wary of discussing compensation arguing that moral values and ethics as well as the conception of psychiatry and rights to sexuality had changed significantly in the past hundred years and it would be inappropriate to judge past practices on the basis of contemporary values.[66]

After a lengthy parliamentary debate, the rejection of a compensation scheme in cases of involuntary sterilisation centred on three key areas of contestation. First, the absence of a national legal framework on sterilisation was argued to affect the legal responsibility of the government. The recurrence of existing provisions for compensation in cases of criminal injury (Victims Compensation Law, *Opferhilfegesetz OHG*, 1991) were thought to be non-applicable as none of the sterilisations had violated a criminal code and were therefore illegal. Second, it was argued that in the

---

[62] In both Sweden and Switzerland political engagement was launched within parliament though in Sweden much more sharply against the backdrop of the international media scandal. In Switzerland, there was no parallel media attention.

[63] Margrith von Felten submitted the parliamentary initiative in 1999 (99.451) which the legal commission of the National Council (RK-N) decided to follow and draft a law for compensation in 2000. This draft was submitted to a consultation process in during 2002 and resulted in a two-part law: the first regulating the future legal basis for sterilisations in accordance with Convention on Human Rights and Biomedicine by the Council of Europe, ETS Nr 164, 1999; and the second creating a legal basis for compensation and redress.

[64] Stellungnahme Bundesrat (SB) *Parlamentarische Initiative Zwangssterilisation. Entschädigung für Opfer (von Felten). Bericht der Kommission für Rechtsfrage des Nationalrates vom 23. Juni 2003*, 99.451: 6355-6368.

[65] As above at 6356.

[66] This social change in attitudes, the Federal Council stipulated, could not only be seen in relation to disabled people's rights to sexuality but also in changing legislation on welfare measures such as administrative internment.

absence of national legislation and the fact that welfare administration was a cantonal matter that the federal government neither could nor should be held accountable. Furthermore, ascertaining with clarity whether sterilisations were fulfilling the condition of 'coercion' was deemed to be 'extremely difficult', therefore hindering a proper assessment of potential applications. In addition, it was thought that the extent of the problem was unclear due to incomplete historical research:

> It can be concluded from the commission report that sterilisations, which took place without informed consent, were based on different situations and practices according to each canton, physician and institution. The boundary between interventions which were evidently based on illegal coercion and whose legitimacy remains controversial today is fluid.[67]

Third, it was feared that a 'dangerous precedent' would be set by installing a compensation scheme which would lead to other reconciliatory demands for past injustices and incur costs, such as in the case of administrative internments and Contract Children before the 1980s.[68] It was also argued that this would 'create different categories of victims of past injustices' — some of which would be compensated and others not — and there was an additional fear voiced that esteemed figures from the past may (retrospectively) be held accountable (morally or legally) for their practices.[69] This is a narrative strategy that Schürer calls 'adventurous', given this is legally not possible.[70] This desire not to judge historical actors acclaimed a rather curious prominence in Federal Council Blocher's (Minister of Justice at the time) final speech to parliamentarians:

> I will tell you: you should reject this also from the heart. It is not merely a juridical question. It is also about people who have in the past acted for socially legitimate reasons and whom you would now condemn for their socially motivated actions.[71]

The final draft had incorporated earlier concerns from the Federal Council and what was presented to a parliamentary discussion was a proposal which had dropped the

[67] Stellungnahme Bundesrat above note 64 at 6357.

[68] Swiss welfare authorities had a range of measures at their disposal to deal with families perceived to be poor or unruly which have come to the attention of the media, the public and politicians since the late 1990s and which have some 20 years later resulted in the Reparation Initiative (*Wiedergutmachungsinitiative*) submitted in December 2014. One of these was the practice of contracting children from poor families out to farmers or placing them in families where they were often subjected to hardship and more. 15.082 Botschaft zur Volksinitiative 'Wiedergutmachung für Verdingkinder and Opfer fürsorgerischer Zwangssmassnahmen (Wiedergutmachungsinitiative)' und zum indirekten Gegenvorschlag (Bundesgesetz ueber die Aufarbeitung der fürsorgerischen Zwangsmassnahmen und Fremdplatzierungen vor 1981) BBL 2016 101 <https://www.admin.ch/opc/de/federal-gazette/2016/101.pdf> Accessed 12 April 2016.

[69] It was argued that past events should not be judged by present ethical standards which would only do injustice to those individuals who, at the time, acted in the interest of society and on the basis of prevalent social norms.

[70] Schürer Stefan *Die Verfassung im Zeichen historischer Gerechtigkeit. Schweizer Vergangenheitsbewältigung zwischen Wiedergutmachung und Politik mit der Geschichte* Chronos Zürich 2009 p 297.

[71] BBI 2004 7265 Blocher.

entitlement of compensation (the proposed 80,000 Sfr) in favour of a symbolic gesture (5000 Sfr), questioning both the principle of compensation and the amount itself. While initially in March 2004 the National Council was supportive, in December 2004 they concurred with the Council of States' rejection.[72] In the following section, some of the narratives and rationales are examined in more detail.

6.1 *Avoiding Precedents, Avoiding National Responsibility*

The Federal Council and the majority of Parliament were strongly driven by legal questions and argued that neither the Victims Compensation Law (OHG)[73] could be applicable nor that a violation of basic human rights was at stake because of the historicity of the concepts. Furthermore, the principle of equality in law would be injured by setting a precedent for one group of people as others could equally launch claims for reparation for historic injustice such as victims of administrative internments,[74] those abused in orphanages and victims of other child welfare measures from the past. As a result, in 2004 Swiss politicians attempted to establish discursively a notion of historical legacy and collective responsibility that lasted merely two years.[75]

However, reparation (as symbolic and material gesture) had been established previously with the compensations program for the victims of the 'Children of the Country Road' program, a privately-initiated but state-supported programme which systematically removed children from Jenisch families to place them in residential or foster care.[76] That reparation debate resulted in the establishment of a Foundation, which was to issue 'solidarity payments', and thus equally avoided the principle of compensation entitlement.[77] This reparation process, however, was felt by victims to lack proper satisfaction and rehabilitation in the decision not to install a principle of compensation, in the administration of the solidarity payments and in the political avoidance of public acknowledgement and recognition.[78]

The position paper on coerced sterilisations recognised the principle of 'recognition owed' but at the same time tried to avert additional financial obligation:[79]

> We would not want to diminish the personal trajectories resulting from practices that today would be considered inacceptable [sic]. But these practices have to be contemplated in the context of a continuously developing society in which we learn from mistakes and

---

[72] This despite an attempt by a group of historians who lobbied parliament to adopt a reparation law after the rejection. BBI 2004 7265 Menétrey-Savary.

[73] Bundesgesetz über die Hilfe an Opfer von Straftaten (Opferhilfegesetz, OHG) 2007 312.5 <https://www.admin.ch/opc/de/classified-compilation/20041159/index.html> Accessed 12 April 2016.

[74] Administrative internment (*administrative Versorgung*) was a means of effecting imprisonment on the basis of the Swiss Civil Code of 1912 rather than through criminal law which had led to widespread abuses of the system in the early parts of the twentieth century, such as in cases of Contract Children.

[75] AB 2004 N 251 BR Blocher.

[76] Huonker above note 18.

[77] AB 2004 N 251 BR Blocher.

[78] Leimgruber et al above note 15 at 11.

[79] Stellungnahme Bundesrat above note 64 at 6359.

> injustices of the past. The recognition which society owes to victims of coerced sterilisation does not necessarily need to be in the form of financial compensation (for many victims this would come too late anyway). Instead of continuously trying to compensate for past injustices, and thereby open old wounds, we prefer to use existing means to support people with cognitive disabilities or who have psychological and social difficulties and who need care in an institution or other institutional support.[80]

The *continuous* attempts to compensate referred, once again, to the *Pro Juventute* practice and the 'Children of the Country Roads' compensation but also to the case of haemophiliacs where responsibility was acknowledged.[81] The phrasing suggests that, contrary to the professed *recognition owed*, there was actually a strong resentment towards the idea of atonement or making amends for past injustices and an attempt to contextualise, perhaps even hide away, support for people within existing welfare structures. In its argumentation, the position paper also implicitly rejected the notion that victims of coerced sterilisations might have undergone two forms of injury: the coerced sterilisation itself as well as the ensuing stigmatisation and management of a *spoiled identity*. Furthermore, it assumes a contemporary notion of *mental ability* to those affected when historical work comprehensively shows that *mental deficiencies* were in fact enmeshed with various marginalised identities.

The reluctance to engage with ideas of responsibility is, I argue, a third form of injury using the idea of reproductive violence within the life trajectory of affected women: in addition to reproductive injuries and the ensuing marked life as a woman without children the rejection of reparation mechanisms constitutes an injury of the present. While there was an acknowledgement that contemporary discussions might open up healed wounds, there was no thought given to the possible effects of a possible rejection in the form of *not just opening wounds but also sticking another knife in them*. Furthermore, what is striking is that although the principle of *past injustice* was verbally acknowledged, the parliamentary discussions were so occupied with establishing whether or not legal responsibility existed that there was never any proposal of an official apology.

6.2 *Unpacking Responsibility*

Any form of collective responsibility, the Federal Council held, was to be placed at local government level if Parliament nevertheless decided on financial retribution, although not so much in legal terms but in social and political terms. This bears an inherent inconsistency in that the collective is both made and unmade as the bearer of responsibility. If the physicians, welfare administrators, priests and other individuals involved in welfare practices and decision-making processes should not be held personally responsible because they acted according to social norms one would assume

---

[80] As above at 6359.

[81] The Swiss government also rectified its wrong doing towards those who helped refugees before and during WWII who were, according to legislation at the time, sentenced to prison. See Schürer above note 70 at 298. Sozialgesetzbuch (SGB) V — Gesetzliche Krankenversicherung — Artikel 1 des Gesetzes 20 December 1988 BGBl I 2477.

that the bigger national bio-social collective bears past and present responsibility. In other words, if these practices were part of a wider regime of care and prevention in the name of the collective then responsibility for breach of care also lay with the collective, in this case the national collective. But the Federal Council took the decision, as did the majority of Parliament later, that responsibility needed to be defined more narrowly:

> It is precisely unproven in the case at hand, and in contrast to the programme 'Children of the Country Roads', that the Federal Government morally, politically or financially supported forced sterilisation, which have been practiced by certain physicians and institutions.[82]

If responsibility towards the past existed at all then it had to be laid, as did welfare administration, with cantonal governments. This argument effaced that it was a national political decision in the first place that welfare support was denominated to be a local responsibility — cantonal and communal — and that a responsibility or a burden towards the past remains incurred. It was a national-political decision *not* to include a national regulation on sterilisation in the criminal law, which was nationalised between the 1890s and 1930s and enacted in 1942. Moreover, if national legislation had had the effect, as did the Vaudois law,[83] of curbing numbers of sterilisations then in fact national responsibility could even more strongly be framed in terms of *not* intervening. Furthermore, the Swiss government did implicitly sanction sterilisations as part of population politics through the government's position on the family article 1944, for instance. Although eugenic arguments were discarded at the last minute from the family protection rationale the Federal Councillor Philipp Etter argued that it was not necessary to include it as such a politics could be carried out in Switzerland without constitutional basis.[84] The Federal government supported eugenic goals and also never spoke against them during the discussions, as members of parliament and social historians have pointed out.[85] Interestingly, the historical commission challenging the previously national narrative of neutrality of Switzerland during World War II, which was prompted by the Nazi Gold scandal, also concluded that 'collective responsibility by the state' can be defined not just by the state's actions but, crucially, by lack of action.[86]

This creates, it could be argued, a much more complex premise for the attempt to relate past (legal) conditions to present responsibility yet a legalistic interpretation of the separation of past and present prevailed. Rather than using the idea of a 'critical genealogy of the present',[87] the attempt to establish whether past law, social norms and

[82] Stellungnahme Bundesrat above note 64 at 6359.
[83] Irrengesetz von 1901 IV. Abschnitt Art 28 3 September 1928 concerning the sterilisation of mentally deficient people. See also Huonker above note 18 at 141.
[84] Bundesblatt *Bericht des Bundesrates an die Bundesversammlung über das Volksbegehren 'Für die Familie' vom 10. Oktober 1944* Jahrgang 96 22 Bd I.
[85] Wecker Regina 'Der Bund hat Zwangssterilisationen begünstigt' *Basler Zeitung* 6 January 2004.
[86] UEK Unabhängige Expertenkommission Schweiz-Zweiter Weltkrieg *Die Schweiz, der Nationalsozialismus und der Zweite Weltkrieg: Schlussbericht* Pendo Zurich 2002.
[87] Visker above note 10.

welfare practices are the principal framing of the reparation question also obscured that reparation is fundamentally attached to the present, or as Schürer argues, reparation is a problem of the present and it is a process of recognition which inevitably incurs recognising a different history and a rupture with those who had been seen as good citizens:[88]

> The responsibility for the victims of the past is a question of the present. Past injury cannot be reversed. The victims of then, however, can be rejected again. What is at stake is thus less the past practices towards those affected than present practices.[89]

In December 2004, a Reparation Bill for coerced sterilisations was rejected driven by centre and right parties who thought it wrong 'to judge the past according to today's measures and knowledge [and] to map our conception of law onto incidents which occurred in different time and under different conditions'.[90] In contrast, Social Democrats and Greens argued for a need to acknowledge past injustices and saw it neither as a shame nor a misjudgment to retrospectively deem certain practices to be illegal and victimising. Furthermore, they contested that there was an absence of regulation and pointed out that physicians were aware of the need to obtain legally valid consent as otherwise they could be brought to justice for grievous bodily harm, though the question might be raised whether marginalised people can ever do that. Left parties emphasised that the mere absence of sentences for committing grievous bodily harm in the form of sterilisations was not indicative of their practice or its contestation.[91] The position of the Federal Council, they argued, was seen to 'lack a sense of history', to be 'constitutionally insensitive and insufficient' and to constitute a form of 'legalistic sidestepping'.[92] Vigorously contesting the majority position, Left parliamentarians argued that the reparation package of 5000 SFr (equivalent to $3850 in 2004) would 'merely be the bunch of flowers that comes with an apology'.[93] In addition, they argued that a parliamentary rejection of the proposal for compensation would legitimise the *wrongs* of the past and reiterate the victimisation and marginalisation of the people who experienced coerced sterilisations, while not mentioning that this was first and foremost women who experienced, I would argue, a threefold form of injury: first, a coerced sterilisation; second, a life managing womanhood without motherhood; and third, a present government that rejects them by neither issuing a clear apology nor a symbolic gesture of compensation.

---

88 Schürer above note 70 at 302.
89 As above at 301–303.
90 AB 2004 N 246 Mathys SVP. See full chronology at <https://www.parlament.ch/en/ratsbetrieb/amtliches-bulletin/amtliches-bulletin-die-verhandlungen?SubjectId=8011> Accessed 3 August 2010.
91 Schürer above note 70 at 301 where he lists an appeal case from 1939 in which the courts in Zurich deemed it illegal to condition the granting of a marriage licence to a voluntary sterilisation.
92 AB 2004 N 253 Kälin SP
93 AB 2004 N 253 Kälin SP

6.3 *Productive Discourses*

Five years later, in November 2009, Switzerland was criticised by the United Nations Human Rights Commission in its third report 'for not having acted "to repair the coerced castrations until 1987"'. The Commission recommended that Switzerland 'undertake reparation for historical injustice in the form of reparation including non-financial means, such as the form of an apology'.[94] Interestingly, the UN text actually said:

> 20. The Committee is concerned at the reluctance of the State party to compensate or otherwise make reparation for forcible castrations and sterilisations conducted between 1960 and 1987 (arts. 2, 7).
>
> The State party should repair this past injustice through forms of reparation, including non-financial means, such as public apology.[95]

In April 2013 a memorial event was attended by 700 people who had experienced coercive welfare measures (including former Contract Children, those put in administrative care and those forcibly sterilised). Federal Councillor Simonetta Sommaruga's speech entailed an apology for the violation of people's dignity and consequent suffering 'in the name of a fellow citizen, as the Minister of Justice and as a member of the Federal Council of Switzerland' adding that 'nothing is more valuable than human dignity'.[96] Her speech — albeit brief — was clear in its intention that the memorial was not a concluding event but the beginning of a collective engagement with the 'dark chapters of Switzerland's social history'.[97] Interestingly, and in stark contrast to the 2004 positioning, a clear collective guilt was acknowledged. Sommaruga stated that 'a society which does not face its past runs the danger of repeating its mistakes' and she added:

> What is at stake here is not merely about the victims and the perpetrators. It is about us all. Because looking away is also an action. Looking away and not wanting to know creates blind spots. And nothing is more dangerous for a society than blind spots.[98]

The UN reprimand together with an increased research output about historical welfare measures more generally, as well as coerced sterilisation specifically, and heightened media attention (in particular to the fate of Contract Children) has created a veritable proliferation of discourses around reparation since 2009 culminating in a public initiative in 2014 and a governmental counter-proposal for a Reparation Law in 2015 in which victims of coerced sterilisations are planned to be included and which was in parliamentary discussion in April 2016.[99]

---

94 <http//www.wiedergutmachung.ch/initiative/ at 7> Accessed 12 April 2016.

95 Concluding Observations of the Human Rights Committee, Switzerland, UN Doc. CCPR/C/CHE/CO/3 (2009) <https://www1.umn.edu/humanrts/hrcommittee/switzerland2009.html> Accessed 12 April 2016.

96 Bundesverwaltung <https://www.news.admin.ch/message/index.html?lang=de&msg-id=48480> Accessed 12 April 2016.

97 Speech Simonetta Sommaruga Gedenkanlass für ehemalige Verdingkinder und Opfer von fürsorgerischen Zwangsmassnahmen Bern 11 April 2013 <http://www.news.admin.ch/NSBSubscriber/message/attachments/30274.pdf> Accessed 12 April 2016.

98 As above.

99 BBL 2016 155 <https://www.parlament.ch/de/ratsbetrieb/suche-curia-vista/geschaeft?AffairId=20150082>Accessed 12 April 2016.

7.0 Conclusion

Switzerland is by no means alone in its slow confrontation with past injustices. The search for a unifying principle of compensation that could reflect reparation for wrongs is now the subject of broad human rights and humanitarian concerns which include criminal actions by the state and breaches of duty of care by state bodies. Australia, for instance, has similarly witnessed a drawn out process of acknowledgement, recognition and reparation around its history of Indigenous oppression and dislocation.[100] An apology was first issued by a state government (South Australia) in 1997 and only more recently has the Federal Government and former Prime Minister Kevin Rudd apologised in 2008, followed by the Stolen Generation Compensation Bill 2008.[101] In late 2015 a $11 million Stolen Generation reparations fund was set up in South Australia although a national compensation scheme remains outstanding.[102] The policy about removing children from their families and cultural traditions in Australia (in place until the 1970s) was based on colonial thinking about the racial inferiority of Aboriginal people and has obvious parallels with the removal of Jenisch children in Switzerland based on eugenic thinking about inferiority.[103] Thus, reparation processes in Australia, as elsewhere, are seen as crucial instruments to pursue meaningful reconciliation between the colonised and the coloniser for historic harms with enduring impact.[104]

Refocusing on coerced sterilisations, there have been apologies as well as compensation payments in various state jurisdictions in the United States. The time lag in those jurisdictions between apology and compensation is indicative of the wider principle that reparation takes time to be implemented. The Swedish and Swiss examples, which have been considered here, have shown similarities — both were driven by politicians rather than victims — but also differences. The Swedish case was shaped significantly by the backdrop of international media attention and the concomitant questioning of its democratic basis. The Swiss case, by contrast, did not receive equivalent media attention and its querying into its past was marked by judicial battle over collective responsibility of contemporary society in the 2004 debates. That a welfare measure should so dramatically affect women negatively was a shocking foundation to the Swedish collective imagination as a democratic state. In Switzerland, by contrast, the gendered nature of coercive sterilisation was barely mentioned whereas the fear of the effects of a successful case in relation to other coercive welfare measures in recent social history dominated the debates.

---

[100] For example, Buti Antonio 'Reparations, Justice Theories and Stolen Generations' (2008) 34 *University of Western Australia Law Review* 168; Reilly Alex 'The Inherent Limits of the Apology to the Stolen Generation' *University of Adelaide Law Research Paper* No 2009–002; Cuneen Chris 'Colonialism and Historical Injustice: Reparations for Indigenous People' (2005) 15 *Social Semiotics* 59; Hocking Barbara Ann 'Confronting the Possible Eugenics of the Past through Modern Pressures for Compensation' (2000) 69 *Nordic Journal of International Law* 501.

[101] <https://www.legislation.gov.au/Details/C2008B00054> Accessed 12 April 2016.

[102] <http://www.statedevelopment.sa.gov.au/news-releases/all-news-updates/reparations-scheme-for-sas-stolen-generations> Accessed 12 April 2016.

[103] Mottier Véronique and Gerodetti Natalia 'Eugenics and Social Democracy: Or, How the European Left Tried to Eliminate the "Weeds" From its National Gardens' (2007) 20 *New Formations* 35.

[104] Cuneen above note 100.

The Swiss response to compensation claims for coerced sterilisations can only be described as a legalistic approach to a gendered historic injustice claim, and defended by lawyer-politicians who made up the steering commission during a period marked by a strong populism in politics and media coverage. The puzzle as to how to litigate past wrongs dominated considerations of transformed historical sensibility, human rights, duties of care or the roles and responsibility of the democratic state. The key concepts were compensation and indemnity rather than, as has been the case in other contexts such as South Africa, reparation and reconciliation. Although the term *reparation* entered the political discussion in Switzerland it was used pragmatically to pursue *compensation claims* rather than being at the basis of a discussion about *collective responsibility* which could lead to wider acknowledgement and a public apology. Crucially, it concerned a claim predominantly affecting women (unlike the removal of Jenisch children who had previously undergone a recognition struggle and since then the Contract Children who are currently undergoing a recognition struggle).[105]

Eugenics can be seen as a utopia with an explicit temporal vision aiming to improve the gene pool of the national collective. The body of thinking and practices emanating from it had a clear future beneficiary, that is, present and future societies. For those trying to separate clearly the past from the present, this is an uncomfortable element and one which incurs a responsibility to present day society. In missing a (first) opportunity at partial restoration, the rejection of either material or symbolic forms of restitution constitute a rejection of recognising gendered welfare injustices and, as Thompson proposes, unremembered, unacknowledged and un-redressed historical injustice cannot help but demoralise the common life of a nation.[106] This is perhaps particularly pertinent to a nation that was reluctant to provide women with basic political rights.[107]

The recognition and compensation of individual injustices is part and parcel of a politics of recognition and reconciliation and redemption, at least in gesture. In terms of being a question of national belonging and citizenship, collective acknowledgement and reconciliation struggles ought not to depend merely on the size and prevalence of discriminatory practices but also on their symbolic value. In this sense, reconciliation debates raise questions about democracies and their understanding of inherited burdens and rights and about whose reparation claims get heard — and succeed — while providing opportunity for collective reflexivity in late modernity about the relationship of the present to our past.

It is, perhaps, worth returning to Nancy Fraser's seminal thinking on the quest for justice and her different ways of conceptualising such undertakings.[108] The dilemmas of justice in what she calls a post-Westphalian world must come to terms explicitly with the central political questions of the *who*: whose interests count; who decides

[105] For a full chronology see also <http://www.fuersorgerischezwangsmassnahmen.ch/de/2015-12-04_mm_botschaft.html> Accessed 12 April 2016.
[106] Thompson above note 30.
[107] Swiss women did not receive full political rights until 1971.
[108] This section arises from a guest talk by Nancy Fraser at the university of Leeds, UK, in a paper entitled 'Who Counts? Dilemmas of Justice in a Postwestphalian World' in 2009 and is more fully developed in Fraser above note 1. See also Fraser and Honneth above note 1; with Axel Honneth *Justice Interruptus: Critical Reflections on the Postsocialist Condition* Routledge London 1997.

who counts; whose voices get heard; who is included among the decision-makers; to whom we have duties and so on.[109] These bare questions have much bearing on ideas and practices of reparation even though, having expanded her conceptual framework from recognition and redistribution to include questions of representation, Fraser's characterisation of 'abnormal justice' is much more focused on justice in relation to changing and challenging spatialities, rather than about justice in relation to temporalities.[110] Adding the dimension of time and past injustices, and alongside that, a critical 'genealogy of the present'[111] has framed the arguments of this paper.

An attempt to answer Fraser's numerous *who* questions yields some gendered answers, and different jurisdictions have had different versions of answering these. Feminist transitional justice approaches have already revealed the ways in which 'webs of gendered harm' have had a more difficult stand in reparation claims.[112] Acknowledging the historic injustices of coerced sterilisations has been a shorter process in Sweden than elsewhere, not surprising perhaps given its general perspective of gender and gender equality. Switzerland's political engagement, by contrast, was more dismissive of reparation yet has found itself having to deal with reparation questions more as a result of having to embark on a much longer and wider framed social and public debate on coerced welfare measures.

The initial Swiss political framing of the reparation claim resulted in an overly legalistic approach making recourse to the (non) applicability of international law and human rights to past practices. The current attempt at reparation has, by contrast, had a wider reception by both media and the public, and has been driven by people who have been affected by past coercive welfare measures. But in addition, it is happening against the backdrop of the attempt of the previous decade which, despite its lack of success, perhaps provided a necessary discursive platform for eventual success. A Swiss law on reparation for coercive welfare measures looks likely to pass in one form or another in 2016 which is billed to have coerced sterilisations included.[113]

Those welfare practices that were explicitly gendered are now subsumed within a larger catalogue of coerced welfare measures. The current situation is much more hopeful with regard to arriving at financial compensation within the next few years, yet at the same time the gendered nature of some practices is now subsumed within a larger category of injustice against marginalised people — with gender barely

[109] Fraser above note 1.

[110] In relation to historic injustices by colonialist regimes and imperial ventures, Fraser's work has been taken to be useful in asking questions about the usefulness of representation and frame-setting *at the time* yet overriding this is the actual exploitation and violation of the colonial and imperial subject population, thereby making it a question of redistribution. Thus, while Fraser undertakes a rethinking of a critical democratic theory of justice and continuously asks questions about the borders and boundaries (and their relevance) of nations, jurisdictions and responsibilities, this question is never expanded, or so it seems, to ask whether this is not merely about spatiality and geographies but also about time and temporalities.

[111] Foucault Michel *Madness and Civilization: A History of Insanity in the Age of Reason* Routledge London 2001 [1961].

[112] O'Rourke above note 34.

[113] 15.082 BBL 2016 101 as above.

mentioned. With gender implicit, rather than explicit, the misrecognised object in a history of the present, using the genealogical critique mapped out by Foucault,[114] remains mapped onto the three forms of injury: one, the coerced sterilisation experienced by women in the context of protectionist welfare measures; second, the concomitant but enduring effects of stigmatisation and the management of a *spoiled identity*; and third, resulting from the long public debate about reparation, a rejection in the present. The question to be posed is perhaps not just whether reparations claims are gendered, but whether gender-based reparation claims take longer.

Disclosure Statement

No potential conflict of interest was reported by the author.

[114] Visker above note 10 at 22.

Civil Society and Gender-Based Violence: Expanding the Horizons of Transitional Justice

*Nicola Henry**

Abstract. The transitional justice field has thus far neglected the nature, scope and impacts of civil society initiatives for addressing gender-based violence. Using a feminist framework of analysis, I examine the role of civil society tribunals as a transitional justice mechanism. Despite their limitations, I argue that civil society tribunals can provide recognition for victim suffering, as well as challenge dominant narratives, explore the underlying individual and structural causes of violence and propose solutions to achieving non-violence and gender equality. Overall, I argue that transitional justice is a useful conceptual framework for examining civil society activity in addressing gender-based harms.

1.0 Introduction

Over the past few decades, feminist scholars, practitioners and activists have begun to examine the usefulness of various practices and processes for securing justice for gender-based violence in the aftermath of armed conflict and politicised violence.[1] Early attention tended to focus on the prosecution of wartime sexual violence under

---

*This work was supported by a La Trobe Asia Grant.

[1] Gender-based violence is a contested term. The Council of Europe Convention (Art 3 (d)) defines it to mean 'violence that is directed against a woman because she is a woman or that affects women disproportionately'. This definition is problematic in treating 'women' as synonymous with 'gender', and implying that women and girls are exclusively victims of violence because of their gender, and equally that women and girls cannot be perpetrators of violence. My use of 'gender-based violence' in this article refers to a wide range of harms that are perpetrated *because of* the targeted victim's gender. It is important to note that gender need not be the only reason for violence and theories of intersectionality are thus useful for critically examining the ways in which victims are targeted or affected on the basis of gender, race, ethnicity, sexuality, age and other factors. For instance, victims may be equally victims of conflict-related sexual violence as well as other gender-based pre-existing realities or post-conflict outcomes, such as socio-economic impoverishment, discrimination, harassment and other harms.

international criminal law,[2] however more recently scholars have sought to examine the efficacy of other justice mechanisms, such as truth commissions, political apologies and local on-the-ground interventions, drawing attention to a range of gender-based harms beyond that of sexual violence.[3] The common goals of feminist practical and analytical work in this field have been to not only problematise the historical silence surrounding gender-based harms, but to also challenge liberal-democratic, state-centric and neocolonial frameworks for addressing these intersecting harms, and the impacts that such processes and mechanisms have on victim-survivors of gender-based violence.[4]

In response to some of the shortcomings of more conventional justice measures, such as international courts or tribunals, non-state civil society organisations have mobilised in innovative ways to seek justice on behalf of, and in concert with, victim-survivors of mass atrocities. Although rarely framed as a transitional justice response, one innovative mechanism of justice is the civil society tribunal, also known as 'people's tribunals' or 'people's courts'. Originating with the International War Crimes Tribunal or 'Russell Tribunal' that was set up in 1966 to investigate American foreign policy and military intervention in Vietnam, civil society tribunals have operated to address various past harms in different geographical locations. In particular, a number of 'women's courts' have been established to respond to past forms of violence against women. Although the tribunals or courts differ in their format and function, some are 'mock' proceedings that are modelled on conventional international war crimes courts, ultimately serving to problematise past impunity for gender-based atrocities, while others function more like truth commissions, whereby victim-survivors publicly bear witness to past and present forms of discrimination and violence. To date, however, civil society tribunals have rarely been examined within the growing field of transitional justice.[5]

---

[2] See Askin Kelly *War Crimes Against Women: Prosecution in International War Crimes Tribunals* Martinus Nijhoff Publishers The Hague 1997; Campbell Kirsten 'The Gender of Transitional Justice: Law, Sexual Violence and the International Criminal Tribunal for the Former Yugoslavia' (2007) 1(3) *International Journal of Transitional Justice* 411; Franke Katherine 'Gendered Subject of Transitional Justice' (2006) 15 *Columbia Journal of Gender and Law* 813; Henry Nicola 'Witness to Rape: The Limits and Potentials of International War Crimes Trials for Victims of Wartime Sexual Violence' (2009) 3(1) *International Journal of Transitional Justice* 114; Meron Theodor 'Rape as a Crime under International Humanitarian Law' (1993) 87(3) *American Journal of International Law* 424.

[3] See, for example, Buckley-Zistel Susanne and Stanley Ruth (eds) *Gender in Transitional Justice* Palgrave Macmillan London 2012; Kent Lia 'Local Memory Practices in East Timor: Disrupting Transitional Justice Narratives' (2011) 5 *International Journal of Transitional Justice* 434; Ross Fiona *Bearing Witness: Women and the Truth and Reconciliation Commission in South Africa* Pluto Press London & Sterling Virginia 2003.

[4] Bell Christine and O'Rourke Catherine 'Does Feminism Need a Theory of Transitional Justice? An Introductory Essay' (2007) 1(1) *International Journal of Transitional Justice* 23; Charlesworth Hillary and Chinkin Christine *The Boundaries of International Law: A Feminist Analysis* Manchester University Press Manchester 2000; O'Rourke Catherine 'Feminist Scholarship in Transitional Justice: A De-Politicising Impulse?' (2014) 51 *Women's Studies International Forum* 118.

[5] Transitional justice refers to different legal and non-legal mechanisms or processes for responding to past wrongdoings, such as genocide, crimes against humanity, war crimes and other harms perpetrated in the context of political violence. It includes criminal prosecutions, truth and reconciliation

This is despite civil society initiatives playing a potentially key role in post-conflict justice.[6]

The twin aims of this article are first, to justify the inclusion of civil society tribunals as a tool of transitional justice, and second, to demonstrate the usefulness of transitional justice to understanding civil society redress activity in response to conflict-related, gender-based violence. The article explores the following two questions: To what extent do civil society tribunals seek to fulfil transitional justice aims, such as perpetrator accountability, victim vindication, collective responsibility, societal reconciliation and establishing a historical record or 'collective memory' of the past? And what are the implications of addressing past forms of conflict-related gender-based violence through a grassroots approach that lacks the punitive powers of arrest, prosecution and conviction of more formal measures of justice?

The first section of the article more broadly describes the role of civil society in responding to mass harm. The second section then draws on transitional justice as an analytical lens from which to examine the potentials and limitations of civil-society tribunals for specifically addressing justice for victim-survivors of conflict-related gender-based violence. Here I use existing feminist critiques of transitional justice to examine the challenges and shortcomings of civil society activity for responding to gender-based harms.

2.0 Civil Society Beyond the State: New Horizons in Transitional Justice

The term 'civil society' (*civilis societas*) is an ambiguous and contested term that has been the subject of much philosophical and political debate over the centuries. According to classical Greek philosophers, political power facilitates rational public debate

commissions, public apologies, memorials, reparations and political and institutional reform. Transitional justice as a field of study has more complex manifestations, encompassing normative or aspirational goals surrounding shifts from a state of conflict to peace, as well as potentially more substantive political and social transformation, such as gender and racial equality, environmental sustainability or socio-economic redistribution. In other words, transitional justice, through these varied mechanisms of justice, can be both individualistic or societal, and short- or long-term. Moreover, transitional justice provides a conceptual framework for bringing together competing discourses on the nature, extent and impact of past injustices, their contemporary effects and the possibilities for future redress measures. See Henry Nicola 'From Reconciliation to Transitional Justice: The Contours of Redress Politics in Established Democracies' (2015a) 9(2) *International Journal of Transitional Justice* 199; Bell Christine 'Transitional Justice, Interdisciplinarity and the State of the "Field" or "Non-field"' (2009) 3(1) *International Journal of Transitional Justice* 5; Teitel Ruti *Transitional Justice* Oxford University Press Oxford & New York 2000.

[6] The few exceptions include Crosby Alison and Lykes M Brinton 'Mayan Women Survivors Speak: The Gendered Relations of Truth Telling in Postwar Guatemala' (2011) 5(3) *International Journal of Transitional Justice* 456; Schmid Evelyne 'Gender and Conflict: Potential Gains of Civil Society Efforts to Include Economic, Social and Cultural Rights in Transitional Justice' *Human Rights in Conflict — The Role of Civil Society* paper presented at SHUR Project Final Conference, Luiss University, Rome, 4–6 June 2009.

and dialogue within civil society, which contributes to the 'common good' of the community.[7] Accordingly, civil society was not seen as separate from political power but rather viewed as a constituent part of a functioning self-governed political association of rulers and citizens who practise the civic virtues of truth, justice and self-restraint.

Some centuries later, philosophers Thomas Hobbes and John Locke, in their respective social contract theories, viewed civil society in a coexistent relationship with the state, where civil society was responsible for maintaining peace and coexistence.[8] This is in contrast to both Georg Hegel and Karl Marx, who saw civil society as a constituent part of a market economy governed by individual rights and private property. Marx, for instance, viewed civil society as a conglomeration of economic relationships within modern industrial, capitalist societies. The state, according to Marx, is the 'superstructure' of social relations that serves predominantly bourgeois interests, whereas civil society constitutes the 'socio-economic base' of the state, which serves to further bolster the division of labour and private ownership. Antonio Gramsci similarly saw civil society as part of the state, where the capitalist state rules through force through 'political society' (the police, army, legal system), and consent through 'civil society' (family, education, trade unions) yet civil society also plays a crucial role in problem-solving.[9]

Modern conceptions of civil society, in contrast, tend to conceptualise the essential elements of civil society as 'autonomous forms of discourse, associations and solidarity [from the state]'.[10] Civil society is the interface between private and public worlds, where ordinary people come together to acquire knowledge, make meaning of the world and make plans of action through engagement with others.[11] Jürgen Habermas's civil society or 'public sphere', for instance, consists of 'more or less spontaneously emergent associations, organizations and movements that, attuned to how societal problems resonate in the private life spheres, distil and transmit such reactions in amplified form to the public sphere'.[12]

That is not to say, of course, that civil society is necessarily separate from both the economy and state in practice,[13] yet civil society can and does constitute non-state actors whose very aim is to critique the role of the state. Although civil society can be supportive or work in collaboration with the state, civil society may be alternatively anti-politics — a site of problem-solving, critique, resistance or subversion. As Aaron Boesenecker and Leslie Vinjamuri note, '[c]ivil society is composed of actors who have varying levels of autonomy not only from the state and the economy but also from

[7] Ehrenberg John *Civil Society: The Critical History of an Idea* New York University Press New York 1999.
[8] Cohen Jean and Arato Andrew *Civil Society and Political Theory* MIT Press Massachusetts 1992.
[9] As above.
[10] As above at viii.
[11] Habermas Jürgen *The Theory of Communicative Action: Reason and Rationalization of Society* trans by McCarthy Thomas Polity Press Cambridge 1987.
[12] Habermas Jürgen *Between Facts and Norms: Contributions to a Discourse Theory of Law and Democracy* trans by Rehg William MIT Press Massachusetts 1996 p 367.
[13] Nielsen Kai 'Reconceptualizing Civil Society for Now: Some Somewhat Gramscian Turnings' in Walzer Michael (ed.) *Toward a Global Civil Society* Berghahn Books Providence 1995 p 41.

both dominant international normative frameworks and deeply embedded local cultural practices'.[14]

Owing to the proliferation of mass communication through online spaces and the transnationalisation or 'postnational constellations' of contemporary 'global' civil societies, it is important to look beyond a territorial, Westphalian frame and explore the role of global civil societies, such as human rights, feminist, indigenous, environmental and other transnational social movements, which have far more autonomy from the state.[15] Nancy Fraser's idea of 'subaltern counterpublics', for instance, embraces a more postmodernist conceptualisation of civil society. She defines this as 'parallel discursive arenas where members of subordinated social groups invent and circulate counterdiscourses, which in turn permit them to formulate oppositional interpretations of their identities, interests, and needs'.[16] Fraser claims that these counterpublics are instrumental in critiquing hegemonic domination in the bourgeois public sphere, contributing to the reduction in socio-economic disparities, and in doing so, helping to redraw the problematic boundaries that exist between public and private spheres.

Despite enormous attention to civil society theory and practice in different disciplinary contexts, the transitional justice field has by and large neglected the nature, scope and impact of civil society justice initiatives, while providing a rich body of literature on a diversity of other conventional and innovative mechanisms of justice, such as war crimes trials and truth commissions. This may in part be attributable to the predominant focus in transitional justice on the state as both actor and remedy for gross human rights violations, and the specific normative goal of *state transition* (for example, the liberalising shifts in state power) in various transitional justice measures from war crimes tribunals to political apologies. As such, many harms have been excluded from transitional justice analysis unless they are somehow connected back to broader forms of state-sanctioned harm (for example, if they occur as part of a pattern of atrocities during warfare) or are part of a prosecuting or redress body that is also indicting (legally or otherwise) individuals who are state-like actors for past wrongdoings. This state-centric focus also potentially renders other transitional justice goals less important, such as victim vindication or perpetrator accountability. Moreover, transitional justice has been limited by the 'constitutive definitions about what constitutes crimes in need of rectification' and 'its applied norms and understandings about what constitutes an adequate practice of *doing justice* for historical violence, abuse, or systemic injustice'.[17] For example, the

14 Boesenecker Aaron and Vinjamuri Leslie 'Lost in Translation? Civil Society, Faith-Based Organisations and the Negotiation of International Norms' (2011) 5(3) *International Journal of Transitional Justice* 364.

15 Fraser Nancy 'Transnationalizing the Public Sphere: On the Legitimacy and Efficacy of Public Opinion in a Post-Westphalian World' (1997) 24(4) *Theory, Culture and Society* 7. See also Kaldor Mary, Anheier Helmut and Glasius Marlies *Global Civil Society* Polity Press Cambridge 2003; Lipschutz Ronnie 'Reconstructing World Politics: The Emergence of Global Civil Society' (1992) 21(3) *Millennium-Journal of International Studies* 389; Walzer Michael *Toward a Global Civil Society* Berghahn Books Providence 1995.

16 Fraser as above.

17 Buckley-Zistel Suzanne and Zolkos Magdalena 'Introduction: Gender in Transitional Justice' in Buckley-Zistel Susanne and Stanley Ruth (eds) *Gender in Transitional Justice* Palgrave Macmillan London & New York 2012 p 9 (original emphasis).

crimes against the so-called 'comfort women'[18] during the Asia-Pacific War, and the civil society tribunal that was established in 2000 to address these wrongdoings, has received minimal attention within the field of transitional justice to date, yet both the harms and the response make it an interesting transitional justice example.

Despite this neglect, as Roger Duthie notes, many transitional justice scholars agree that civil society plays an important role in transitional justice processes.[19] For instance, civil society organisations have been instrumental in 'promoting and supporting transitional justice experiments around the world'.[20] Moreover, the success of transitional justice measures in part can be attributed to the organisation, expertise and participation of civil society organisations.[21] Yet, according to Iavor Rangelov, while civil society actors are crucial for developing, adapting and contesting transitional justice processes and structures, as well as normative justice goals, '[f]ew attempts have been made to develop analytical frameworks that may be useful for approaching a wider set of civil society encounters and engagements with transitional justice'.[22] Rangelov defines civil society as:

> the range of non-state actors that engage with justice discourses and processes ... and seek to influence them in some way, whether they be NGOs or civic associations or more loosely organised social movements and networks, media or individuals who shape the public conversation.[23]

---

[18] The term 'comfort woman' is a euphemism to refer to between 50,000 to 200,000 women and girls who were kidnapped, rounded up, coerced, lured, tricked, sold and otherwise recruited into military 'prostitution' for the Japanese military during the Asia-Pacific War (1931–45). While the majority of comfort women were Korean, a large number were also from China, as well as from other South-east Asian, Pacific Island, American and European countries. The comfort women issue and the redress responses to sexual enslavement are discussed in further detail below. See, for example, Hicks George *The Comfort Women* W.W. Norton & Company New York & London 1997; Qui Peipei, Zhiliang Su and Lifei Chen *Chinese Comfort Women: Testimonies from Imperial Japan's Sex Slaves* UBC Press Vancouver 2013; Soh C Sarah *The Comfort Women: Sexual Violence and Postcolonial Memory in Korea and Japan* University of Chicago Press Chicago & London 2008.

[19] Duthie Roger *Building Trust and Capacity: Civil Society and Transitional Justice from a Development Perspective* Research Unit International Center for Transitional Justice New York 2009.

[20] Brahm Eric 'Transitional Justice, Civil Society, and the Development of the Rule of Law in Post-Conflict Societies' (2007) 9(4) *International Journal of Not-for-Profit Law* 62.

[21] Hayner Priscilla 'Responding to a Painful Past: The Role of Civil Society and the International Community' in Bleeker Mô and Sisson Jonathan (eds) *Dealing with the Past: Critical Issues, Lessons Learned, and Challenges for Future Swiss Policy* KOFF Series Working Paper Swiss Peace Bern 2005 p 45. See also Backer David 'Civil Society and Transitional Justice: Possibilities, Patterns and Prospects' (2003) 2(3) *Journal of Human Rights* 297 at 302–305; Crocker David A 'Transitional Justice and International Civil Society' (1998) 14 *Social Philosophy Today* 147; Rangelov Iavor and Teitel Ruti 'Global Civil Society and Transitional Justice' in Albrow Martin and Seckinelgin Hakan (eds) *Global Civil Society 2011: Globality and the Absence of Justice* Palgrave Macmillan London 2011 p 162.

[22] Rangelov Iavor 'Civil Society and Transitional Justice in the Balkans: Three Models of Interaction' (2015) 1 *Security in Transition* 3–4.

[23] As above at 5.

His ambivalent conception includes both supporters and critics of the state and/or the justice processes. He usefully proposes three different models of civil society interaction with transitional justice as:

> a) 'participation' in formal transitional justice mechanisms established by states and international actors; b) 'contestation' over questions of justice in the public domain; and c) 'mobilisation' of civil society itself outside formal justice processes.[24]

While some transitional justice scholars have explored the role that non-state actors, such as non-governmental organisations, have played in the establishment, development and critique of transitional justice processes and outcomes (for instance, in: data collection; monitoring human rights abuses; representation and advocacy; consultation; service delivery; research and education; and a range of other roles),[25] the third model (the mobilisation of civil society *outside formal justice processes*) has attracted the least amount of attention in the transitional justice field to date. The remainder of this article therefore concentrates on this model through an examination of civil society tribunals, arguing that these tribunals represent a worthy site of investigation in the study of transitional justice.

In the analysis below, I take a broad approach to 'transitional justice', where first 'transition' is defined as both a justice process and an outcome: as 'gradual, cumulative, contested and perhaps incomplete',[26] and as encompassing a wide range of different goals, including that of state transition. Second, I include historical injustices, such as the crimes against the so-called comfort women or colonialism, as viable objects of study within the transitional field. Third, I use transitional justice as a unifying framework for bringing together competing discourses on the nature and extent of past injustices, and the nature of historical and contemporary response to these harms.[27] Finally, although my conceptualisation of transitional justice decentres both law and the state, I nonetheless retain the importance of state transition or a shift in state power as *one* of a number of key normative goals of transitional justice. I also retain the importance of organised political violence and 'extraordinary' crimes carried out by political entities[28] in order to circumvent an over-extended definition of transitional justice that could potentially include just about anything.[29] Ultimately, I seek to demonstrate the importance of transitional justice frameworks for the analysis of civil society responses to conflict-related gender-based violence.

---

24 As above at 3–4.

25 See Backer above note 21 at 302–305. See also Boesenecker and Vinjamuri above note 14; Hovil Lucy and Okello Moses Chrispus 'Editorial Note' (2011) 5(3) *International Journal of Transitional Justice* 333; Simić Olivera and Volčič Zala *Transitional Justice and Civil Society in the Balkans* Springer New York Heidelberg Dordrecht & London 2014.

26 Winter Stephen 'Towards a Unified Theory of Transitional Justice' (2013) 7(2) *International Journal of Transitional Justice* 231.

27 Henry above note 5.

28 See Luban David 'A Theory of Crimes against Humanity' (2004) 29 *Yale Journal of International Law* 85.

29 See Henry above note 5.

3.0 Responding to Mass Harm: Civil Society Tribunals

Responding to so-called 'ordinary' crimes in domestic, peacetime contexts is almost always exclusively the province of the state. The state prosecutes the accused person, the violator of community norms, on behalf of the community. The offence is against both the state and the afflicted community. In Aristotelian terms, this community is essentially *koinōnía politikḗ* — a 'civil society' with a set of norms and values which are shared by citizens on an equal footing under the rule of law. Citizens then have a shared interest in the prosecution of the offender. Yet who and what should bear the responsibility of criminal prosecution for crimes against humanity; crimes that are 'organized attacks of the gravest and most barbaric kind carried out by political entities against groups under their control'?[30] David Luban argues that offences against the 'laws of humanity' are international crimes that must be criminally tried by the international community: '[t]he analogy is straightforward', he suggests:

> states are to be the community of states as individual subjects are to their own state; international criminal laws are norms of the international community in the same way that domestic criminal laws are norms of the state that enacts them.[31]

But this positions the state, or the collection of states, as the central source of remedy for past harm. Moreover, the injustice emanating from the failure of states or the international community to prosecute grave violations renders the state as a particularly flawed mechanism of justice, and paves the way for alternative approaches to not only address the lacunae of conventional justice measures, but also actively critique the 'misrecognition' perpetuated by such measures.[32]

Civil society tribunals are one innovative, alternative approach to addressing the past wrongdoings of the state or state-like actors that have not been addressed by formal justice mechanisms. The first known civil society tribunal was the 1966 Russell-Sartre Tribunal that was set up by British philosopher and Nobel Prize winner Bertrand Russell, and hosted by French philosopher and writer Jean-Paul Sartre. The Russell-Sartre Tribunal convened two sessions in Sweden and Denmark with representatives from 18 different countries. The main aim was to conduct an investigation into American acts of aggression against Vietnam, Cambodia and Laos, and war crimes against civilians and prisoners of war under international law. The Tribunal examined different sources of evidence and unanimously found that the US government had committed acts of aggression and that government and armed forces were guilty of the 'deliberate, systematic and large-scaled bombardment of civilian targets'. It also found the US guilty of genocide against the people of Vietnam.[33]

---

[30] Luban above note 28.

[31] As above at 124.

[32] Fraser Nancy 'Social Justice in the Age of Identity Politics: Redistribution, Recognition and Participation' in Peterson Grethe (ed.) *The Tanner Lectures on Human Values XIX* University of Utah Press Salt Lake City 1998 p 1.

[33] Duffett John (ed.) *Against the Crime of Silence: Proceedings of the Russell International War Crimes Tribunal, Stockholm, Copenhagen* O'Hare Books New York 1968; Falk Richard 'The Rights of

Similar tribunals were set up in the decades that followed, including the Russell Tribunal II on Latin America that held three meetings in Rome and Brussels between 1973–76 concerning predominantly the military dictatorships of Argentina, and Brazil. In 1979, the Permanent Peoples' Tribunal was established as an international opinion tribunal, independent of state authorities. It examined a wide variety of cases, including the Armenian Genocide and the Bhopal disaster. Similar tribunals were established in Berlin in 2001 (on human rights in psychiatry), Brussels in 2005 (on Iraq) and Barcelona from 2009–12 (on Palestine). The most recent hearing of the Russell Tribunal took place in Venice in September 2014 on human rights issues in the East Ukraine war, finding the presidents of the Ukraine and the US, as well as NATO and the European Commission leaders, guilty of war crimes in Eastern Ukraine (albeit receiving limited mainstream media coverage).

A number of women's civil society tribunals have also been established over the past four decades. Some examples include the 1976 International Tribunal on Crimes Against Women;[34] the 2010 International Tribunal on Crimes Against Women of Burma;[35] and the 2010 Tribunal of Conscience for Women Survivors of Sexual Violence During the Armed Conflict in Guatemala.[36] The most recent example is the 2015 Women's Court that was established by activists from different countries and organisations from the former Yugoslavia. The Court, held in Sarajevo, was set up in order to provide 'a space for women's voices and women's testimonies about the daily injustices suffered during the war and now, in peace'. It documented violence perpetrated during the 1990s conflicts in the former Yugoslavia, as well as 'everyday' violence experienced since the end of the conflicts. The different forms of violence included: ethnic violence; military violence; gender-based violence (including sexual violence and intimate partner violence); exploitation; political repression; and structural, socio-economic violence. Described as a 'feminist approach to justice', the aims of the Court were to 'write an alternative history', collect women's experiences of violence and 'strengthen global feminist-pacifist alliances and coalitions' with the aim of encouraging punishment, influencing international justice institutions and contributing to the documentation of gender-based violence and inequality. The Court's activities included meetings, seminars, workshops, conferences, roundtables, various publications, documentary screenings, performances, exhibitions and personal testimonies from victim-survivors.[37] This Court reflects what M. Brinton Lykes and Alison Crosby describe as transformative, embodied and creative methodologies of justice.[38]

Peoples (In Particular Indigenous Peoples)' in Crawford James (ed.) *The Rights of Peoples* Oxford University Press New York 1988 p 17.

[34] See Russell Diana and Van de Ven Nicole *Crimes Against Women: Proceedings of the International Tribunal* Les Femmes Publications California 1976.

[35] See <http://www.burmalibrary.org/docs20/Nobel_Tribunal-burma-2010-en-op.pdf> Accessed 11 March 2016.

[36] Lykes M Brinton and Crosby Alison 'Creative Methodologies as a Resource for Mayan Women's Protagonism' in Hamber Brandon and Gallagher Elizabeth (eds) *Psychosocial Perspectives on Peacebuilding* Springer Cham Heidelberg New York Dordrecht & London 2014.

[37] See <http://www.zenskisud.org/en/> Accessed 11 March 2016.

[38] Lykes and Crosby above note 36 at 147.

Most scholarly attention to date has focused on the 2000 Women's International War Crimes Tribunal on Japanese Military Sexual Slavery.[39] The Women's Tribunal was instigated by the Violence against Women in War Network, Japan (VAWW-Net) and supported by NGOs throughout Asia. Like the Women's Court in Sarajevo, the Tribunal was established to hear the testimonies of the suffering endured by victim-survivors, but was premised more squarely on a legal model of redress in order to determine the criminal liability of leading military figures, political officials and the Japanese state for the systematic enslavement of up to 200,000 'comfort women' in military brothels for the Japanese military during the Asia-Pacific War (1931–45). The Women's Tribunal was specifically modelled on a conventional international war crimes trial and operated as a continuation of the post-WWII Tokyo war crimes trial that failed to adequately address the enslavement of comfort women. The Tribunal, however, lacked the legal authority to enforce its verdicts.[40]

In analysing these women's courts, it is useful to consider a number of well-identified shortcomings of conventional forms of post-conflict justice (such as war crimes courts) in terms of responding to gender-based violence (which have been explored in transitional justice feminist critiques). In summary, they include: a failure to articulate the individual and structural causes of conflict-related gender-based harms; the failure to provide a safe space for victims to tell their stories; the failure to attribute perpetrator accountability beyond that of individual criminal responsibility; and the failure to establish a historical record of the past. These deficits correspond with the stated goals of women's courts which attempt to explore underlying causes of gender-based violence, provide a safe space for victims, consider both individual and collective forms of responsibility, consciously contribute to the collective memory of the past, raise awareness of gender-based violence and discrimination and propose strategies and recommendations for future action.

Overall then, the strength of civil society tribunals is that they seek, by and large, to value *redistribution* (breaking the cycle of socio-economic disadvantage as a result of past wrongdoing), *recognition* (promoting respect, dignity and worth), *transformation* (accommodation of difference and structural change) and *participation* (ensuring full social and political participation in representations of the past and how to redress wrongdoing in the present and future).[41]

[39] See, for example, Chinkin Christine 'Women's International Tribunal on Japanese Military Sexual Slavery' (2001) 95(2) *The American Journal of International Law* 335; Chinkin Christine 'People's Tribunals: Legitimate or Rough Justice' (2006) 24 *Windsor Yearbook of Access to Justice* 201; Dolgopol Tina 'The Judgment of the Tokyo Women's Tribunal' (2003) 28 *Alternative Law Journal* 242; Sakamoto Rumi 'The Women's International War Crimes Tribunal on Japan's Military Sexual Slavery: A Legal and Feminist Approach to the "Comfort Women" Issue' (2001) 3 *New Zealand Journal of Asian Studies* 49; Women's International War Crimes Tribunal for the Trial of Japan's Military Sexual Slavery *Judgement on the Common Indictment and the Application for Restitution and Reparation* 4 December 2001 The Hague The Netherlands <http://www1.jca.apc.org/vaww-net-> Accessed 11 March 2016 p 19.

[40] Chinkin as above.

[41] Fredman Sandra *Discrimination Law* Oxford University Press Oxford 2011 p 25. This is based on Nancy Fraser's three dimensional model of justice as recognition (acknowledging the status of others); redistribution (fair distribution of benefits and burdens); and representation (symbolic representation through language) (discussed in further detail below). See Fraser Nancy 'Reframing

Operating outside the realm of the state, these women's courts or tribunals are an example of Fraser's 'counterpublics' in that they actively seek to honour the dignity of victim-survivors, articulate alternative discourses on the past, fill in the gaps in formal avenues of justice and provide an important critique of the state and hegemonic, masculine power. But to what extent do civil society tribunals fill the gaps left by conventional transitional justice mechanisms? Do civil society tribunals achieve specific transitional justice goals such as accountability, reconciliation, peace, victim vindication and collective memory? And do civil society tribunals fall into the similar traps of more conventional forms of transitional justice mechanisms, such as war crimes tribunals? In the subsection below, I analyse some of the benefits and shortcomings of civil society mechanisms for addressing gender-based violence, focusing on civil society tribunals.

3.1 Feminist Critiques of Civil Society and Transitional Justice

Lucy Hovil and Moses Chrispus Okello claim that there is a 'dearth of strong civil society critiques' in transitional justice analyses, and that future analysis of civil society activity should consider 'the dynamics in the relationship between civil society actors and those they claim to represent; between civil society and the state; among various civil society actors; and between civil society and those who fund it'.[42] They claim that civil society activity too often escapes scrutiny because it is perceived as a mechanism to keep in check the power of the state and as such 'civil society evokes an overwhelming faith in its benefit to society simply by virtue of its existence'.[43]

The various women's courts discussed above in this article have curiously been the subject of little critique, perhaps owing to the benevolence in which civil society initiatives are attributed, as well as the fact that they have received significantly less public attention than national or international official justice mechanisms, such as international criminal courts.

Although it may seem politically insensitive to critique well-meaning civil society initiatives, it is vital to do so in order to use these innovative processes as a source of inspiration or as a lesson for future justice responses to sexual violence — regardless of forum or context. Hovil and Okello implore that questions are asked about civil society activity, including whether civil society 'delivers the goods in practice', and whether civil society actors are 'genuinely inclusive'.[44] This, they argue, is important given that 'transitional justice civil society activity has proliferated and remains relatively unmonitored'.[45]

The benefit of using transitional justice as a conceptual framework for understanding the processes and outcomes of civil society tribunals for addressing gender-based

Justice in a Globalizing World' in *Global Inequality: Patterns and Explanations* Held David and Kaya Ayse (eds) Polity Press Cambridge 2007 p 252.

[42] Hovil and Okello above note 25 at 334.

[43] As above at 334.

[44] As above at 333.

[45] As above at 336.

harms is that such a framework can bring together competing discourses on the nature, scope and impacts of redress activity, including civil society redress activity.[46] These debates are important conversations about justice and power in the aftermath of conflict. This approach is supported by other transitional justice scholars. For instance, Suzanne Buckley-Zistel and Magdalena Zolkos suggest that although there are limits to transitional justice as a concept due to its restrictive parameters, they nonetheless encourage a critical gender perspective to examining the exclusions and inclusions, the global operations of power, the shaping of norms and the ideological constructs of gender within transitional justice. They write:

> critical gender analysis traces the processes whereby gendered subjectivity is constructed in social and political life, and how this subjectivity is formed and perpetuated though diverse systems of knowledge ... It thus draws attention to the subjects at the margins of political communities — those that on the basis of gender, class, ethnicity, or other categories of social differentiation tend to be regarded as 'invisible' or 'silent', or unable to exert political participatory agency.[47]

Exploring the shortcomings, problems and ambivalent effects, as well as benefits, of civil society redress activity, can be guided by critiques proffered by feminist and transitional justice scholars. Some feminist scholars, for instance, claim that transitional justice is another powerful global project that is constructed around a false, apolitical universalism that is restricted to specified 'extraordinary' events, with the effect of framing justice in narrow, rights-centric terms, and in doing so, overlooking structural forms of violence and inequality.[48] Others claim that transitional justice is androcentric. Bell and O'Rourke,[49] for instance, argue that the emphasis of democratic transition in transitional justice prioritises 'male-defined political violence', including violations of civil and political rights as opposed to socio-economic and cultural rights.[50]

While these critiques more broadly concern transitional justice as a field, feminist scholars have been also instrumental in pointing to the shortcomings of transitional justice *practice*, mostly with a focus on what I term representational deficits or shortcomings. For instance, scholars have pointed to the problematic effects relating to demands for, or promises of, catharsis and closure that transitional justice mechanisms offer.[51] Ruti Teitel writes that transitional justice promises a kind of closure but does so at a cost:

> These rituals attempt to relegate to the past the worst of this century, while also propounding a workable shared narrative for the future. By these practices, a line is drawn delineating the parameters of that collective memory to be preserved: what is to be

[46] Henry above note 5.
[47] Buckley-Zistel and Zolkos above note 17 at 19.
[48] Nagy Rosemary 'Transitional Justice as Global Project: Critical Reflections' (2008) 29(2) *Third World Quarterly* 275.
[49] Bell and O'Rourke above note 4.
[50] See also Buckley-Zistel and Zolkos above note 17 at 1; Schmid above note 6.
[51] Orford Anne 'Commissioning the Truth' (2006) 15(3) *Columbia Journal of Gender and Law* 851.

> remembered and what repressed; what is to be abandoned and what validated; what is to be rendered incontestable and what will remain controverted … As such, transitional practices have an ambivalent character, the resort to these practices in political flux is in the service of unity; yet, there is also a loss.[52]

Others have argued that transitional justice approaches to addressing mass harm serve to consolidate the notion of perpetual victimhood. Victim narratives of suffering may also be co-opted for other agendas, such as serving nationalistic goals.[53] Some scholars have pointed to the exclusions of men and boys from redress activity for gender-based harms,[54] while others have problematised the hegemony of international law and the neocolonial impulses of justice, even in unofficial, non-state mechanisms.[55] It is claimed, for instance, that the reliance on political and intellectual elites is a further source of power imbalance between victims, activists and intellectual experts.[56] Moreover, regardless of the forum, transitional justice measures may promote a false universalism as well as generate problematic representations of suffering.[57] This in turn runs the risk of creating a spectacle of pain and suffering.[58] Finally, the reinforcement of a false dichotomy between conflict and post-conflict contexts may in turn reinforce the notion that gender-based violence only happens in wartime, by strangers and not in times of so-called peace.[59]

To what extent do civil society tribunals embody or enact these representational problems? In reflecting on the 2010 Tribunal of Conscience for Women Survivors of Sexual Violence During the Armed Conflict in Guatemala, Crosby and Lykes explore many of these limitations, while also acknowledging the benefits of civil society activity to victim-survivors and their communities:

> Truth-telling processes, in which documentation relies on the personal testimonies of survivors who have been directly or indirectly affected by the violations under consideration, tend to be framed within the liberal language of human rights and emphasize the experience of individuated harm, particularly bodily harm. They also focus on this harm as a particular 'event', rather than as part of the broader structural relations of power that shape and inform the construction of the subject within her social context. Such rights-based discourse is rooted in the assumption that, as [Fiona] Ross puts it, '"violation" necessarily produces "victims,"' and this is a gendered relation. Violence produces women victims, the underlying assumptions being that victims are gendered female, that women are all the same and that, within the individuated framework of rights violations and bodily harm, the harm they experienced was sexual violence. Thus, sexual harm is reified as the gendered face of war.[60]

52 Teitel above note 5 at 229–230.
53 Franke above note 2 at 813.
54 Buckley-Zistel and Zolkos above note 17.
55 Dhawan Nikita 'Transitions to Justice' in Buckley-Zistel Susanne and Stanley Ruth (eds) *Gender in Transitional Justice* Palgrave Macmillan London & New York 2012 p 264.
56 Chinkin above note 39.
57 Ross above note 3 at 332; Soh above note 18.
58 Lykes and Crosby above note 36.
59 Valji Nahla *Gender Justice and Reconciliation* Friedrich-Ebert-Stiftung Berlin 2007.
60 Lykes and Crosby above note 6 at 462.

Although it is crucial to examine the array of representational deficits, shortcomings or issues in the analysis of the processes and outcomes of transitional justice redress activity, it is equally important to address the extent to which civil society tribunals, or women's courts in particular, contribute to two other important justice goals as articulated by the critical theorist Nancy Fraser: recognition and redistribution.[61]

First, according to Fraser, recognition entails acknowledgement of the identity or status of the 'other' and the cultural injustices against these groups which are 'rooted in social patterns of representation, interpretation, and communication'.[62] Such injustices include the 'everyday' and the 'extraordinary' and in fact, potentially merge them together: cultural domination by one culture by another; non-recognition or invisibility within one's own culture; and disrespect through disparaging stereotypes and representations in everyday life. The mass sexual enslavement of comfort women, for instance, is not simply about the daily abuse that women and girls endured in the military brothels throughout the Asia-Pacific War, but it also concerns a much broader story about impoverishment and abuse prior to their incarceration, as well as after their release back into their communities.[63] The Women's Tribunal that was set up in 2000 as a civil-society, mock war-crimes tribunal, was an attempt to further consolidate respect, dignity and worth to the former comfort women as 'collective subjects of injustice'.[64] As the Women's Tribunal was set up to adjudicate gendered crimes that the Tokyo Tribunal failed to address, and the Tribunal sat 'as if it were a continuation of the [1946] IMTFE [Tokyo Tribunal] and the subsidiary trials held in the Asia-Pacific',[65] it served to address not only the misplaced stigma and shame of past violence, but also the injustice of what Fraser calls 'misrecognition';[66] namely, cultural, social, political and legal amnesia and denial that has plagued this issue since the end of World War Two.

In addition to this, the Women's Tribunal sought to provide a clear statement about individual and collective criminal responsibility using the language of international law and the trial format to condemn the wrongdoings against the comfort women. This had the effect of raising further awareness of the issue specifically, but also brought international attention more broadly to the prevalence and impacts of wartime sexual violence. The Tribunal also contributed to a collective memory of the past through its creation of a permanent public record (including a lengthy judgment as well as other documents and materials). Finally, the Tribunal provided a space for victim-survivors to come together to tell their stories in a non-adversarial context, where the multiple physical, psychological, financial and social harms that they suffered were duly acknowledged.[67]

---

[61] Fraser above note 41. See also Henry Nicola 'The Law of the People: Civil Society Tribunals and Wartime Sexual Violence', in Powell Anastasia, Henry Nicola and Flynn Asher (eds), *Rape Justice: Beyond the Criminal Law* Palgrave Macmillan Basingstoke 2015b.
[62] Fraser as above at 7.
[63] Soh above note 18.
[64] Fraser above note 32 at 8.
[65] Women's International War Crimes Tribunal above note 39.
[66] Fraser above note 32.
[67] Henry above note 61.

Second, Fraser defines 'redistribution' as the fair distribution of benefits and burdens which, as a practical socio-economic tool, is not distinct from that of recognition.[68] A reparative model that seeks to provide victims with an array of redistributive remedies may include restitution (restoring victims to their original situation where possible) and monetary compensation for material and emotional damages. Compensation for past wrongdoings, for instance, helps to acknowledge not simply the psycho-social harms, but also the socio-economic and intergenerational impacts of egregious acts. But individual reparative measures are not the only means of redistribution in the context of gross human rights violations. Redistribution would also entail economic restructuring; the reorganisation of the division of labour; and other fundamental transformations to the political economy.[69]

As a mock, civil-society tribunal, the Women's Tribunal could not make arrests and could only provide recommendations for redress to governments; however, it was able to avoid some of the problems inherent in more conventional transitional justice mechanisms, such as international war crimes courts, including an almost exclusive focus on individual criminal responsibility. The Tribunal was nonetheless premised on the articulation of legal harms using international criminal law as the benchmark and it did therefore focus on proving charges laid out in the indictments against named individuals for rape and sexual slavery as crimes against humanity. Although the Tribunal judgment did outline the structural injustices, such as the comfort women's vulnerability to 'recruitment' into the comfort stations (whether that was kidnapping, coercion or some other method), the fixation on legal harms was largely at the expense of exploring the more deeply embedded structural factors underlying the systematic sexual enslavement of comfort women, such as colonialism, patriarchy and capitalism.[70]

By way of contrast, the more recent 2015 Women's Court in the former Yugoslavia specifically includes a much more expansive definition of wrongdoing to include socio-economic disadvantage and discrimination, in addition to gender-based harms

---

[68] Fraser above note 7.

[69] Fraser above note 32 at 7. It is interesting to note that in December 2015, a bilateral agreement was reached between Japan and South Korea regarding the comfort women issue. Under the agreement Japan promised to pay South Korea 1 billion yen to set up a foundation to support the few surviving comfort women, and to provide a stronger apology to the comfort women. South Korea in return promised to consider the matter 'finally and irreversibly' resolved and to consider the removal of the comfort women statue outside the Japanese Embassy in Seoul. While this redress example does not concern the 2000 civil-society Women's War Crimes Tribunal as such, it is an important reminder about the importance of *processes* of transitional justice. While the agreement, for instance, attempts to strike a deal that recognises the harm against the comfort women in clear and unambiguous terms, as well as provide some sort of redistribution in the form of monetary compensation, it has been criticised by various groups such as Amnesty International and the UN Committee on the Elimination of Discrimination Against Women (CEDAW) because political leaders failed to consult victim-survivors about the details of the agreement, and many victims want both a direct apology and direct compensation. See Sasazawa Kyoichi and Yomiuri Shimbun 'U.N. Panel Criticizes "Comfort Women" Deal' *The Japan Times* 8 March 2016 <http://the-japan-news.com/news/article/0002797179> Accessed 11 March 2016; Tiezzi Shannon 'South Korea's "Comfort Women" Reject Deal with Japan' *The Diplomat* 30 December 2015 <http://thediplomat.com/2015/12/south-koreas-comfort-women-reject-deal-with-japan/> Accessed 11 March 2016.

[70] Sakamoto above note 39.

perpetrated during the armed conflicts in the former Yugoslavia. However, this court is quite different to the Women's Tribunal which resembled a conventional criminal trial for crimes against humanity. There are of course strengths and weaknesses associated with both forms of justice. A mock trial, for instance, may be heavily focused on questions of individual criminal responsibility and the direct crimes perpetrated during the period under examination. While this approach may diminish the role that broader structural forces play, existing legal frameworks and decisions are able to be drawn on as a source of legitimacy and authority. Broader civil society mechanisms without this mandate essentially lack this power. Regardless of form, like any other civil-society-led justice measures, or indeed formal justice mechanisms, the key justice question concerns both the *processes* of justice (for example, the extent and nature of victim participation and inclusion), and also the actual *outcomes* and impacts that such measures have on achieving transformation and change. The latter of course will depend largely on the broader publicity that such courts attract, and the ways in which governments will take on board their claims and recommendations.

Although participants' voices are often heard in innovative, supportive and respectful ways in civil society tribunals addressing gender-based violence, especially compared to conventional justice measures, little is currently known about the impacts of women's courts since there have been very few studies to date exploring the impacts on victim-survivors.[71] As such, little is known about how these courts function as a truth-telling forum or to what extent they provide relief or catharsis to victims. Moreover, while civil society tribunals seek to promote recognition of past injustices, as well as the injustices of other formal mechanisms that have failed to address these harms, it is difficult to measure their influence on states or international bodies, nor whether their activity has led to shifts in state power.[72] In fact, transnational civil society entities may have weaker influences on the state in some circumstances, as civil society tribunals lack the authority and force to fully contribute to political transition and structural change, or to implement reparative measures, such as compensation, restitution or other symbolic acts (such as apologies) to victims.

Despite the varied uncertainties surrounding the efficacy of women's courts, they do, however, play an important role in contributing to the documentation of victim (and sometimes perpetrator) experiences, and provide institutional recognition of the pain and suffering endured. For many of course this will never satisfy justice needs in the absence of national or international criminal prosecution and punishment, or in the absence of a full and frank apology from perpetrators and the state, or owing to the failure of the state to introduce a compensation scheme. Indeed, civil society tribunals should not be viewed as a replacement for formal and conventional justice measures, or as a panacea for victim-survivors in terms of recovery and healing.

Overall, while civil society tribunals lack the authority and force that can contribute to transformative political transition and structural change (which some might

---

[71] One exception is Lykes and Crosby above note 36.

[72] Van der Merwe Hugo, Baxter Victoria and Chapman Audrey (eds) *Assessing the Impact of Transitional Justice, Challenges for Empirical Research* United States Institute for Peace Washington DC 2009.

argue is the primary goal of transitional justice), these tribunals nonetheless have the capacity to contribute to shifts in state power and bring awareness to historical injustices. Yet the goals of transitional justice go beyond that of the state. At an individual level, such measures may provide support and validation for victims of gender-based violence. At a societal level, these tribunals can challenge dominant narratives, explore the underlying individual and structural causes of violence and propose solutions to achieving non-violence and gender equality.

Furthermore, while civil society justice measures are an important signal of the limits as well as possibilities of justice, like conventional justice measures, they too should not be immune from critical inquiry if lessons are to be learnt and the transitional justice field is ultimately to be strengthened.

4.0 Conclusion

Civil society initiatives for responding to the past injustices of gender-based violence have rarely been analysed within the transitional justice field. This is in part due to the state-centric focus of transitional justice measures to date. This article, however, has sought to demonstrate the ways in which transitional justice is a useful theoretical lens through which to examine non-state forms of institutionalised redress. First, a transitional justice framework provides the analytical tools to examine the nature and extent of both historical and contemporary forms of gender-based violence. Second, as Bell and O'Rourke claim, transitional justice can help to challenge the legitimacy of the state and advocate for more radical transformative change in achieving equality and social inclusion.[73] Third, transitional justice is a useful conceptual framework for examining the range of discourses on injustices, providing the necessary discussions about the what, who, how and why of justice. In particular, transitional justice provides a way for critically examining the norms, structures, processes, outcomes and impacts of civil society initiatives, drawing on the invaluable feminist and other scholarly critiques of transitional justice as both an analytical field and a practice.

While it is inherently difficult to measure the efficacy or impacts of civil society tribunals in terms of socio-economic redistribution, recognition of historical and contemporary injustices, transformation and structural change or participation of victim-survivors and others,[74] more empirical research on the experiences of participants might yield important insights into the potentials and limitations of such forums. Further, more scholarly attention to the shortcomings of civil society activity can and should be undertaken. Although far from perfect, civil society tribunals serve as a lesson for future justice mechanisms — formal and informal, during peacetime or in post-conflict contexts, and for a whole range of egregious harms. Both their potential benefits and shortcomings are a reminder that justice itself is ongoing, complex, piecemeal and never complete, but nonetheless vitally important to the dignity and memory of survivors. Overall, discussion and critique should not undermine the processes and outcomes, or the civil society actors, many of whom work tirelessly to create

---

[73] Bell and O'Rourke above note 3.

[74] See Henry above note 61.

an alternative and supportive space for victim-survivors to be heard. Rather, critique should serve to strengthen both future civil society initiatives as well as more conventional forms of justice in responding to gender-based and other forms of violence.

Disclosure Statement

No potential conflict of interest was reported by the author.

ORCID

Nicola Henry http://orcid.org/0000-0002-5462-341X

'THEY SAY THAT JUSTICE TAKES TIME': TAKING STOCK OF TRUTH SEEKING IN PERU, ARGENTINA AND SERBIA

*Olivera Simic**

Abstract. What is the role of arts and artists in transitional justice? What role do artists play in the aftermath of political violence? What can artists offer to people still searching for their loved ones? This paper will bring together three artistic projects from Peru, Argentina and Serbia; geographical spaces that have all experienced mass human rights violations. While art cannot replace formal judicial mechanisms or material reparation, this paper argues that grassroots artistic initiatives offer a significant and distinct reparative contribution to transitional justice processes.

> My memory. It is endless. I can forget nothing. I alone have more memories than the whole of mankind. They have cut me off from my future. And they totally cut off my sense of continuity. By remembering, I bring back my sense of continuity. Because without memory, continuity does not exist.[1]

> Man fears to discover a hidden truth about himself, in the same way that the nation, or part of it, is afraid to accept a tragic and unjust reality in its past and present.[2]

Transitional justice is a plethora of judicial and non-judicial measures that seek to promote accountability and redress for massive violations of human rights that occurred in the era of dictatorship or armed conflict. Truth seeking, prosecutions, lustration and vetting are amongst some of the mechanisms that may be implemented in order to redress legacies of past human rights abuses. There is a general acknowledgement among transitional justice scholars and policymakers

*I would like to thank to Dr Lia Kent and three peer reviewers for their constructive feedback on the previous draft of this paper. I would also like to extend my thanks to Maricarly Escalona for her research assistance and an invaluable insight into Latin America's past and present. The title of this article comes from an actor from Yuyachkani Theatre Group 'Rosa Cuchillo' performed by Ana Correa, at Brown University's Brown International Advanced Research Institutes 11 June 2013 https://www.youtube.com/watch?v=i7U9NsRpjXcyoutube.

[1] *The Shivering of the Rose* Performance Text *Dah Theater* on file with author.

[2] Guardiola Manuel Prendes 'Constantes Tematicas en Tres Novelas Peruanas Sobre la Epoca del Terrorismo' (2010) 50(2) *Romance Notes* 229.

that '[t]he question today is not whether something should be done after atrocity but how it should be done'.[3]

Using only one transitional justice mechanism, according to Olsen et al, rarely gives satisfactory results.[4] Still, even when two or more of these mechanisms are used simultaneously, they can only address a fraction of all political violence while impunity and amnesia prevails in most cases.[5] The overarching goal of any transitional justice strategy, and a component of most of its judicial and non-judicial mechanisms, is seeking truth about the past. The specific mechanisms that focus solely on the right to truth are commonly labelled as 'truth seeking' mechanisms.[6] Perhaps the most well known amongst these are truth and reconciliation commissions (TRCs); official, non-judicial bodies of limited duration established to determine the facts, causes and consequences of past human rights violations.[7] Due to the necessity of an institutional commitment to operationalise them, Ruti Teitel argues that truth commissions act as nothing less than a 'bureaucratic response to bureaucratic murder'.[8]

TRCs, as institutional and political mechanisms, have swept across the globe since the early 1980s. The first TRC was established in Argentina in 1981; Cote d'Ivoire, Thailand and Nepal are amongst the latest countries to establish TRCs.[9] Most recently, the Venezuelan government and opposition agreed to establish a TRC.[10] While TRCs have been used by many countries emerging from state repression or armed conflict, often this mechanism is embedded within larger processes that include other forms of transitional justice.[11] They may be established prior to trials, as in the case of Argentina, or established concurrently with reparation programmes, such as in South Africa. However, once established and operational, generally there is a poor record of the implementation of the TRC recommendations, in particular when

[3] Nagy Rosemary 'Transitional Justice as Global Project: Critical Reflections' (2008) 29 *Third World Quarterly* 275.

[4] Olsen Tricia, D Payne Leigh A, Reiter Andrew G, Wiebelhaus-Brahm Eric 'When Truth Commissions Improve Human Rights' (2010) 4 *International Journal of Transitional Justice* 457.

[5] Bakiner Onur *Truth Commissions: Memory, Power, and Legitimacy* University of Pennsylvania Press Philadelphia 2016 p 2.

[6] Boutruche Theo 'Seeking the Truth About Serious International Human Rights and Humanitarian Law Violations: The Various Facets of a Cardinal Notion of Transitional Justice' in Matthee Marielle, Toebes Brigit and Brus Marcel (eds) *Armed Conflict and International Law: In Search of the Human Face* TMC Asser Press The Hague 2013 p 318.

[7] Hayner Priscilla B *Unspeakable Truths: Transitional Justice and the Challenge of Truth Commissions* 2nd ed Routledge New York 2010; Teitel Ruti G 'Human Rights in Transition: Transitional Justice Genealogy' (2003) 16(69) *Harvard Human Rights Journal* 69; Freeman Mark *Truth Commissions and Procedural Fairness* Cambridge University Press New York 2006.

[8] Teitel Ruti G *Transitional Justice* Oxford University Press Oxford 2000 p 77.

[9] Cote d'Ivoire and Thailand established TRCs in 2010. Nepal established a TRC in 2015.

[10] Ministeriode Relaciones Exteriores y Movilidad Humana 'The Venezuelan Government and Opposition Achieved Progress in the Dialogue Under UNASUR Support' 2014 <http://www.cancilleria.gob.ec/the-venezuelan-government-and-opposition-achieved-progress-in-the-dialogue-under-unasur-support/> Accessed 11 January 2016. A TRC is also being negotiated in Northern Ireland. See, for example, Brewer John D Mitchell David and Leavey Gerard *Ex-Combatants, Religion, and Peace in Northern Ireland* Palgrave MacMillan Hampshire 2013 p 127.

[11] Wiebelhaus-Brahm Eric, Dancy Geoff and Kim Hun Joon 'The Turn to Truth: Trend in Truth Commission Experimentation' (2010) 9 *Journal of Human Rights* 45 at 25.

it comes to reparation programmes.[12] Some scholars argue though that overall social transformation — building the rule of law, reconciliation and reform — is not entirely possible without reparations.[13]

Sometimes in parallel, but often as an alternative form of justice, civil society and artists have initiated non-official, grassroots ways of seeking truth for victims of mass violations of human rights. Louis Bickford employs the notion of 'unofficial truth projects' to refer to non-governmental truth-finding initiatives organised at the sub-state level.[14] The notable rise of local level practices of memorialisation, remembrance and commemoration could be seen, as Lia Kent argues, as 'attempts to remember and make narrative sense of the past… as well as struggles for official recognition' of those groups and individuals who feel they have been left out of the processes of nation-building.[15]

In this paper I analyse the importance of such alternative, grassroots artistic projects by drawing on three case studies from Peru, Argentina and Serbia. Although dealing with different historical and political contexts, these geographical spaces have all experienced mass human rights violations in which artists share the same goal: to raise awareness about past atrocities through artistic projects that call for memory and truth seeking. While their artworks have been created independently of one another, there are commonalities in the artists' motivations to create and deliver projects that transcend their own contexts and speak to the power of art in transitional justice processes at a universal level.

The three case studies drawn upon in this paper are: Grupo Cultural Yuyachkani from Peru and their work with the TRC in Peru and the performance *Rosa Cuchillo*; the work of Argentinian photographer Gustavo Germano on disappeared people (two photo exhibitions/projects: *Ausiencias* and *Busquedas*); and Dah Theater from Serbia and its performance *The Shivering of the Rose*. All three projects concern missing people. All make a call for keeping memories alive and underscore the necessity of knowing the truth about victims' fates.

This article draws on media, documentary and audio-visual sources, including local and international Spanish and Serbian newspapers and articles, media and online interviews with the Peruvian theatre group Yuyachkani. It also draws upon personal correspondence with Gustavo Germano, including his personal files on photo exhibitions that he shared via email. I have a long-term personal and professional relationship with Dah Theater, Belgrade, and have received permission from its director, Dijana Milošević, to draw upon an original text from the performance *The Shivering of the Rose*. All materials from Spanish and Serbian were translated by me.

---

[12] Knuckey Sarah *The Transformation of Human Rights Fact-Finding* Oxford University Press Oxford 2016 p 292.

[13] Minow Martha 'The Hope for Healing: What Can Truth Commissions Do?' in Rodberg Robert and Thompson Dennis (eds) *Truth v Justice: The Morality of Truth Commissions* Princeton University Press New Jersey 2000 p 252.

[14] Bickford Louis 'Unofficial Truth Projects' (2007) 29(4) *Human Rights Quarterly* 994.

[15] Kent Lia *Truth Seeking and Memory Politics in Post Conflict East Timor* Paper presented at the 17th Biennial Conference of the Asian Studies Association of Australia, Melbourne, 1–3 July 2008 p 14 <http://artsonline.monash.edu.au/mai/files/2012/07/liakent.pdf> Accessed 13 December 2015.

Although the three projects differ in genre (two are theatre plays and two are photo installations), given they share common concerns, my interest was to bring them together and analyse what they can offer to truth seeking and symbolic reparation. The study of these arts and drama projects has, to date, largely been confined to their national contexts. Analyses have also tended to be in languages other than English (Spanish and Serbian respectively). Bringing them into one space can exemplify the unique yet universal yearning for truth seeking by victims of enforced disappearances regardless of which corner of the globe they reside.

I first provide an overview of the right to truth in international law. I then turn to analyse the role of art in the process of truth seeking. I then discuss art as an alternative and potential reparative mechanism of truth seeking in transitional justice, and situate the three case studies within this discussion. I argue that art can make a significant contribution to these processes and play a prominent role as a tool of symbolic reparation.

1.0 Truth Seeking in International Law

> I have to know what has happened, to know what they did to him, to know how they killed him, to know where they threw him. They must tell me that.[16]

Although the right to the truth has not been an object of specific convention, the core elements of this right are well accepted. A report by the Office of the United Nations High Commissioner for Human Rights defines the right to truth about gross human rights violations and serious violations of human rights law as an 'inalienable and autonomous right, linked to the duty and obligation of the State to protect and guarantee human rights, to conduct effective investigations and to guarantee effective remedy and reparations'.[17] The same report specifies that this right is 'closely linked with other rights and has both an individual and a societal dimension and should be considered as a non-derogable right and not be subjected to limitations'.[18]

The visibility of the right to truth has come about due to an increase in truth commissions and other truth-seeking mechanisms around the globe.[19] The right to truth has been elaborated in international treaties, the national legislations of some countries and through international jurisprudence. It has been recognised by international judicial bodies and legal systems in several countries.[20] While the right to the truth applies to serious human rights violations, it is most explicitly associated

---

[16] *Shivering of the Rose* above note 1.

[17] United Nations Economic and Social Council, Office of the High Commissioner for Human Rights *Report: Promotion and Protection of Human Rights: Study on the Right to the Truth* UN Doc E/CN.4/2006/91 p 2 (8 February 2006).

[18] At 2.

[19] Hayner above note 7; Bickford above note 14; Borer Tristan Anne (ed.) *Telling the Truths: Truth Telling and Peace Building in Post Conflict Societies* University of Notre Dame Press Indiana 2006.

[20] Inter-American Commission on Human Rights and Inter-American Court of Human Rights have confirmed the right to truth established by the American Convention on Human Rights in a series of cases. See, for example, *Velásquez Rodríguez Case* Inter-AmCtHR Ser C No 4 (29 July 1988); *Bámaca Válesquez Case* Inter-AmCtHR Ser C No 91 (22 February 2002) at 77; *Myrna Mack Chang Case* Inter-AmCtHR Ser C No 101 (25 November 2003) at 274–275.

with the issue of enforced disappearances. Victims and their families have the 'imprescriptible right' to know the truth about human rights violations and in which circumstances these took place.[21] There are also explicit treaty references to the right to know certain facts, such as the Additional Protocol I to the Geneva Convention[22] and the International Convention for the Protection of all Persons from Enforced Disappearances[23] which both establish the right of victims and relatives of the missing or disappeared to learn the fate and whereabouts of their loved ones.

Although it is considered one of the key rights, and despite moral obligation and international pressure, not all governments are willing to fully reveal the truth.[24] There are a number of reasons why states are reluctant to reveal the truth about the past. One argument often used by governments is that the publication of documents and data relating to past human rights abuses will compromise national security.[25] Another reason why governments may be reluctant to open files is that they may perceive this could endanger their security, especially if some of the people involved in past crimes are still part of the ruling government.[26] During the apartheid era, the South African government was not only reluctant to reveal data and documents but also destroyed massive amounts of documentation. This was recognised in the TRC report, which stated:

> the mass destruction of records ... has had a severe impact on South Africa's social memory ... ultimately, of course, all South Africans have suffered the consequences — all are victims of the apartheid state's attempted imposition of a selective amnesia.[27]

The destruction of documents is contrary to the principles accepted under international law, in which 'the state has a duty to preserve documentary evidence for commemoration and remembrance'.[28] Still, whether a country establishes a truth-seeking mechanism is a decision that rests upon 'the country itself'.[29] These mechanisms are not only important for acknowledging the victims' rights to truth but also because they give the community 'as complete a version of history as possible'.[30] The truth can

---

21 United Nations Commission on Human Rights, Independent Expert Diane Orentlicher *Report: Updated Set of Principles for the Protection and Promotion of Human Rights through Action to Combat Impunity* UN Doc E/CN.4/2005/102/Add.1 (8 February 2005) at Principle 4.

22 *Protocol Additional to the Geneva Conventions of 12 August 1949 and Relating to the Protection of Victims of Internal Armed Conflicts (Protocol I)* adopted at Geneva 8 June 1977, 1125 UNTS 3 (entered into force 7 December 1948).

23 *International Convention for the Protection of all Persons from Enforced Disappearances* UN Doc E/CN.4/2005/WG.22/WP.1/Rev.4 (20 December 2006). As of 1 February 2016, 95 states have signed the convention and 51 ratified or acceded it.

24 Hayner above note 7 at 23–25.

25 Naqvi Yasmin 'The Right to Truth in International Law: Fact or Fiction?' (2006) 88(862) *International Review of the Red Cross* 245 at 265.

26 Hayner above note 7 at 227.

27 Truth and Reconciliation Commission *Report* 1998 vol 1.

28 United Nations Commission on Human Rights above note 21 at Principle 3.

29 Hayner above note 7 at 197.

30 Bosire Lydiah *Overpromised, Underdelivered: Transitional Justice in Sub-Saharan Africa* International Center for Transitional Justice New York 2006 p 13.

assist in healing processes after traumatic events and act as a safeguard against impunity and public denial.[31]

According to international law, truth seeking is closely related to reparations. In 2005, the UN General Assembly adopted and proclaimed the 'United Nations Basic Principles and Guidelines on the Rights to a Remedy and Reparation for Victims of Gross Violations of International Human Rights Law and Serious Violations of International Humanitarian Law' (Basic Principles) which identify 'mechanisms, modalities, procedures, methods' to put in operation existing obligations in respect to redress and reparation.[32] Article 24 of the Basic Principles includes '[v]erification of the facts and full and public disclosure of the truth' as an example of satisfaction. The Inter American Court of Human Rights in *Gelman v Uruguay* confirmed this right when ordering a factual investigation and the immediate 'localization' of the remains of a disappeared victim 'as a form of reparation the victim's right to the truth'.[33] The updated set of principles for the protection and the promotion of human rights through action to combat impunity (the Impunity Principles) echo and confirm 'the inalienable right to truth', 'the duty to preserve memory' and 'the victims' right to know'.[34] States are obliged to preserve 'collective memory from extinction … guarding against the development of revisionists and negationist arguments'.[35]

According to the reparations expert Feyter Koen, however, justice and truth recovery need to be part of the process if reparations are going to be 'good enough' by victims. If reparations are not integrally linked with the process of uncovering the truth and seeking justice, they run the danger of being seen by survivors as a governmental strategy to close the chapter of the past too early.[36]

In the next section I introduce a discussion of different kinds of truths since the notion of truth is complex and manifold. Different types of truths, such as collective, hegemonic or selective truths, may reveal and construct the past in particular ways. The various processes of truth telling entail and produce types of truths that can affect communities in numerous ways. However, due to the limits of the scope of this paper, I focus my discussion on the two most popular truth-seeking mechanisms: trials and TRCs. In the next section I juxtapose these truth-seeking mechanisms with the truth seeking employed by the artists studied in this paper.

---

[31] Gonzales Eduardo and Varney Howard (eds) *Truth Seeking: Elements of Creating an Effective Truth Commission* International Center for Transitional Justice New York 2013 p 4.

[32] *Basic Principles and Guidelines on the Right to a Remedy and Reparation for Victims of Gross Violations of International Human Rights Law and Serious Violations of International Humanitarian Law* GA Res 60/147 UN OHCHR 60th sess 64th plen mtg UN Doc A/RES/60/147 (16 December 2005) Preamble and Article 1 emphasise that they do not create any new international or domestic legal obligations.

[33] *Gelman v Uruguay (Judgement — Merits and Reparations)* Inter-AmCtHR Ser C No 221 (24 February 2011) para 259.

[34] See United Nations Commission on Human Rights above note 21 at Principles 2–4.

[35] At Principle 3.

[36] Feyter Koen *Out of the Ashes: Reparations for Victims of Gross and Systematic Human Rights Violations* Intersentia Oxford 2005 p 140.

2.0 Kinds of Truth

What kind of truth does a TRC or trial aim to establish? The Chilean Commission Final Report defined truth as four distinct concepts.[37] The first is factual or forensic truth based on the legal and scientific notion of presenting corroborated evidence obtained through objective and impartial procedures. The second, personal or narrative truth, is premised on a culmination of individuals' subjective stories to provide a multilayered set of experiences. The third, social or dialogue truth, is constructed through the debate and discussion of facts on a collective level. Finally, the fourth, healing and restorative truth, is truth that places given facts 'in context' in an attempt to acknowledge individual experiences. These overlapping notions of truth are meant to inform the working of TRCs, combining subjective stories with objective fact-finding in order to create a *new* truth, one that was made and owned *by* people not *for* people [original emphasis].[38]

The fact that the South African TRC attempted to acknowledge personal narratives should have ensured that it had a certain degree of legitimacy amongst the South African people.[39] Yet, although it provided a forum for diverse views and acknowledged personal suffering, it also left South Africans 'ultimately unsatisfied'.[40] This is in part because the master narratives of TRCs are based on strict mandates, are written in legal language and focus on individual victims of human rights violations at the expense of perpetrators. Truth telling and truth seeking in these contexts are seen as a minimum requirement of justice from the stake holders in power.[41]

Matt Matravers argues that the purpose of the trial is to 'get the right answer'[42] and it uses victims and witnesses to reach that answer. Still, there are situations in which truth is not paramount; plea bargaining, for example, does not aim at truth although it might be legally justified.[43] For Summers there is a difference between the actual truth, which he calls 'substantial truth', and the 'formal legal truth', which is 'whatever is found as fact by the legal fact-finder'.[44] The goals of trials are more complex than discovering the 'truth'. Trials are concerned with due process, procedural fairness, protection of privacy and judging on innocence and guilt, among others.[45]

---

[37] Truth and Reconciliation Commission above note 27 at 29–45.

[38] Stanley Elizabeth 'Evaluating the Truth and Reconciliation Commission' (2001) 39(3) *Journal of Modern African Studies* 525 at 528.

[39] At 530.

[40] Rosenburg Tina 'Prologue: Confronting the Painful Past' in Meredith Martin (ed.) *Coming to Terms: South Africa's Search for Truth* Perseus Books New York 1999 p xi.

[41] Arthur Paige 'How "Transitions" Reshaped Human Rights: A Conceptual History of Transitional Justice' (2009) 31(2) *Human Rights Quarterly* 321 at 354.

[42] Matravers Matt '"More Than Just Illogical": Truth and Jury Nullification' in Duff Antony Farmer Lindsay Marshall Sandra and Tadros Victor *The Trial on Trial: Truth and Due Process* Hart Publishing Oxford 2004 vol 1 p 71.

[43] Duff Antony, Farmer Lindsay, Marshall Sandra and Tadros Victor 'Towards Normative Theory of the Criminal Trial' in Duff et al as above at 26.

[44] Summers Robert 'Formal Legal Truth and Substantive Truth in Judicial Fact-Finding: Their Justified Divergence in Some Particular Cases' (1999) 18 *Law and Philosophy* 497 at 498.

[45] Griffin Lisa Kern 'Narrative, Truth, and Trial' (2012) 101 *Georgetown Law Journal* 281 at 289.

Too often 'trial truth' cements the victim/perpetrator dichotomy. Although the concept of truth depends on the various perspectives of individuals (and thus is relative) this should not become an excuse for not seeking it.[46] As Florence Hartmann argues, 'reconciliation without truth' is not possible; it is 'a false illusion'.[47] In trials, witnesses have to be careful about telling their story in a way that fits the legally prescribed framework and responds to the demands of criminal justice.

A handful of people will see justice through the courts and TRCs but even they may continue to be victimised at the hands of incumbent governmental officials. In addition, only a small number of those most responsible for serious human rights abuses will be held accountable, which in turn prevents the settling of accounts which may help in building shared understanding and truth. Likewise, only a small number of victims will be selected to testify before the courts or tell their story before TRCs.[48] The majority of victims will feel deprived of the whole truth since international criminal justice chooses to blame only a handful of individuals.[49]

'Truth' in both legal proceedings and TRCs is an obligation of the state to investigate and establish the facts about the past.[50] Artists, on another hand, may feel an 'aesthetic responsibility' to act on injustice. This requires the attention of committed artists, an attention that exceeds the limits of time and space and transcends boundaries between artists and audience.[51]

3.0 The Alternative Ways of Truth Seeking: Art

The field of transitional justice has recently seen an upsurge of literature concerning art and its role in post-conflict justice processes.[52] This literature has acknowledged that it is necessary to pay attention to 'the cultural and individual dimensions of

[46] Putnam Hilary *Reason, Truth and History* Cambridge University Press Cambridge 1981 p 51–54.
[47] Hartmann Florence 'A Slipping Memory: Can the International Criminal Tribunal be a Bulwark Against Oblivion?' in Spini Dario, Elcheroth Guy and Biruski Dinka Corkalo (eds) *War, Community and Social Change* Springer-Verlag New York 2014 p 202.
[48] Siddiqui Nadia *Theater and Transitional Justice in Afghanistan: Creating Space for Change* International Center for Transitional Justice New York 2010.
[49] Drumbl Mark A 'Sands: From Nuremberg to The Hague: The Future of International Criminal Justice' (2005) 103 *Michigan Law Review* 1295.
[50] Klep Katrien 'Transitional Justice and Local Memory: Commemoration and Social Action in Londres 38, Espacio de Memorias' in Brants Chrisje, Hol Antoine and Siegel Dina *Transitional Justice: Images and Memories* Ashgate Surrey 2013 p 107.
[51] Knill Paolo J, Levine Ellen G and Levine Stephen K *Principles and Practice of Expressive Arts Therapy: Towards a Therapeutic Aesthetics* Jessica Kingsley London 2005 p 140.
[52] See, for example, Bisschoff Lizelle and van de Peer Stefanie *Art and Trauma in Africa: Representations of Reconciliation in Music, Visual Arts, Literature and Film* IB Tauris London 2013; Rush Peter D and Simić Olivera (eds) *The Arts of Transitional Justice: Culture, Activism, and Memory after Atrocity* Springer New York 2014; Mengel Ewald and Borzaga Michela (eds) *Trauma, Memory, and Narrative in the Contemporary South African Novels* Rodopi Amsterdam 2012; Ramírez-Barat Catherine (ed.) *Transitional Justice, Culture and Society: Beyond Outreach* Social Science Research Council New York 2014; Bell Vikki *The Art of Post-Dictatorship: Ethics and Aesthetics in Transitional Argentina* Routledge New York 2014.

transitional processes'.[53] Artistic exhibitions have become one of the various communicative acts that strive to bring forward survivors' experiences of war and violence to larger audiences in order to break that silence and denial. These 'unofficial truth-telling' or 'alternative truth-telling' processes are informed by 'official truth-telling' accounts but are independent of them.[54] Although reparations 'are proving to be an essential transitional justice measure'[55] and a 'necessary complement' to its processes, there is still little research done on the potential of art as symbolic reparation.[56]

Art can enhance public awareness of the reality of human rights violations and the suffering that resulted from these violations. Artists can strive to engage the public on multiple levels and create the *potential* for confronting both injustice and historical narratives that need to be challenged. Art can raise questions of justice, explore alternative historical narratives, give a voice to those far too often ignored individual experiences and ensure that these stories do not disappear altogether from the national memory. In his work on 'justice as recognition', Frank Haldemann talks about a human need for validation and recognition.[57] He argues that feelings of being ignored and a failure to recognise another's dignity or equal worth are internalised as a lack of respect.[58] Art can provide a form of recognition and validation of individual human experiences of pain and suffering in times of political violence.

While the criminal trial is the process of calling to account, 'artistic truth', as expressed in the three case studies in this article, calls for reflecting, rethinking and sharing. It calls for recognition and validation of victims' personal experiences. Art can transcend the temporal limits of legal justice. Vikki Bell argues that art serves to work against the notion that transition can be 'over';[59] that is the time to move on from the past as something that is resolved. Art can serve as a reminder that wounds are still open and healing is not yet over and has the potential to problematise the present. With their work, artists may blur the line between past and present and make the idea of a 'completed transition' complex and contentious. As Adorno argues, 'the past will have been worked through only when the causes of what happened then have been eliminated'.[60]

Art can appeal to a collective sense of community as it can invite audiences to construct parts of the narrative, and speak language free from legal and professional jargon. Artists can use plain, everyday language or rituals and symbols with which

---

[53] de Greiff Pablo 'On Making the Invisible Visible: The Role of Cultural Interventions in Transitional Justice Processes' in Ramírez-Barat above note 52 at 14.

[54] Bilbija Ksenija, Fair Jo Ellen, Milton Cynthia E and Payne Leigh A *The Art of Truth-Telling About Authoritarian Rule* University of Wisconsin Press Madison 2005 p 2–4.

[55] Laplante Lisa J and Theidon Kimberly Susan 'Truth with Consequences: Justice and Reparation in Post-Truth Commission Peru' (2007) 29(1) *Human Rights Quarterly* 228 at 249.

[56] Simić Olivera and Daly Kathy '"One Pair of Shoes, One Life": Steps Towards Accountability for Genocide in Srebrenica' (2011) 5(3) *International Journal of Transitional Justice* 477.

[57] Haldemann Frank 'Another Kind of Justice: Transitional Justice as Recognition' (2008) 41(3) *Cornell International Law Journal* 675.

[58] As above.

[59] Bell Vikki 'Contemporary Art and Transitional Justice in Northern Ireland: The Consolation of Form' (2011) 10(3) *Journal of Visual Culture* 324 at 325.

[60] Adorno Theodor W 'The Meaning of Working Through the Past' in Adorno Theodor W *Critical Models: Interventions and Catchwords* Columbia University Press New York 2005 p 103.

people are familiar, and deliver truth in ways law cannot; it can express individual truths that appeal and affect the broader community. Alternately, art may blend official and unofficial histories and memories, and with visual and bodily language, transmit and transcend the individual and reach the collective and universal.

Theatrical performances, exhibits and artistic installations are transportable and, as such, can be staged or displayed in isolated and remote areas where communities may not necessarily engage with the press, Internet and formal judicial language.[61] This is where grassroots theatres concerned with social justice, such as Yuyachkani and Dah Theater, focus their audience outreach. With his photo exhibition, Gustavo Germano also aims to pay respect to victims, and acknowledge their victimisation, since acknowledging the facts and the wrongfulness of the violations is a precondition to 'de-victimization'.[62] As Albie Sachs comments, there is a need 'to move from knowledge to acknowledgment ... Knowledge is just knowing the facts, the details, but it's abstract ... [A]cknowledgment means it enters into your emotional world, your world of responsibility'.[63]

Experiencing artistic installations and bearing witness to past harms is of significance for the law. Performances, and art more generally, can create a complex yet accessible language 'to speak the seemingly unspeakable'.[64] Not only does an audience bear witness, but its presence also indicates public acknowledgement of crimes committed. This public acknowledgement is important for rebuilding trust among communities: acknowledgement of crimes is a break from the narrative of denial, which is often followed by strong feelings of shame and guilt for what has been perpetrated by group members.

Art can confront the culture of denial, silence or rationalisation in multiple ways.[65] It can open space for collective acknowledgement of the past, for empathy, solidarity and truth seeking. Local art projects are capable of 'making private grief public', and demanding recognition from the state as acts of 'political mourning'.[66]Artistic installations have the potential to create narratives that strengthen the social fabric of the nation, even if this narrative acknowledges the horrors of the past. They can create narratives of social trauma through aesthetic choices that privilege the mutual negotiation of conflicting narratives and appeal for the recognition of different individual experiences of violence.

---

[61] Simić Olivera and Milošević Dijana 'Enacting Justice: The Role of Dah Theater Company in Transitional Justice Processes in Serbia and Beyond' in Rush and Simić above note 52 at 99.

[62] Lawry-White Merryl 'The Reparative Effect of Truth Seeking in Transitional Justice' (2015) 64(1) *International and Comparative Law Quarterly* 141 at 151.

[63] Cited in Lawry-White as above.

[64] Varea Roberto Gutierrez 'Fire in the Memory: Theater, Truth, and Justice in Argentina and Peru' in Cohen Cynthia E, Varea Roberto Gutierrez and Walker Polly O (eds) *Acting Together: Performance and the Creative Transformation of Conflict* Volume I: *Resistance and Reconciliation in Regions of Violence* New Village Press Oakland 2011 p 154.

[65] Weaver James and Colleran Jeanne 'Whose Memory? Whose Justice? Personal and Political Trauma in Ariel Dorfman's Death and the Maiden' (2011) 16(1) *Performance Research: A Journal of Performing Arts* 31.

[66] Humphrey Michael and Valverde Estela 'Human Rights, Victimhood, Impunity: An Anthropology of Democracy in Argentina' (2007) 51(1) *Social Analysis* 179 at 181.

4.0 Yuyachkani (Peru)

I think the best thing that can happen to us is realizing the importance of the truth.[67]

The struggle of people against power is the struggle of memory over forgetting.[68]

Peru's most important theatre collective, Grupo Cultural Yuyachkani (Yuyachkani) has been working since 1971 as an independent institution at the forefront of theatrical experimentation, political performance and collective creation. Yuyachkani is a Quechua word that means 'I am thinking, I am remembering'. It is one of Latin America's oldest theatre collectives with a 40-year history of performing 'in reaction to, and in defiance of, politics in Peru'.[69] The theatre group has devoted itself to the collective exploration of embodied social memory, reconstruction of the past and negotiating private and public histories, particularly in relation to questions of ethnicity, violence and memory in Peru. It is well known for embracing both cosmopolitan and indigenous forms of theatre, while addressing broader issues of social and post-dictatorship Latin American aesthetics.

Yuyachkani has a strong commitment to grassroots community issues, mobilisation, social justice and advocacy. Its members see the group, and its performances more generally, as a space for self-reflection and social intervention. One of their principal goals is to contribute to the development and strengthening of public memory.[70] Yuyachkani wants audiences to collectively share time and physical space in ways that may open up possibilities for dialogue and interaction, for sharing thoughts and feelings. They use the stage to re-enact acts of mourning, and to provide testimony of past events, through the actors' bodies and narration.

The Peruvian TRC was established in 2001 to investigate two decades of armed conflict between the government of Peru and the insurgent People's Guerrilla Army (1980–2000), when Peru was plagued by the worst political violence in the history of the republic. The Communist Party of Peru began its campaign to overthrow the Peruvian state by initiating a reign of terror with the aim of ushering the nation toward a communist utopia.[71] The government response was a brutal counter-insurgency in which Andean peasants became conflated with terrorists.[72] According to the TRC, 75% of the indigenous population, in particular Quechua-speaking peasants and farmers, had been killed or disappeared, making it one of the country's most deadly conflicts.[73] The poor and illiterate constituted the majority of the victims of

67 Yuyachkani Theatre Group 'Rosa Cuchillo' performed by Ana Correa, at Brown University's Brown International Advanced Research Institutes 11 June 2013 <https://www.youtube.com/watch?v=i7U9NsRpjXcyoutube> Accessed 13 November 2015.

68 Kundera Milan *The Book of Laughter and Forgetting* Harper Perennial New York 1999 p 4.

69 'Historia' Yuyachkani Cultural Group <http://www.yuyachkani.org/historia.html>; 'Historia del Grupo' Yuyachkani Cultural Group <http://hemisphericinstitute.org/cuaderno/yuyachkani/group.html> Accessed 6 January 2016.

70 As above.

71 Palmer David Scott (ed.) *The Shining Path of Peru* 2nd ed Palgrave MacMillan Hampshire 1994.

72 Laplante and Theidon above note 55.

73 Comisión de la Verdad y Reconciliación, *Final Report* (2003) General Conclusions para 2.

the conflict.[74] More than 80% of women who reported sexual violence were indigenous — the majority of them Quechua.[75]

The TRC focused on forced disappearances, massacres, human rights violations, terrorist attacks and violence against women during the internal armed conflict, abuses that were committed by both the rebel groups and the military of Peru. Many sectors of civil society were appointed as members of the TRC, including scholars, journalists, sociologists, priests and artists.

To facilitate the truth-gathering process, as well as to publicly honour and remember the dead, five members of Yuyachkani were invited by the TRC to stage a series of performances as 'preparation for the public hearings'.[76] According to Salomon Lerner Febres, Yuyachkani 'contributed to the fostering of an apt context in which to carry out the process — to the solemnity and ceremony appropriate to an act of symbolic reparations to the victims'.[77] The TRC recognised the power of art to reach much wider and more diverse audiences than legalese ever could. As Chilean-born artist Alfredo Jarr has said: 'Enough of me speaking to you and you speaking to me, me applauding to you and you applauding to me — let's get out, let's reach a larger audience'.[78] Margaret Urban Walker also highlights the importance of the truth reaching diverse populations with different experiences and perceptions of the repression, armed conflict and violence under investigation.[79]

Yuyachkani travelled to the mountainous regions of the Andes most affected by the conflict. There, over a period of eight months, the group held workshops, performed in the streets and participated in local demonstrations. Through a range of performances and street-art installations, they converted ordinary streets and plazas into ritual spaces for reflection and remembrance. As Ana Correa, a Yuyachkani troupe member, reported:

> The Commission in Peru organised meetings where families of disappeared could come to testify … We met with people everywhere, in markets, public squares, churches … we emotionally supported people and families who suffered and testified … . We needed to be in this moment of flowering memory, contributing from our modest space of art and culture.[80]

Rosa Cuchillo was a performance that was brought to the streets of Huamanga in preparation for the public hearings. It tells the story of a mother searching for her

74 At paras 5–7.

75 As above.

76 Febres Salomon Lerner 'Memory of Violence and Drama in Peru: The Experience of Truth Commission and the Yuyachkani Theatre Group' Keynote speech presented at the Just Performance: Enacting Justice in the Wake of Violence Symposium, Brandeis University, USA, 1–2 December 2011 p 16.

77 As above.

78 Interview with Alfredo Jaar *The Gramsci Trilogy* 11 March 2007 <http://www.art21.org/texts/alfredo-jaar/interview-alfredo-jaar-the-gramsci-trilogy> Accessed 6 November 2015.

79 Walker Margaret Urban 'How Can Truth Telling Count as Reparations?' in Neumann Klaus and Thompson Janna (eds) *Historical Justice and Memory* University of Wisconsin Press Madison 2015 p 142.

80 Yuyachkani Theatre Group above note 67.

disappeared son. In accordance with Andean eschatology, she continues her search in other worlds even after her death. Yuyachkani sees ghosts of victims as 'repositories of national memory' that help Peru to collectively confront its past and shape the future.[81] The act was based on a novel with the same name by Oscar Colchado Lucio.[82] The Yuyachkani troupe used a personal story to connect with their audience. Art often uses individual stories to portray personal and unique experiences that transcend and become universal. This is important since transitional justice measures seek to provide recognition to victims as individuals and as bearers of rights.[83] (Figures 1 and 2)

> There, we found mothers with their dead babies, children with their hands tied to their backs. And there, turning over corpses, pulling out hands, arms, and legs, I left dying of sadness ... telling myself that even after death I would continue to look for my son.[84]

The Yuyachkani troupe member reported on his experience in Huamanga:

> This experience in Huamanga, of accompanying and enforcing the work of public agencies, is so important for the country's reconciliation and the healing of the people ... Many people would approach us as we were representatives of truth. They would thank us for the work we have done on the streets, and then, they would start giving us their personal testimonies.[85]

In Peru, the TRC recommendations have not been implemented and new human rights violations against indigenous people are committed on an ongoing basis. Yuyachkani's work serves as a constant reminder that there are 'deep truths that have gotten lost among the facts'[86] and that families who still wait for justice are not forgotten.

5.0 Gustavo Germano (Argentina)

During the military dictatorship in Argentina, from 1976 to 1983, nearly 30,000 people disappeared without trace. Like Peru, Argentina decided to establish a TRC to seek the truth and give space to victims to tell their stories. After democracy was restored in 1983, then President Raul Alfonsin created the National Commission on the Disappearance of Persons (CONDAEP). In 2006, following the upholding of the repeal of amnesty laws and pardons in Argentina, survivors regained public visibility when domestic investigation recommenced and trials against military junta officials restarted.[87] Still, the renewed trials against the

---

[81] 'Plays' Yuyachkani <http://www.yuyachkani.org> Accessed 6 December 2015.
[82] Colchado Oscar Lucio *Rosa Cuchillo* Universidad Nacional Federico Villarreal Lima 1997.
[83] de Greiff Pablo 'Theorizing Transitional Justice' (2012) 51 *Nomos* 31 at 42.
[84] Yuyachkani Theatre Group above note 67.
[85] As above.
[86] Febres, the former president of Peru's Comisión de la Verdad y Reconciliación, above note 76.
[87] Micus Annelen *The Inter-American Human Rights System as a Safeguard for Justice in National Transitions* Brill Hijhoff Leiden p 242; Gandsman Ari 'The Ex-Disappeared in Post-Dictatorship

Figure 1. Ana Correa as Rosa Cuchillo. Reproduced with permission of the theatre group.

military and its collaborators were held in an atmosphere of fear, intimidation and threats, including the disappearance of a key witness, Julio Lopez, in the first set of cases to be held in 2006. Miguel Etchecolatz was the Commissioner General of

Figure 2. Ana Correa as Rosa Cuchillo. Reproduced with permission of the theatre group.

Buenos Aires provincial police during dictatorship and was the second to be prosecuted.[88]

Lopez, a key witness who testified about his disappearance and torture at the hand of Etchecolatz, disappeared two days before the verdict was announced. His abduction and disappearance has been described as a 'second disappearance' and is seen as an effort to intimidate future witnesses in order to prevent them testifying and to prove that 'the repressive apparatus has not been dismantled'.[89]

In such a socio-political context, in which 'healing is still work in progress',[90] Argentine photographer Gustavo Germano decided to restage snapshots of Brazilian and Argentine families whose loved ones are among the disappeared; the people who were tortured and murdered by dictatorial regimes in Latin America from the 1960s to 1980s. *Ausencias* [Absences] is a photographic exhibition that deals with disappearances from that period. The exhibition reconstructs black and white family photos from the 1970s, in which the disappeared was/were present. Germano recreates these photos in the same place and condition as the originals, and then juxtaposes the original black and white photos from the past against new colour photos of the family, taken more than 30 years later, in order to highlight the absence of the disappeared. Germano created 14 pairs of such photos as testimony to the time and void that will never be filled. He describes this series of work as an exercise of reflection on temporality, and as a threshold that brings viewers into an illusory parallel dimension where a viewer can sense what the disappearance of a human being means. Germano reported:

> *Ausencias* are reflected in fourteen cases ... in fourteen faces is the story of all who are 'absent'. In absences, each picture is an absence itself but also the whole story ... I think it is very important that people identify with faces, with specific people and by reading a few stories to comprehend the magnitude of the tragedy ... If *Ausencias* conveys something, it's the attitude of the portraits. They with their attitude denounce the space that should be occupied, but they do it with serenity, with the conviction of a lack of hatred, which is what moves the people.[91] (Figures 3–8)

Argentina: The Work of Testimony and Survivors at the Margins' in High Steven (ed.) *Beyond Testimony and Trauma: Oral History in the Aftermath of Mass Violence* University of British Columbia Press Vancouver 2015 p 45.

[88] Julio Simon was the first to be convicted on 4 August 2006 for the kidnapping and torture of the Poblete-Hlaczik couple. See Niell Paz Rodríguez 'Histórica Condena por Crímenes de la Dictatura' *La Nacion* 5 August 2006 <http://www.lanacion.com.ar/829171-historica-condena-por-crimenes-de-la-dictadura> Accessed 5 February 2016.

[89] Trigona Marie 'Long Standing Impunity Challenges Argentina: 4 Years Without Julio Lopez' *Upside Down World* 27 September 2010 <http://upsidedownworld.org/main/argentina-archives-32/2709-long-standing-impunity-challenges-argentina-4-years-without-julio-lopez> Accessed 28 October 2015.

[90] Varea above note 64 at 154.

[91] Secretaría de Cultura y Educación Rosario *Interview with Gustavo Germano* 22 October 2009 <https://www.youtube.com/watch?v=QGhtvGLKBIo> Accessed 13 October 2015.

Figure 3. Gustavo Germano, *Ausencias*. Reproduced with permission of the photographer.

Figure 4. Gustavo Germano, *Ausencias*. Reproduced with permission of the photographer.

Ausencias strives to make visible those who are not, and bring private experiences of disappearance into the public, institutional and artistic frame.[92] The images bring attention to lifetimes that the victims of repression have missed, and the span of time that their families have lived through without their presence. The motivation

[92] Fortuny Natalia 'Memoria Fotografica: Restos de la Desaparicion, Imagines Familiars y Huellas del Horror en la Fotografia Argentina Posdictatorial' ['Photographic Memory: Remains of the Disappearance, Family Pictures and Fingerprints of the Post-Dictatorship Argentina Horror Picture'] (2012) 2 *Amerika: Mémoires, Identités, Territoires* 31.

Figure 5. Gustavo Germano, *Ausencias.* Reproduced with permission of the photographer.

Figure 6. Gustavo Germano, *Ausencias.* Reproduced with permission of the photographer.

for this work comes from Germano's personal experience of searching for a missing brother. When he was 11, his brother Eduardo, who was 18 at the time, was abducted.

In December 2014, *Ausenicas* was inaugurated as an exhibition in Washington DC at an event that marked 31 years since the overthrow of the military dictatorship and the birth of democracy in Argentina. Germano could not be present at this event since, paradoxically, he was receiving the remains of his missing brother at the time, which had been found and identified by the Argentine Forensic Anthropology team.[93]

[93] 'La Muestra "Ausencias" Arriba a la Sede de la OEA en Washington' ['The Exhibition "Absences" Top OAS Headquarters in Washington'] *Telam* 2 December 2014 <http://www.telam.com.ar/notas/201412/87453-arte-muestra-oea-fotos.html> Accessed 2 October 2015.

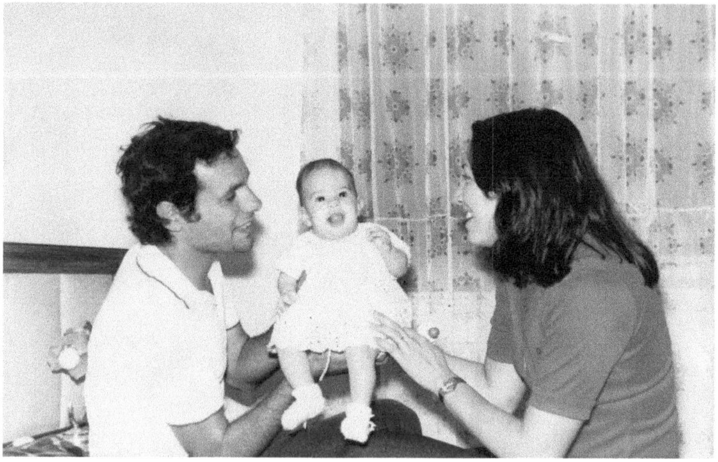

Figure 7. Gustavo Germano, *Ausencias.* Reproduced with permission of the photographer.

Figure 8. Gustavo Germano, *Ausencias.* Reproduced with permission of the photographer.

To Germano, *Ausencias* enabled victims of the regime to stand up and say: 'I am here to show you who is not here anymore. I practice memory in order to avoid silence. This is why I expose myself and I let the photographer take pictures of me.'[94] Horacio Verbitsky commented on *Ausencias*, suggesting that 'more than criminal trials, journalistic investigations or philosophical essays, art realises the searing emptiness that causes inexplicable absence'.[95]

[94] Cited in van Dembroucke Celina 'The Absences Made Visible: The Case of Ausenc'as, Gustavo Germano's Photographic Exhibition' (2010) 4 *InTensions Journal* 1 at 19.

[95] Verbitsky Horacio *Blog: Ausenc'as Exposición Fotográfica, Gustavo Germano* 25 April 2009 <http://ausencias-gustavogermano.blogspot.com.au/2009/04/prologo-horacio-verbitsky.html> Accessed 3 November 2015.

Germano's second exhibition, entitled *Busquedas* [Search], has not yet been inaugurated.[96] This project is about seeking the truth about the whereabouts of missing children in Spain and Argentina. It builds upon *Ausencias* in the sense that it is concerned with the desires of families of the missing to know the truth about the circumstances of their disappeared newborn babies. Each of the photographs are accompanied by a caption with the name of the family member and a brief description of the family's search.

There are allegations that in Spain, between 1940 and 1990, in hospitals throughout the country, medical personnel were assisted by nuns from different orders to steal newborn children, or give them away to other families. These children were told that their mothers died during or shortly after giving birth.[97] Around 2000 official cases of this nature have been filed with Spanish prosecutors, but there could be thousands more to come.[98] These children grew up without knowing who they were, who their parents were and the circumstances of their birth. These facts and their magnitude suggest that these abductions were part of an organised campaign that deserves a search for explanations. Today, thousands of mothers, fathers and brothers look for these children and they encounter silence, obstacles and impossibilities.

Similarly, the kidnapping of minors was a systematic state practice that lasted throughout the military dictatorship in Argentina, between 1976 and 1983, and which included the abduction, disappearance and changing of children's identities. These children belonged to parents who were detained and later disappeared.[99] According to some estimates, around 500 children were victims of kidnapping under these circumstances. The search for the children has been spearheaded by the Abuelas de Plaza de Mayo (Grandmothers of Plaza de Mayo) and, in recent years, the state has also participated. Their work helped to recover an identity for 119 children.[100] According to Germano:

> *Busquedas* portrays mothers, fathers, brothers and sisters who interrogate, question, seek ... trying to find something of babies. They told them 'they were born dead.' They are seeking to their eyes in all directions and who should complete their incomplete picture.[101] (Figure 9)

---

[96] Material from Germano Gustavo (Personal email correspondence 25 January 2016).

[97] Graham Helen *The War and its Shadow: Spain's Civil War in Europe's Long Twentieth Century* Sussex Academic Press Eastbourne 2012 p 148. See also Adler Katya 'Spain's Stolen Babies and the Families Who Lived a Lie' *BBC News* 18 October 2011 <http://www.bbc.com/news/magazine-15335899> Accessed 15 November 2015; Minder Raphael 'Spain Confronts Decades of Pain over Lost Babies' *New York Times* 6 July 2011 <http://www.nytimes.com/2011/07/07/world/europe/07iht-spain07.html>; Tremlett Giles 'Victims of Spanish Stolen Babies Network Call for Investigation' *The Guardian* 27 January 2011 <http://www.theguardian.com/world/2011/jan/27/spain-alleged-stolen-babies-network>.

[98] Shubert Atika 'Stolen Babies Scandal Haunts Spain' *CNN News* 26 April 2012 <http://edition.cnn.com/2012/04/25/world/europe/wus-spain-stolen-babies/> Accessed 15 January 2016.

[99] Staff Indy 'Abuelas de Plaza de Mayo Recover 119th Missing Grandchild' *The Argentina Independent* 30 November 2015 <http://www.argentinaindependent.com/currentaffairs/newsfromargentina/abuelas-de-plaing-grandchild/> Accessed 4 January 2016.

[100] As above.

[101] Material from Germano Gustavo (Personal email correspondence 29 January 2016).

Figure 9. Gustavo Germano, *Busquedas*. Reproduced with permission of the photographer.

Portraits of family members have been made in Madrid, Valencia, Barcelona and San Sebastian. The individual stories become part of the same large story that acquires a social and also universal dimension. The exhibition is proposed as a linear path, a story with two 'moments'. In the first part, families of the missing (mothers, fathers, brothers, sisters) are photographed alone. This account of incomplete images finishes with photographs of happy endings, in which families find what they sought for for so many years. The second set of images comprises portraits of the meetings. A happy ending allows confirmation that in truth and in justice, other ways of social, political and human construction is possible.[102] (Figure 10) According to Germano, these two projects are fused and interact with each other:

> while the *Ausencias* started with a 'complete' photograph of the whole family it goes to impossibility of completion in the second photo. In *Busquedas* it is a reversed path. It starts with [an] 'incomplete' photo [portrait of one person who searches for another] with a desire of, and above all, the real possibility that it can be 'completed'.[103]

6.0 Dah Theater (Serbia)

Dah Theater (Dah) was created in Belgrade by Dijana Milošević and Jadranka Anđelić in 1991, at the beginning of the fall of former Yugoslavia. At the time,

[102] As above.
[103] Material from Germano Gustavo (Personal email correspondence 4 February 2016).

Figure 10. Gustavo Germano, *Busquedas*. Reproduced with permission of the photographer.

Milošević and Anđelić were driven 'perhaps subconsciously, to oppose the destruction with creation; to create, in the midst of a world falling apart, a microcosmos of theatre'.[104] They envisioned that their theatre would last for 15 to 20 years, but 25 years later Dah is still engaged in vital cultural work.

The war in former Yugoslavia started in Slovenia and quickly spread to Croatia, Bosnia and Herzegovina (Bosnia) and, later on, to Kosovo. The whole region was affected by armed conflict directly or indirectly and is still recovering from the destructive mayhem that gripped the country between 1991 and 2001. In May 1993, the UN Security Council established the International Criminal Tribunal for Yugoslavia (ICTY) to bring to trial those responsible for violations of international humanitarian law in the territory of the former Yugoslavia since 1991. As of today, the ICTY has indicted 162 people for crimes committed. Serbia established a War Crimes Chamber in 2003 in order to try war crimes cases in its national courts.[105] Unlike Peru and Argentina, Serbia has seen only one attempt at establishing a TRC, in 2001, which was abolished six months after its inauguration due to political turmoil within the TRC Committee. The Committee never published a report. While the processes of 'dealing with the past' in Serbia are multilayered, they have barely gone beyond retributive justice and continuous demands for prosecution.

Dah's three performances, which engage with questions of our responsibility to the past — *Crossing the Line*, *Story about Tea* and *The Shivering of the Rose* — draw extensively on historical facts and documentary material about the war. Dah Theater is a theatre that raises the question of accountability for crimes in its performances. As Milošević argues:

---

[104] Knežević Dubravka 'Till the Last Breath' (1995) 5–6 p 12 *Scena*.

[105] Human Rights Watch *Justice at Risk: War Crime Trials in Croatia, Bosnia and Herzegovina, and Serbia and Montenegro* Human Rights Watch New York 2004 vol 16 p 7.

> There have been lots of theater performances who had for their subject the dissolution of Yugoslavia but it seems to me that they did not raise the question of accountability in the right way. To be honest, I do not expect that from an institutional mainstream theater that is financed by the government. It is an unfortunate fact that many theaters are financed because they follow party lines. In that way, the artists' freedom of expression is significantly restricted.[106]

In *The Shivering of the Rose* Dah uses authentic testimonies from Bosnian women, but also personal diaries and literature from Argentina and Chile. The performance deals with the post-traumatic memories of missing family members, especially women, who have lost their loved ones. Dah sees itself as a theatre that can open doors to victims to seek justice and as a space where people can reconsider their views. As a theatre, it employs techniques that allow the crossing of borders between the rational and the irrational, between reality and metaphor. These border-crossing techniques inherent to transformational theatre can at times open up a much larger space for potential reconciliation than the formal justice mechanisms. According to Milošević, *The Shivering of the Rose* was well received by its audience because of the:

> specificity and relevance of the topic that opens the possibility of the universal. People disappear in all parts of the world for various reasons and we wanted to work on the constant presence of 'absence' and look for answers as to how that happened, who is responsible, and in whose name that happened. [107]

As in the case of Yuyachkani, the audience responded enthusiastically. According to Maja Mitić:

> The truth and memory are important themes to work with in order to move on ... People were thanking us for telling the truth about wars which all bring the same human misery regardless where they are fought.[108]

Artistic projects, such as Dah's performance, can uncover hidden traumas, and artists can create 'a time and a space to remember, to mourn, to forgive, to heal, and to glimpse a new future'.[109] (Figures 11 and 12)

The subject of missing people in Serbia is marginalised and not yet tackled by the government. The UN Committee on Enforced Disappearances issued its concluding observations in February 2015 and recommended that Serbia 'conduct a thorough and impartial investigation into all cases of enforced disappearance in the context of the previous armed conflicts, and adopt necessary legislative measures ... in order to adequately address the legal situation of disappeared persons and their

[106] Gočanin Sonja 'Intervju: Rediteljka Dijana Milošević: Teatar nije pijaca' ['Interview: The Director Dijana Milošević: The Theatre is Not a Market Place'] *Buka* 25 July 2012 <http://www.6yka.com/novost/26271/rediteljka-dijana-milosevic-teatar-nije-pijaca> Accessed 9 September 2015.
[107] 'Dah teatar istražuje Sardiniju' ['Dah Theatre Explores Sardinia'] *Politika* 24 July 2014 <http://www.politika.rs/scc/clanak/300163/Dah-teatar-istrazuje-Sardiniju> Accessed 15 February 2016.
[108] Maja Mitić (Personal email correspondence 8 February 2016).
[109] de Bruyne Paul and de Maeseneer Yves 'Secret and Sacred Places: The Role of Art in Processes of Reconciliation' (2013) *Concilium: International Review of Theology* 24.

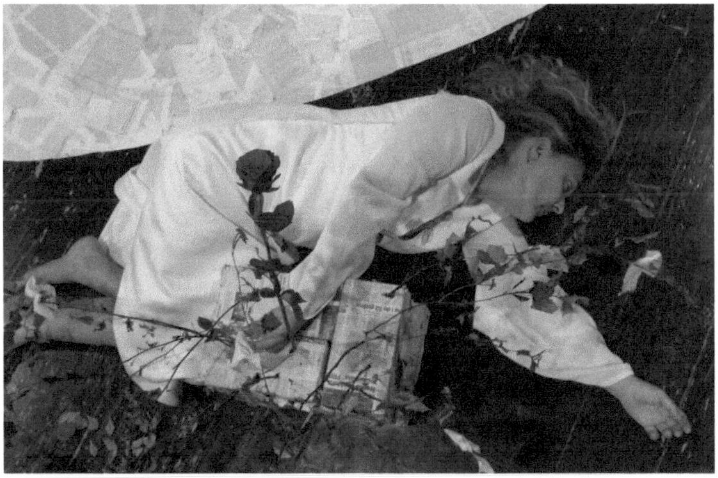

Figure 11. Maja Mitić, *The Shivering of the Rose*, Dah Theater. Reproduced with permission of theatre director. Photographed by Una Škandro.

Figure 12. Zašto! [Why!]. Maja Mitić, *The Shivering of the Rose*, Dah Theater. Reproduced with permission of theatre director. Photographed by Una Škandro.

relatives'.[110] Despite these suggestions Serbia has not yet shown any determination to resolve the fate of persons who are listed as missing or to discover locations of

[110] *Concluding Observations on the Report Submitted by Serbia under Article 29, paragraph 1, of the Convention* UN Committee on Enforced Disappearances 8th sess UN Doc CED/C/SRB/CO/1/1049043 (2–13 February 2015) <http://tbinternet.ohchr.org/Treaties/CED/Shared%20Documents/SRB/INT_CED_COC_SRB_19624_E.pdf> Accessed 11 November 2015.

mass graves on its own territory.[111] In their performance *The Shivering of the Rose*, Dah Theater raises the question of enforced disappearance at a universal level:

> Families whose closest relatives disappeared from Serbia, Kosovo, Bosnia, Rwanda, Argentina are no longer celebrating their important dates, holidays, birthdays, graduations, and anniversaries because life has stopped for them. They are frozen in their waiting.[112]

Perhaps, more than the other two case studies, Dah Theater brings to a profound level the theme of the 'universality' of human suffering and the need to search for the truth. By transcending physical borders and fusing personal experiences from various parts of the world, the theatre brings all these geographies of loss together. Their work helps audiences to place their local realities in a global perspective and enhances their capacities to see their experiences not in isolation but connected with others.

7.0 Untapped Potential of Art

Throughout this paper I have discussed grassroots arts projects that are striving for a more open and participative approach to commemoration and collective memory, and tirelessly challenging official discourses on the past. They open new spaces for people to voice their memories and broaden their perspectives on corrupted regimes.[113] They collectively emphasise that, as Stephen Levin argues, 'there is no erasing the past, but different ways of living it'.[114]

In Peru, Yuyachkani accompanied the official truth-seeking processes and has been recognised as an important mechanism that can assist people in preparation for telling their stories. The necessity to preserve memory and speak the truth is an integral part of Yuyachkani's work. In Argentina, Gustavo Germano calls for the missing not to be forgotten and serves as reminder of the necessity of long-awaited justice. While the Yuyachkani group has been embraced, recognised and invited by officials to help in seeking the truth and preserving memory, Dah Theater works largely in isolation and fills the vacuum left by the lack of state initiatives to address the problem of missing people and their families. And while the symbolic forms of reparation offered by artists discussed in this paper are not enough without material reparations (financial compensation, rehabilitation or restitution),[115] they are of significant importance to transitional justice processes. They allow a country to

---

[111] 'Serbia 2015 Progress Report: The Humanitarian Law Center Contribution' (2015) *Humanitarian Law Center* 5 <http://www.hlc-rdc.org/wp-content/uploads/2015/11/2015-Progress-Report-Humanitarian-Law-Center-Contribution.pdf> Accessed 5 November 2015.

[112] *The Shivering of the Rose* above note 1.

[113] Klep above note 50.

[114] Levine Stephen K 'Art Opens the World: Expressive Arts and Social Action' in Levine Ellen G and Levine Stephen K *Art in Action: Expressive Arts Therapy and Social Change* Jessica Kingsley Publishers London 2011 p 27.

[115] Carranza Ruben Correa Cristián and Naughton Elena *More Than Words: Apologies as a Form of Reparation* International Center for Transitional Justice New York 2015 p 3 <https://www.ictj.org/sites/default/files/ICTJ-Report-Apologies-2015.pdf> Accessed 13 October 2015.

develop a common and shared memory thereby creating a sense of unity. They are rooted in the need of people to mourn and commemorate victims and to honour the dead, which is imperative for remembrance.[116]

Art can have instrumental, intrinsic and extrinsic effects on people, and can inspire them to self-reflection and acknowledgement of the knowledge they possess about the crimes committed in their community. The experiences of others/victims in that sense may become integrated into the experiences of the viewer/witness. Art has intrinsic value in that the 'charismatic power of the work of art itself' can 'ennoble and inspire political thinking and action'.[117] It encourages people to participate in open, interactive and participative debate. As Susanne Buckley-Zistel argues, transitional justice in post-conflict societies is always a political process, and we have to maintain a critical stance towards the political implications of its application.[118]

While Peru, Argentina and Serbia have employed transitional justice measures such as trials, they are still a long way from achieving justice for victims of gross human rights violations. Artists from these three case studies may bring that justice a step closer by striving to keep memory alive, continuing to ask for justice and defying the denial and silence pervading their communities. The artists discussed bring calls for justice into public spaces, and their art serves as a reminder that memory and truth will not be discarded. They create new political and social spaces and within them they plant a seed of hope while providing an opportunity for a community to engage in collective remembrance and truth seeking.

Disclosure Statement

No potential conflict of interest was reported by the author.

[116] Ashplant TG, Dawson Graham and Roper Michael *The Politics of War Memory and Commemoration* Routledge London 2000.
[117] Baudot Barbara 'Art in International Relations' in Denemark Robert A *International Studies Encyclopedia* Blackwell Publishing Hoboken 2000 p 2.
[118] Buckley-Zistel Susanne *Transitional Justice in Divided Societies — Potentials and Limits* Paper presented at the 5th European Consortium for Political Research General Conference, Potsdam University, Germany, 10–12 September 2009. See also Angelovska Despina '(Mis)Representations of Transitional Justice: Contradictions in Displaying History, Memory and Art in the Skopje 2014 Project' in Rush and Simić (eds) above note 52 at 183.

Prosecuting the Khmer Rouge Marriages

*Maria Elander**

Abstract. At the Extraordinary Chambers in the Courts of Cambodia (ECCC), the trial against the two surviving leaders of the Khmer Rouge charged in Case 002 is about to deal with the 'regulation of marriage'. This is the name given by the ECCC to the Khmer Rouge-instigated marriages also known as 'red weddings' or 'forced marriage'. In this symbolically laden case, the charges relating to the marriages stand as the only alleged crime of sexual and gender-based violence after no charges were brought for the many rapes committed in security centres and work cooperatives. As such, the charges have been described as 'the Court's best last chance to contribute to the ever-evolving body of law aimed at better responding to perpetually neglected sexual and other gender-based crimes in times of conflict and atrocity'. In this article, I examine the ways in which the marriages so far have appeared at the ECCC. One aim in writing this is to simply bring to attention what is about to unfold at trial. But in reading the representations of the marriages, the difficulties in prosecuting gender-based harms also come into view. Thus, the charges relating to the 'regulation of marriage' raise a question about the limits of symbolic value in any one trial.

1.0 Introduction

Trials do many things. Trials bring people together, bring attention to acts and roles held in the past and present. Memories are narrated as testimonies, events are presented as evidence. This is the dramatisation of truth, of events, of facts. During the trial, stories are contested, but, as Cornelia Vismann points out, 'the main task of a trial is not to investigate the truth — since this can be done outside of the courtroom, behind the scenes — but to dramatize, and hence to register in discourse, the violation of an instituted legal frame'.[1] While the trial may register harms and responsibility, the work to articulate these, and to frame them, often occurs elsewhere.

This type of dramatisation of the 'truth' is about to take place at the Extraordinary Chambers in the Courts of Cambodia (ECCC), or the Khmer Rouge Tribunal as it is

*For comments and feedback, I wish to thank Olivia Barr, Dianne Otto, Peter Rush, Christoph Sperfeldt and the two anonymous reviewers.

[1] Vismann Cornelia '"Rejouer les crimes" Theater vs Video' (2001) 13 *Cardozo Studies in Law and Literature* 119 at 124–125.

also called. Here, the long-awaited trial segment relating to the so-called 'regulation of marriage' is finally scheduled to appear.[2] While marriage is always in some way 'regulated', this is the name given by the ECCC to the Khmer Rouge-instigated marriages also known as 'red weddings' or 'forced marriage'. It has been a long wait: the alleged crimes were committed between 1975 and 1979,[3] an agreement to establish the Court was signed in 2003,[4] and charges were brought against the then four surviving leaders of the Khmer Rouge in 2010.[5] This massive 'Case 002' covers everything from forced population movement to internal purges to treatment of specific groups such as the Buddhist, Vietnamese and Cham, acts for which the former leaders are charged with crimes against humanity, Grave Breaches against the Geneva Conventions and genocide. Here, the regulation of marriage is presented as alleged crimes against humanity.[6]

In this symbolically laden case against the leaders, the charges relating to the marriages stand as the only alleged crime of sexual and gender-based violence. Despite evidence of rapes in security centres and work cooperatives, no charges were brought against the leaders.[7] As such, the representation of the marriages as crimes against humanity have been described as 'the Court's best last chance to contribute to the ever-evolving body of law aimed at better responding to perpetually neglected sexual and other gender-based crimes in times of conflict and atrocity'.[8] The stakes seem, in other words, high.

---

[2] At the time of writing (March 2016), this segment is planned for May 2016.

[3] There is some controversy over the exact relationship between the Khmer Rouge and the Communist Party of Democratic Kampuchea with suggestions that this is more complex than first appears. The name 'Khmer Rouge' was given to the group by Prince Sihanouk. See Linton Suzannah 'Putting Cambodia's Extraordinary Chambers into Context' (2007) 11 *Singapore Year Book of International Law and Contributors* 195. On the Khmer Rouge period more generally, see, for example, Becker Elizabeth *When the War was Over: The Voices of Cambodia's Revolution and its People* Simon and Schuster New York 1986; Chandler David *Voices from S-21: Terror and History in Pol Pot's Secret Prison* University of California Press Berkeley Los Angeles & London 1999; Alexander Laban Hinton *Why Did They Kill? Cambodia in the Shadow of Genocide* University of California Press Berkeley 2005; Kiernan Ben *The Pol Pot Regime: Race, Power and Genocide in Cambodia under the Khmer Rouge, 1975–79* 3rd ed Yale University Press New Haven 2008; Ben Kiernan *Genocide and Resistance in Southeast Asia: Documentation, Denial and Justice in Cambodia and East Timor* Transaction Publishers New Brunswick 2008.

[4] *Agreement Between The United Nations and The Royal Government of Cambodia Concerning the Prosecution under Cambodian Law of Crimes Committed During the Period of Democratic Kampuchea* signed 6 June 2003 (entered into force 29 April 2005) ('*ECCC Agreement*').

[5] *Prosecutors v Nuon Chea, Ieng Sary, Khieu Samphan and Ieng Thirith (Closing Order)* (ECCC Trial Chamber Case No. 002 15 Sep 2010) ('Closing Order'). Since the charges were issued, two of the charged persons have died: in 2013 Ieng Sary and two years later his wife, Ieng Thirith. Left accused for the 'regulation of marriage' are 'Brother No 2', Nuon Chea, and former Head of State, Khieu Samphan.

[6] Closing Order at 1430 and 1442.

[7] See discussion below.

[8] de Languis Theresa 'A Missed Opportunity, a Last Hope? Prosecuting Sexual Crimes under the Khmer Rouge Regime' (2014) 2 *Cambodia Law and Policy Journal* 42. Also available at http://cambodialpj.org/article/a-missed-opportunity-a-last-hope-prosecuting-sexual-crimes-under-the-khmer-rouge-regime/ Accessed 22 March 2016.

In this article, I examine the ways in which Khmer Rouge marriages have been represented so far at the ECCC. One aim in writing this is to simply bring to attention what is about to unfold. I suggest that the representation of the marriages as crimes against humanity illustrates the difficulties in prosecuting gender-based harms as well as the dangers in putting too much symbolic weight in any one trial. I begin with situating the ECCC in the international attention given to crimes of sexual and gender-based violence. Second, I turn to some background on the Khmer Rouge marriages. In the third part, I examine in depth the presentation of the marriages as crimes at the ECCC.

2.0 Prosecuting Sexual Violence

Certain questions and concerns travel. For feminists interested in the international as a site in which to address atrocity-related sexual and gender-based violence, the ways in which international courts and tribunals have successfully prosecuted forms of rape and sexual violence as war crimes, crimes against humanity and genocide are familiar.[9] For many, these stand as recognitions of the violence perpetrated particularly against women during wars and conflicts. Others have been less optimistic and have instead seen signs of worry in the ways in which sexual violence has been prosecuted. For example, Karen Engle argued that the ways in which rape and sexual violence were prosecuted at the International Criminal Tribunal for the Former Yugoslavia reinforced the image of women as passive victims while also reifying ethnic differences;[10] Doris Buss expressed concern that the approach by the International Criminal Tribunal for Rwanda to rape as a 'weapon of war' foreclosed seeing other potential forms of sexualised violence;[11] and Janet Halley warned against assuming a lack of consent in a conflict situation as this would foreclose any type of lawful sex occurring between different parties in a conflict.[12] In all of this lies a story of the rise and travels of judicial attention to what is often called sexual and gender-based violence but is more often (only) sexual violence.[13] In one reading, this attention can be linked to

[9] See, for example, *Prosecutor v Jean-Paul Akayesu* (*Judgment*) (ICTR Chamber 1 Case No. ICTR-96-4-T 02 September 1998) (*'Akayesu Judgment'*); *Prosecutor v Ante Furundzjia (Judgment)* (International Criminal Tribunal for the former Yugoslavia Trial Chamber Case No: IT-95-17/1-T 10 December 1998); *Prosecutor v Dragoljub Kunarac, Radomir Kovac and Zuron Vukovic (Judgment)* (International Criminal Tribunal for former Yugoslavia Trial Chamber Case No: IT-96-23-T& IT-96-23/1-T 22 February 2001); *Prosecutor v Sesay, Kallon & Gbao* (*Judgment)* (Special Court for Sierra Leone Trial Chamber I Case No. SCSL-04-15-T 2 March 2009).

[10] Engle Karen 'Feminism and its (Dis)Contents: Criminalizing Wartime Rape in Bosnia and Herzegovina' (2005) 99 *American Journal of International Law* 778.

[11] Buss Doris 'Rethinking "Rape as a Weapon of War"' (2009) 17 *Feminist Legal Studies* 145.

[12] Halley Janet 'Rape in Berlin: Reconsidering the Criminalisation of Rape in the International Law of Armed Conflict' (2008) 9 *Melbourne Journal of International Law* 78.

[13] For purposes of clarity, I am not referring to the feminist technic of 'world travelling', which, in contrast to the phenomenon I am describing here, is thoroughly grounded in experience. See, for example, Lugones Maria 'Playfulness, "World"-Traveling, and Loving Perception' (1987) 2 *Hypatia* 3; Charlesworth Hilary 'Feminist Methods in International Law' (1999) 93 *America Journal of International Law* 379 at 383–385.

and explained as a form of feminist governance.[14] Another way to read it would be as a selective appropriation of, or engagement with, certain feminist strands that align with other interests and agendas.[15] Regardless of how one explains the attention to atrocity-related sexual violence, some conflicts 'have virtually become synonymous with rape in part due to the attention given to these crimes'.[16] Notably, the Khmer Rouge period is not one of these conflicts, and any consideration of sexual or gender-based violence came late at the ECCC.

The ECCC was set up through an agreement between the United Nations and the Cambodian government 'to bring to trial senior leaders' and 'those who were most responsible for the crimes' committed during the period when Cambodia was known as Democratic Kampuchea.[17] When the Court began operating in 2006, the general understanding was that while killings, torture and forced labour had been widespread in Democratic Kampuchea, sexual violence had not. The assumption was that the strict moral codes of the Khmer Rouge and its emphasis on gender neutrality had meant that any and all non-marital sexual encounters had been subjected to punishment, regardless of whether between non-married lovers or instances of rape. This in turn would have deterred any widespread occurrence of sexual violence.[18] So when investigations began at the ECCC, sexual and gender-based violence was not a priority.[19] In a country with 'tens of thousands of criminal episodes', the Co-Prosecutors[20] had to make the cases manageable and chose to address only a

---

[14] Halley et al 'From the International to the Local in Feminist Legal Responses to Rape, Prostitution/Sex Work, and Sex Trafficking: Four Studies in Contemporary Governance Feminism' (2006) 29 *Harvard Journal of Law and Gender* 335.

[15] See Charlesworth Hilary 'The Woman Question in International Law' (2011) 1 *Asian Journal of International Law* 33; Fraser Nancy 'Feminism, Capitalism and the Cunning of History' (2009) 56 *New Left Review* 56; Otto Dianne 'Exile of Inclusion: Reflections on Gender Issues in International Law over the Last Decade' (2009) 10 *Melbourne Journal of International Law* 10.

[16] Henry Nicola 'The Fixation on Wartime Rape: Feminist Critique and International Criminal Law' (2014) 23(1) *Social & Legal Studies* 93 at 94.

[17] Law on the Establishment of the Extraordinary Chambers, with inclusion of amendments as promulgated on 27 October 2004 (NS/RKM/1004/006) (Unofficial translation by the Council of Jurists and the Secretariat of the Task Force. Revised 26 August 2007) ('*ECCC Law*').

[18] See, for example, Jacobsen Trudy *Lost Goddesses: The Denial of Female Power in Cambodia* NIAS Press Copenhagen 2008; Nakagawa Kasumi 'Gender-Based Violence During the Khmer Rouge Regime: Stories of Survivors from the Democratic Kampuchea (1975–1979)' 2nd ed March 2008 <http://gbvkr.org/publications-and-materials/research-and-documentation/> Accessed 22 March 2016; Studzinsky Silke 'Neglected Crimes: The Challenge of Raising Sexual and Gender-Based Crimes before the Extraordinary Chambers in the Courts of Cambodia' in Buckley-Zistel Susanne and Stanley Ruth (eds) *Gender in Transitional Justice* Palgrave Macmillan Basingstoke 2011 p 92; Williams Sarah and Palmer Emma 'The Extraordinary Chambers in the Courts of Cambodia: Developing the Law on Sexual Violence' (2015) 15 *International Criminal Law Review* 452 at 456.

[19] Amongst internationalised courts and tribunals, the ECCC is unique in that it follows the French inquisitorial model whereby investigation and its initiation are split between the prosecution and independent investigative judges. Prosecution is initiated by the Co-Prosecutors and on the basis of their Introductory Submission, the Co-Investigative Judges carry out the main investigation. (See ECCC Law, art 25 on the independence of Co-Investigative Judges and Internal Rule 49)

[20] As a result of its internationalised feature, all main posts at the ECCC are held by one national and one international staff. Hence, Co-Prosecutor etc.

'representative sample' of the criminal acts.[21] Notably, all investigators and translators at the ECCC were male at that time, and there was no training into how to investigate sexual and gender-based crimes.[22] While former Co-Prosecutor Andrew Cayley claims that the Office of the Prosecutor never 'ignored gender-based crimes' and that 'female victims were not forgotten',[23] former Civil Party Lawyer Silke Studzinsky argues that these words never translated into action.[24] Studzinsky, who spent seven years at the ECCC representing victims, many of whom had suffered sexual and gender-based violence, maintains that the Co-Prosecutors and later the Co-Investigative Judges 'followed the common historical record without question',[25] which, as mentioned above, had never focused in depth on sexual and gender-based violence.[26] The marriages were first brought to the attention of the ECCC by Studzinsky and her colleague Ny Chanda when four of their clients filed complaints arising from marriages to which they had been subjected.[27] During the main investigation conducted by the Co-Investigative Judges, Civil Party Lawyers filed a number of Supplementary Investigative Requests, alongside the Co-Prosecutors' Supplementary Submissions, for the investigation to broaden and encompass a wider range of sexual violence. Most of these were dismissed.[28]

In the resulting Closing Order — the legal document prepared and written by the Co-Investigative Judges that charges an accused and provides a description of the material facts and their legal characterisation — for Case 002,[29] attention is paid to forms of sexual and gender-based violence both in security centres, worksites and

[21] 'On International Criminal Justice: Interview with Andrew Cayley' *Global Brief* 9 September 2011 (Andrew Cayley was International Co-Prosecutor 2009–2013).

[22] Studzinsky above note 18 at 101.

[23] Cayley Andrew 'KR's Female Victims Were Not Forgotten' *Phnom Penh Post* (Phnom Penh) 1 June 2012.

[24] Studzinsky Silke *Challenges to a Successful Prosecution of Sexualized and Gender-Based Crimes* paper presented at the International Conference on Bangladesh Genocide and the Issue of Justice, Heidelberg, Germany, 4–5 July 2013 <http://www.civilparties.org/?page_id=48> Accessed 22 March 2016.

[25] As above at 3.

[26] There were exceptions, for example, Kalyanee Mam 'Evidence of Sexual Abuse During the Rule of Democratic Kampuchea' (March 2001) 15 *Searching for the Truth* 2.

[27] Chanda Ny and Studzinsky Silke 'Four Victims of Forced Marriage under the Khmer Rouge Regime File their Complaint to the ECCC' Press Release 16 October 2008 <http://www.civilparties.org/?p=295> Accessed 30 March 2016.

[28] *Second Request for Investigative Actions Concerning Forced Marriages and Forced Sexual Relations* dated 15 July and filed on 23 July 2009; *Co-Lawyers for the Civil Parties' Fourth Investigative Request Concerning Forced Marriages and Sexually Related Crimes* dated 4 December 2009 and filed on 9 December 2009; *Decision on Appeal of Co-Lawyers for Civil Parties Against Order Rejecting Request to Interview Persons Named in The Forced Marriage and Enforced Disappearance Requests for Investigative Action* (ECCC Pre-Trial Chamber Decision, 21 July 2010); *Appeal of Co-Lawyers for Civil Parties Against Order Rejecting Request to Interview Persons Named in The Forced Marriage and Enforced Disappearance Requests For Investigative Action* (ECCC Pre-Trial Chamber Decision, 21 July 2010) at 2, 3.

[29] In accordance with the Internal Rules, the Closing Order 'sets out the identity of the Accused, a description of the material facts and their legal characterisation by the Co-Investigating Judges, including the relevant criminal provisions and the nature of the criminal responsibility'. ECCC, *Internal Rules* (*Rev 9*) (adopted 16 January 2015) r 67(2).

cooperatives, and in the context of 'the regulation of marriages'. Only acts within the context of marriage led to charges against the accused leaders. While the Co-Investigative Judges note that rapes were committed in 'diverse circumstances' during the regime,[30] they found that these cannot be characterised as crimes against humanity committed by the accused leaders because there was no policy to rape.[31] In contrast, 'the regulation of marriage' led to charges of crimes against humanity.[32]

3.0 The Khmer Rouge Marriages

Before I look at the Closing Order and its description of the marriages and their criminality, I want to pause and spend some time on these marriages in their broader context during the Khmer Rouge period. What characterised these marriages and made them potential *crimes*? As is generally known, part of the Khmer Rouge revolution was a radical upheaval of previous orderings of life. Cities were evacuated and religion abolished. No longer was society to be structured into small family units,[33] but into larger village cooperatives, where life and work were organised according to gender, age and work ability. Here, women, men and children often lived separately, and bonds and loyalty previously tied to the immediate family were now meant for *Angkar* — the 'organisation'.[34]

In accordance with this collectivisation of life and the dismantling of the strong bonds of family, marriage and its initiation became the responsibility of *Angkar* and its village representatives. Sometimes soldiers were given a spouse of their choice as a reward for their service;[35] at other times both spouses were chosen by *Angkar*. In this general atmosphere of fear, marriage proposals became near impossible to refuse since this raised a risk of being sent for 're-education'.[36] Couples who wed during this period often met for the first time at the ceremony itself. Ceremonies

---

30 Closing Order at 1426.

31 For critiques of this reading, see De Langis Theresa '"This Is Now the Most Important Trial in the World": A New Reading of Code #6, the Rule Against Immoral Offenses under the Khmer Rouge Regime' (2014) 3 *Cambodia Law and Policy Journal* 61; and Elander Maria *Figures of the Victim in International Criminal Justice* (forthcoming).

32 Closing Order at 1430, 1442.

33 Heuveline Patrick and Poch Bunnak 'Do Marriages Forget their Past? Marital Stability in Post-Khmer Rouge Cambodia' (2006) 43(1) *Demography* 99, 101.

34 Becker above note 3 at 240; Mam Kaylanee 'The Endurance of the Cambodian Family under the Khmer Rouge Regime: An Oral History' in Susan E. Cook (ed.) *Genocide in Cambodia and Rwanda: New Perspectives* Transaction Publishers New Brunswick 2006 p 119 at 123–133. For a slightly different reading of the policies directed towards women and mothers, see LeVine Peg *Love and Dread in Cambodia: Weddings, Births and Ritual Harm under the Khmer Rouge* National University of Singapore Press Singapore 2010 p 107. For a description of traditional marriages and family organisation, see Jacobsen above note 18 at 131–144, 223.

35 Nakagawa above note 18 at 15.

36 'Re-education' was a euphemism used by the Khmer Rouge and would usually mean either imprisonment or death. Jain Neha 'Forced Marriage as a Crime Against Humanity, Problems of Definition and Prosecution' (2008) 6 *Journal of International Criminal Justice* 1013 at 1024; Strasser et al *A Study about Victims' Participation at the Extraordinary Chambers in the Courts of Cambodia and Gender-Based Violence under the Khmer Rouge Regime* Transcultural Psychosocial Organisation Phnom Penh September 2015 p 53–54.

were brief and almost always conducted collectively, with the number of couples involved sometimes reaching 300 at any one time. After the wedding, there would be prearranged private sleeping huts for the newly-weds to spend a couple of nights together and consummate the marriage.[37] After this was done, the spouses would return to their previous work and living units, and some, like all couples, would only meet intermittently. Many of the couples who wed through these weddings have remained together,[38] because they had children and/or because they developed close relations.[39] Others separated as soon as the regime fell.

How should these marriages be represented? While some call them *red weddings*,[40] they are generally described as instances of *forced marriage*.[41] The epitaph of 'forced' is in common use, also by the ECCC, but not all agree that it captures the distinct nature of the marriages.[42] Peg LeVine, an anthropologist who spent a decade interviewing people who wed during this period, vehemently dismisses the epitaph 'forced'. She describes them instead as 'conscripted', in that 'the Khmer Rouge conscripted (drafted) young people into matrimony', something that she sees gives a language for cases of 'conscientious objectors'. She claims that the people she met 'used the word "forced" to describe work conditions, but no one used the same word to describe their marriage'.[43] Without entering the debate on whether or not the marriages were 'forced' but still wanting to capture their distinctiveness, I refer to them, as can be noted so far, as the *Khmer Rouge marriages*, or simply, *the marriages.*

4.0 Marriages as Ceremonies and Relations

About to reach trial are thus alleged crimes against humanity in the context of marriages. There is something rather radical about this: a (possible) legal recognition that marriage can be harmful, that certain imposed conjugal relations can be considered to be of similar gravity as, for example, murder and enslavement. That it is

[37] Studzinsky above note 18 at 93; Ye Beini 'Forced Marriages as Mirrors of Cambodian Conflict Transformation' (2011) 23 *Peace Review: A Journal of Social Justice* 23.

[38] See in particular Heuveline and Poch above note 32 at 118 who, on the basis of a quantitative study, found a 'striking … *lack* of a notable difference' in marriage stability between the Khmer Rouge and post-KR weddings. (118). Also see LeVine above note 33 at 87, who interviewed 192 persons who were wed during this period. 153 or 80% of these are still with their assigned partner. While her sample, assembled through snowballing, cannot be generalised for the larger population, it does suggest that many couples have stayed together.

[39] LeVine above note 33; Strasser et al above note 35 at 56–58.

[40] See, for example, the documentary *Red Wedding* (Directed by Lida Chan and Guillaume Suon Bophana Production Bophana Center Tipasa Production 2012).

[41] See, for example, Becker, above note 3 at 267; Jain above note 35; Nakagawa above note 18 at 14–15; Mam above note 33; Mam Kaylanee 'An Oral History of Family Life under the Khmer Rouge' *Working Paper Yale University* 1999 p 17; Ye above note 36. Also the ECCC describes them as forced marriages.

[42] See, for example, LeVine above note 33 in particular at 26–29, 175; Peg LeVine 'Weddings under the Khmer Rouge: How Has "Forced" Been Decided?' *Phnom Penh Post* 4 November 2014 <http://www.phnompenhpost.com/weddings-under-khmer-rouge-how-has-forced-been-decided> Accessed 16 February 2016.

[43] LeVine above note 33 at 26–29, 175.

a *crime* to force people to live in accordance with certain predetermined genders and gender roles. What is further notable with the charges is that in contrast to many other sexual and gender-based crimes, both persons in the imposed relations — the couples — figure here as victims. The perpetrator does not face the victims and does not take part in the imposed relation. Since this is a crime in which men and women were forced to marry each other, the fact that both spouses were victimised brings a gender neutral aspect to what is often within sexual and gender-based crimes a focus on female victims. This is also reflected somewhat amongst the group of victims who are now active in the criminal proceedings. At the ECCC, victims can apply to participate as civil parties,[44] and amongst the 3866[45] civil parties admitted to Case 002, 780 are so in relation to the marriages. Within this group are both men and women.[46]

While the marriages will be presented and contested during trial, much work of their representation as crimes is done already in the Closing Order. As noted above, the Closing Order is the result of investigation conducted first by the prosecution and then the investigating judges, and the ways in which crimes are presented (or dismissed) there sets out a frame for what can be narrated and challenged. The trial and subsequent judgment are to some extent bound by the Closing Order. The legal characterisation of a crime may change, but only 'as long as no new constitutive elements are introduced'.[47] Furthermore, no new facts can be presented as the judgment is 'limited to the facts set out' in the Closing Order.[48] It matters then how the Closing Order represents the events, the facts, the crimes.

In the Closing Order, the marriages are referred to in two separate counts of crimes against humanity: as rape and as other inhumane acts.[49] However, despite rape being enumerated in the ECCC Law as an underlying offence,[50] the defence successfully challenged the legality of classifying rape as a constitutive underlying offence of crimes against humanity given that the act was committed in the 1970s.[51] As a result, rape — within the context of the marriages — was re-characterised into 'other inhumane acts'.[52] It seems that what is proceeding to trial are two counts of

[44] ECCC Internal Rules r 23.

[45] 'Reaching Out to Newly Admitted Civil Parties' (Aug 2011) 39 *ECCC Court Report* 1.

[46] Strasser et al above note 35 at 33.

[47] ECCC Internal Rules r 98(2).

[48] The meaning of this is disputed. Civil party lawyer Silke Studzinsky has argued that the Trial Chamber is not bound by the Closing Order conclusion that rapes in security centres could not be linked to the accused persons. However, the Trial Chamber found that including these rapes would amount to adding new facts, something it is not authorised to do. See discussion by Studzinsky 'Comments in Response to International Co-Prosecutor's Supplementary Submission in Case 004 Requesting the Investigation of Sexual or Gender-Based Violence' 31 May 2013 <http://www.civilparties.org/?p=1716> Accessed 22 March 2016.

[49] Closing Order at 1430 and 1442. In order to be characterised as an international crime, the marriages must meet the criteria of both the chapeau elements of the crime (here crimes against humanity) and the underlying offences (here the separate categories of rape and other inhumane acts).

[50] ECCC Law Art 5.

[51] I.e. *Nullum Crimen sine lege. Ieng Thirith Appeal Against Closing Order* (18 Oct 2010) at 61; *Ieng Sary's Appeal Against Closing Order* (25 Oct 2010) at 218; *Decision on Appeals by Nuon Chea and Ieng Thirith Against the Closing Order* (ECCC Pre-Trial Chamber Case 002 15 February 2011) at 154.

[52] *Decision on Appeals by Nuon Chea and Ieng Thirith Against the Closing Order* (ECCC Pre-Trial Chamber Case 002 15 February 2011) at 154.

other inhumane acts of crimes against humanity, where one focuses on rape (in the context of forced marriage) and the other forced marriage *per se*.

So how is this other inhumane act of forced marriage *per se* described? One of the descriptions centres on the wedding ceremonies: '[P]eople were typically married in mass ceremonies',[53] the Closing Order notes, and 'followed a similar pattern'.[54] Here, 'family members were not present',[55] and a 'traditional Cambodian ritual such as the participation of monks' was absent.[56] It concludes that at the weddings, '[t]here was no respect of the traditional rituals'.[57] In other words, what supports the characterisation of the marriages as crimes against humanity is the way the weddings broke with tradition. What is noticeable with this presentation of a break with traditions and rituals as inflicting 'serious ... suffering or injury'[58] is that it suggests that the victimised were not only the individuals who wed, but also the relations that hold society together.

This presentation of the Khmer Rouge wedding ceremonies as rupturing important societal bonds resonates with the work on the marriages by LeVine. According to her, the Khmer Rouge approach to traditional practices and wedding rituals was 'erratic ... attending to some, omitting some, including some, revamping some, and violating many sacred rites'.[59] The Khmer Rouge ignored the traditional referrals to horoscopes for appropriate wedding days[60] and mothers were not allowed to participate in their children's weddings. This, LeVine claims, 'violated the culture'.[61] In LeVine's writing, the wedding ceremonies conducted during this period became part of a larger 'ritualcide'[62] and a 'cosmic betrayal'[63] of the Cambodian population. They cannot be considered separate but instead, distorted the way an entire generation became adults through weddings, pregnancy, births and parenthood.[64] This 'ritualcide'[65] eroded peoples' 'psycho-emotional, familial, cultural and spirit-based infrastructures',[66] and altered the way people engaged with spirits and ancestors, something that severed their sense of predictability and safety.[67] Her concept of 'ritualcide', while not a legal term, is nevertheless akin to one of the issues the Closing Order represents as injurious in the marriages. And affected by the ritualcide were not only individuals but also 'infrastructures' of society, the relations to the past and to others that make community.

---

[53] Closing Order at 844.
[54] At 855.
[55] At 856.
[56] At 855.
[57] At 1447.
[58] For a discussion on other inhumane acts, see *Decision on Appeals by Nuon Chea and Ieng Thirith Against the Closing Order*, above note 51 at 158–164.
[59] LeVine above note 33 at 175.
[60] As above at 61.
[61] As above at 175.
[62] As above at 183.
[63] As above at 183
[64] As above at 181.
[65] As above at 182–183.
[66] As above at 181.
[67] As above at 183.

The suggestion that not only individuals but also the community can be considered to have suffered due to the weddings is challenging. On the one hand, there is the danger that a representation of the community as victim would undermine the suffering inflicted on the individual. For example, feminists have fought hard to disassociate acts such as rape from ideas of communal harm.[68] On the other hand, there is also a feminist critique against the assumption that individuals are completely autonomous beings, figuring independently of each other.[69] Take, for example, the work by Judith Butler who, in examining the way processes of mourning and loss constitute subjects, has emphasised the significance of relations and attachments. According to her, we are 'socially constituted bodies, attached to others'.[70] Her conception of the social as held together through attachments provides a way of appreciating that we are 'at risk of losing those attachments, exposed to others, at risk of violence by virtue of that exposure'.[71] And so, to sever the attachments upon which society is constituted would inflict violence on *both* the individuals and the relations. If then, the ways in which the Khmer Rouge wedding ceremonies disrupted the relations past and present is the 'truth' that will be dramatised during the trial, it would challenge the current emphasis in international criminal law on bodily harm and seeing gender-based harm as primarily one of sexualised violence.

The ECCC is not the first international(ised) court or tribunal to be called upon to articulate forms of marriage as crime. While the ECCC is not bound by the decisions in these other courts and tribunals, the Special Court for Sierra Leone (SCSL) dealt with forced marriage in the case against Brima, Kamara and Kanuet (the AFRC case). There, the Appeals Chamber found in its judgment that the forced marriages to which women had been subjected during the Sierra Leonean conflict were not sufficiently characterised by the crime of 'sexual slavery' but rather consisted of a distinct 'other inhumane act'. Whereas the Trial Chamber[72] found the suffering women had experienced resonated with practices of slavery and, more particularly, a form of slavery that was sexual in nature, the Appeals Chamber disagreed. Experts before the Court argued that forced marriage was not simply characterised by rape, sexual slavery, forced pregnancy or forced domestic labour and that the forced marriage had constituted something more than the sum of all these together. Ultimately, the

[68] See, for example, Askin Kelly D 'Prosecuting Wartime Rape and Other Gender-Related Crimes under International Law: Extraordinary Advances, Enduring Obstacles' (2003) 21 *Berkeley Journal of International Law* 288; Charlesworth above note 13; Chinkin Christine 'Rape and Sexual Abuse of Women in International Law' (1994) 5 *European Journal of International Law* 326.

[69] See, for example, Nedelsky Jennifer *Law's Relations: A Relational Theory of Self, Autonomy, and Law* Oxford University Press Oxford & New York 2011; West Robin 'Jurisprudence and Gender' (1988) 55 *University of Chicago Law Review* 1.

[70] Butler Judith *Precarious Life* Verso London & New York 2004 p 20.

[71] As above.

[72] *Prosecutor v Brima, Kamara and Kanu* (*AFRC* case) (*Judgment*) (Special Court for Sierra Leone Trial Chamber II SCSL-2004-16-T, 20 June 2007) ('AFRC Trial Judgment') found no distinct issues, translating the suffering of forced marriage into the underlying offence of sexual slavery, an enumerated act under the SCSL statute but not at ECCC. See also Frulli Micaela 'Advancing International Criminal Law: The Special Court for Sierra Leone Recognizes Forced Marriage as a "New" Crime Against Humanity' (2008) 6 *Journal of International Criminal Justice* 1033 at 1036.

Appeals Chamber found the forced marriage to be a distinct act under other inhumane acts and, importantly, 'not predominantly a sexual crime'.[73]

Notwithstanding the reference in the Closing Order description of the marriages to the non-sexual act of wedding ceremonies, it seems that the ECCC is taking a different approach from the SCSL. Of course, there are fundamental differences between the two situations: in Sierra Leone, women were forced by men to marry them, whereas in Democratic Kampuchea, both women and men were forced to marry by a third party, the regime. But this does not explain the radical difference between the two tribunals in their approaches to the relation between forced marriage and sex. Although there are two counts relating to the marriages in the ECCC Closing Order, they are in fact rather similar. That is, apart from the description of the wedding ceremonies in one of them, both counts focus on the 'consummation of marriage' — in other words: sex. Or, rather, rape.

The definition of rape employed by the Closing Order ensures that both men and women could have been raped. Rape here is a 'physical invasion of a sexual nature against a victim in coercive circumstances in which the consent of the victim was absent'.[74] In using the concept of 'invasion', the Closing Order draws on the definition of the *actus reus* of rape adopted in international criminal law by the *Akayesu* case before the ICTR in 1998 and the ICC Elements of Crime.[75] At the ICC, it is explicitly noted that 'invasion' is meant to ensure gender neutrality.[76] This definition will then hopefully make superfluous any discussion of whether penetration has 'actually' occurred, and hopefully allow for the narrations of the harms suffered by both the man and the woman in the consummation of marriage. What is worrying in the Closing Order, and further reasons to play close attention to the forthcoming trial, is the way the consummation of the marriage comes to dominate the description of the crime of 'the regulation of marriage'. Given that there is a separate count focusing on the rapes within the marriages, why does the second count also turn to the consummation of marriage?[77] The only difference is that here, 'consummation of their union'[78] appears alongside the 'imposition of sexual relations aimed at enforced procreation'.[79] While the addition of 'procreation' could indicate a concern with forced pregnancy, it is still the sexual act that is in focus.

This emphasis in the Closing Order on the sexual act is both curious and problematic. It is curious because it goes directly against the SCSL insistence that forced marriages are *not* primarily sexual. As mentioned, the ECCC is not bound by the SCSL, but the difference is curious nevertheless. The emphasis is also problematic.

[73] *AFRC case* above note 72 at 195.
[74] Closing Order at 1431.
[75] 'The central elements of the crime of rape cannot be captured in a mechanical definition of objects and body parts.' *Akayesu Judgment* above note 9 at 597. Celebrated by many feminists, the term was successfully lobbied for at the ICC, and now appears in International Criminal Court *Elements of Crimes* Doc No ICC-ASP/1/3 (part II-B) (adopted and entered into force 9 September 2002) ('ICC Elements of Crime').
[76] ICC Elements of Crime art 7(1)(g)-1.1 Fn 15.
[77] At 1447.
[78] At 1447.
[79] At 1445.

This is not because sex and rape appear in the description of the marriages — for some who married, the rapes took up a central role in their suffering and if one believes that crimes should somehow also reflect the experiences and suffering of the victim then excluding consummation/rape would have been similarly problematic. Rather, at issue here is the way that the emphasis on the sex produces a narrow understanding of and focus on the injured and sexualised body. In reading the Closing Order on the marriages, the body that is visible is the one which is raped and/or childbearing. This resonates all too well with stereotypical images of the female subject in law and war. See, for example, the early human rights documents with their focus on the mother, 'valued for [her] chastity ... and domesticity'.[80] From here, it is not far from the 'women and children' references, with all their connotations of passivity, innocence and need for protection. What differs in the context of the marriages is that men are included in the representation. But how this will be reflected, I cannot at this point say.

Sometimes, as Cynthia Enloe put it, making rape visible can be 'dangerously easy'.[81] This was not the case with rapes committed in security centres and worksites, the exact nature of which remains contested. However, it does seem easy to point to the rapes within the marriages. Why is that? Are sexualised harms easier to narrate than gender-based ones? This more difficult question I save for later but at this point I will say that if this emphasis on sex and rape remains during the trial and in the subsequent judgment, we will have a parsimonious account of the complex relations and the multifaceted suffering imposed through these marriages.

5.0 Conclusion

Trials do many things, but they are not *tabulae rasae*. Much work of framing and presenting facts and events occur elsewhere, such as during investigations and in the characterisation of the charges. The story of how the Khmer Rouge marriages will soon appear at trial at the ECCC demonstrates just that — how certain issues never even reach trial but then how a forthcoming trial is framed to narrate a certain version of the events. Of course, many things may still happen during the hearings. Testimonies by witnesses and civil parties may challenge the written texts, or the prosecutors may come to emphasise something else in the marriages. We, the observers, the listeners, will hopefully learn something more about what happened during these four years of the Khmer Rouge regime and how this has affected the lives of people. While the trial cannot depart too far from what has already been written, it can at least shift the emphasis in a way that means the marriages will not be equated with rape.

Trials do many things, but they cannot do it all. Nor should they. Regardless of whether the trial and the subsequent judgment will come to provide a more

[80] Otto Dianne 'Lost in Translation: Re-scripting the Sexed Subjects of International Human Rights Law' in Anne Orford (ed.) *International Law and its Others* Cambridge University Press Cambridge & New York 2006 p 318 at 325.
[81] Enloe Cynthia *Maneuvers: The International Politics of Militarizing Women's Lives* University of California Press Berkeley Los Angeles & London 2000 p 109.

complex representation of the marriages, it would be mistaken to place too much hope or symbolic value in the legal events. The trial is significant: former leaders of the Khmer Rouge stand accused of horrific crimes and the ways in which the Court represents the marriages will have effects on whether victims will feel recognition for their suffering and on the ways in which academics and lawyers discuss international criminal law. Yet, although the charges relating to the marriages are the only crimes of sexual and gender-based violence appearing in this case, these should not be placed to represent, in the sense of standing for, all sexual and gender-based violations during the regime. Furthermore, the belief that a legal event or law would be able to hold it all, to represent complex and at times contradictory experiences, events and suffering, will remain a fantasy. It is the belief that law, in offering recognisable names, also provides justice and healing. Perhaps the trauma of the marriages is exactly that, a trauma, and thus cannot be represented in the symbolic order. Perhaps this partly explains why the marriages slip in the Closing Order into rape. As a societal trauma then, the marriages — state-imposed conjugal relations — will resist any complete recognition in law.

The Transitional Heart: Writing Poetry on War, Grief and the Intimacy of Shared Loss

Robyn Rowland; Mehmet Ali Çelikel, translations

Abstract. A personal note on the creation of *This Intimate War: Gallipoli/ Çanakkale 1915 — İçli Dışlı Bir Savaş: Gelibolu/Çanakkale 1915* by Robyn Rowland, Turkish translations by Mehmet Ali Çelikel, published by Five Islands Press: Melbourne, Australia, 2015 and Bilge Kultur Sanat, Turkey, 2015. Republished Spinifex Press, Melbourne, Australia, 2018.

My brother did me an unpredictable favour in marrying a Turkish-Australian woman, Sevil. Our shared love of archaeology and her great capacity for history and cooking cemented our friendship. In 2009 I took my younger son, almost 16, and headed for Turkey. We spent six weeks travelling around the ruins and museums, which barely touched the surface of what is held there.

I fell in love with a golden period of Ottoman history under the great Sultan, Suleiman Kanuni, 'The Lawgiver', whom the West called 'The Magnificent'. I was awarded a Literature Board grant, and began my work. On a second trip aimed at studying the period I'd adopted, I was shocked and captured by an experience in Çanakkale. Visiting the Naval Museum there, I learned the Gallipoli story from the Turkish viewpoint and the history of the Battle of Çanakkale, of which I was ignorant. It was uncomfortable to find myself identified with the enemy, the aggressor.

When I was in primary school, I grew up with the story every Anzac Day about the brave boys who went to war. I knew nothing about politics or different cultures. I knew nothing about the Ottoman Empire. (We still celebrated 'Empire Day' with fireworks.) Once a year we gathered at dawn to remember them — 'lest we forget'. Then the film 'Gallipoli' starring Mel Gibson came out in 1981, and the story became a tragedy perpetrated by British leaders who used 'our boys' as fodder. There was no mention of 'their boys'.

I did not know that before Gallipoli, on 18 March 1915, the Ottomans, with few resources, defeated the British Navy, then the greatest navy in the world. After this, they knew the war would advance by land, an invasion Churchill estimated would take four days from landing to arrival in Constantinople. I didn't know that the story of Troy fired Britain's attempt. That historical context is in my narrative documentary poem, 'The Folly of Myth: Prologue 1915'.[1] After that, it is the personal journeys that take centre stage.

The Ottoman Empire had been brilliant in the sixteenth century under Suleiman the Lawgiver but gradually diminished itself through lack of coordination and modernisation. By 1915 it was exhausted from four years of war in the Balkans and unwilling to enter into another. At that point the British were advising the Sultanate on the development of its navy and the Germans on the development of its army. The Ottomans had raised money from public subscription to buy two new battleships from the British. When they refused to ally themselves with the British and enter the war, the British refused to hand over the ships. The Germans offered two ships that were available in the harbour. So began Turkey's angry entrance into the war.

And it marked the end of empires. Australia learned an identity; the British Empire began its disintegration in places like India; the Austro-Hungarian Empire was dissolving; the Russian Revolution was about to change that country. And in Ireland, massive political change was creating hope in many, confusion in some as the Easter Rising of 1916 eventually led to Independence. While the Irish fought for the British in the hope that it might show their worth as an independent country, Ireland itself was changing and unwilling to remember those who fought for the 'enemy'. As Patrick MacGill, the solider-writer wrote in the 1917 poem 'Lament': 'They'll call me coward if I return. But a hero if I fall.'[2]

For Turkey, the War of Independence followed immediately on from World War I, led by Mustafa Kemal Atatürk, its first president. An officer who led at Gallipoli, he was widely read and keen for change. His astonishing leadership finished the Sultanate which had been ready to allow Turkey to be carved up by the allies. Under his leadership, the most incredible rate of social change occurred. He created an extensive education system, opened up the lives of women and girls, gave women the vote and banned the wearing of the Fez and of the headscarf in public institutions. He modernised Turkish clothes, he introduced surnames and modernised the economic and industrial systems. He reshaped the armed forces, private publishing and social behaviour. Most strikingly he changed the language itself, taking out many Persian words and replacing the Arabic alphabet with a Latin one, allowing people three months in which to learn it. They did. Literacy increased from 10% to 90%. He remade a dissolving empire into the modern secular democracy Turkey is today.

War forces countries and individuals into transition in powerful and multifaceted ways. It impacts on every single person from the country involved. I could write 100 books with 1000 stories and still not plumb the depths of the experiences and tales of World War I. Soldiers, sailors, airmen, nurses, doctors, the women who were involved in munitions manufacture, the child soldiers, women who lost husbands,

[1] Rowland *This Intimate War: Gallipoli/Çanakkale 1915* Five Islands Press Melbourne 2015 p 20.
[2] MacGill Patrick *Soldier Songs* Herbert Jenkins London 1917 p 31.

father, sons or saw their men return totally damaged in mind and body; the painters, musicians, poets, composers lost. No one was left unscathed.

I wrote them all into my book, *This Intimate War: Gallipoli/Çanakkale 1915 —İçli Dışlı Bir Savaş: Gelibolu/Çanakkale 1915*, a book of poems reflecting the experiences of both Australians and Turks during the Çanakkale/Gallipoli campaigns. The book is historically accurate. But it is not a history. It is poetry out of history. It is my attempt to put balance into the Anzac story and to create a book that Australians, the Allies and the Turks will relate to. I had to work hard to find a publisher and funding for it in bilingual form as I believed so strongly that both English and Turkish should be together side-by-side in this book. Clare Rhoden writes in her review: 'The decision to face each poem with its Turkish translation ... is a sharp and provocative representation of the anomaly of the Gallipoli campaign itself.'[3]

With many Turkish friends now, I'm always amazed at the forgiveness Turkey expresses towards Australia. That friendship continues too with my translator, Mehmet Ali Çelikel, and with the painter, Fehmi Korkut Uluğ, who allowed us to use his painting on the cover of the first edition. 'Mehmetçik ve Johnny Mehmetçik' represents so well the unusual relationship created during the Gallipoli/Çanakkale wars because 'at first glance it is not clear which is the Turk and which the invader, or who is supporting whom'.[4] He agreed for Spinifex to use 'KanlıSırt', 'The Bloody Hill', capturing the violent, bloody chaos and the glint of bayonet. My coming across his Gallipoli series, my inclusion of a poem on it and the fact of his grandfather having fought at Gallipoli and survived, form one of the notable and mystic stories that accompanied the writing and production of this book.

It is impossible to grasp that the total number of military and civilian casualties in World War I was over 37 million: over 16 million deaths and 20 million wounded. The total number of deaths includes about 10 million military personnel and about 7 million civilians. Those soldiers left at a least 3 million widows and 10 million orphans, of those who could be counted.

It was appalling carnage, with the introduction of a kind of warfare unknown before and one for which nurses and doctors could not have been prepared. Trained to heal, they now found themselves facing the savagery of mechanised war. As nurse Ellen Newbold La Motte (1873–1961) wrote: 'Thus the science of healing stood baffled before the science of destroying.'[5]

Militaries call it mopping up — killing the last vestiges of an army.
Women mean, cleaning up, repairing, making spotless.
Florence taught what they all learned, west and east —
compassion is the salve beneath the gauze that heals.
Yet for some pain, *morphia, good as it is, is not as good as death.*

[3] Rhoden Clare '"Poppy-Hunters, Poppy-Picking": Review of Robyn Rowland *This Intimate War: Gallipoli/ Canakkale 1915*' (2015) 19(2) *Text* <http://textjournal.com.au/oct15/rhoden_rev.htm> Accessed October 2015.

[4] As above.

[5] Newbold La Motte Ellen *The Backwash of War: The Human Wreckage of the Battlefield as Witnessed by an American Hospital Nurse* G P Putnams & Son New York & London 1916 republished 1934 p 55. See the poem 'Mopping up' below and Rowland Robyn 'The Other Hero of Anzac' (2014) 24(20) *Eureka Street*.

They stitched, cleaned gastric away, gagged on gangrene stench,
soiled their own skin with blood and spit, shit and foul language.
They held eyes that dangled, shot out; pressed their elbows into holes in backs
blown away by mortars; stuffed their fists into spurting arteries.
They saw through to the bone in every way.

They learned a deeper pain in nursing, not for health,
but to refit an armed force with patched-up husbands and sons,
knowing that ripped apart in body and mind, as soon as flesh was
repaired, they'd shrug up their rifles and packs, strap their faces
into the resignation of obedience, and go back to be shattered again.

from 'Mopping up' in *This Intimate War.*

This was a difficult work to write. It took over two years and the search for Turkish voices and history in English. It involved many days scanning the web for footage or photos hidden in obscure places, in order to get the details right. It meant tracing films and diaries. Often, after intense periods of research and writing, I had to stop to recover from the onslaught of that story: the loss, the horror, the stupidity, the waste. From the first moment it was hand-to-hand killing, shocking physical violence, the physical closeness of its soldiers unmasking the depersonalisation of the propaganda of war. In the end, I found it hard to let go, to let go of all those voices that have disappeared into the earth, particularly the 'boys' from all countries. I felt I knew many of them, and wanted them here still.

2015 was the centenary of Gallipoli/Çanakkale, and coincided with a special year to celebrate relationships between Turkey and Australia. In 2012 the then Prime Ministers, Julia Gillard (Australia) and Recep Tayyip Erdoğan (Turkey), agreed that 2015 would be proclaimed the *Year of Turkey in Australia and the Year of Australia in Turkey, to be marked by a series of cultural and other events.* From the demonised 'other' and the enemy, to friendship — a strange and compassionate transition after such a war.

A selection of poems follow from the book *This Intimate War Gallipoli/Çanakkale 1915 - İçli Dışlı Bir Savaş: Gelibolu/Çanakkale 1915* by Robyn Rowland, with translations by Mehmet Ali Çelikel. It was published initially in 2015 in Australia by Five Islands Press and in Turkey by Bilge Kultur Sanat in the centenary year, funded by the Municipality of Çanakkale, attesting to the continuing close relationship between the two countries post-war. The cover image 'Mehmetçik ve Johnny Mehmetçik' was from a series of war paintings by modern Turkish artist, Fehmi Korkut Uluğ. 'The image intriguingly blends the shapes, emotions and motives of the two soldiers pictured, so that at first glance it is not clear which is the Turk and which the invader, or who is supporting whom (Clare Rhoden, 'Poppy-hunters, Poppy-picking', *Text*, Vol 19 No 2 October 2015. http://www.textjournal.com.au). In addition, a poem in the book on Fehmi Korkut Uluğ's work, includes the story of a regiment of which his grandfather was the only survivor. The current publication by Spinifex Press, Melbourne, Australia, features his 'KanlıSırt', 'The Bloody Hill', capturing the violent, bloody chaos and the glint of bayonet.

From 'The Folly of Myth: Prologue, 1915'

Part I Desire and myth

> *Think of fighting ... on the plains of Troy itself! I am going to take my Herodotus as a guide-book.*
>
> — Patrick Shaw-Stewart, poet and soldier at Gallipoli

Three small boys, ten years old, careen among torpedoes, mines,
in green grounds around Çimenlik Kalesi, stone fortress
built by Mehmet the Conqueror, to stop Crusaders, Venetians,
protect the Dardanelles. Mimosa sweetens a grey sea of weapons.
Valerian, deep pink and white, flowers between stones of its high walls.
In orange T-shirt, the tallest has a smile bigger than a cannon's mouth.

They climb steel-net anchors used to stop allied subs with
black-and-white arrowhead hooks to dig into sand.
If all three boys splayed along the huge shank from its throat
they would fit with room to spare. They love the camera.
Fearless they quiz and laugh repeating, 'hello', 'hello'.
Go serious. Pose for destiny. Think of wars and heroic deeds.

Troy is just down the road. Bone-house of heroes.
When my boy stood there he saw Achilles and Hector,
armies over a hundred thousand, blood on their spears.
I smelt fear, heard the scurry to hide girls. At that crumbled gate
Priam watched his son's body dragged ragged behind horses.
I prayed to any god that my sons navigate manhood without war.

When the British came they sailed in the wash of Agamemnon.
Every English Officer and Gentleman grew up with
Homer in his hand, unruined Troy on his horizon.
Greek history was furrowed ground where skeletons of immortal
dreams sprout to life. From a country where the rich built
fake ruins for their 'follies', they longed for ancient valour.

Bred on the classics, lusting for another Troy, they camped
in castle grounds on Tenedos and dreamed at night
of sending their ships up the straits to the city of gold.
Straddling present and past above the cove in which the Greeks
waited for a signal that the Trojans had accepted the horse,
modern pride swelled to think they would follow in their wake.

They carried their empire with them — the defeated, the colonised,
the unaware. They so desired Constantinople, mythic, it floated as a
jewelled palace in their minds; like forbidden fruit, it stirred their
loins; exotic, it wove gauzy dreams of riches, of women, wanton,
depraved, eager to be unveiled. *To Constantinople and the Harems*
screamed one Australian troopship's banner.

'Mitos Aldanması: Giriş, 1915'

I Arzu ve Mitos

Vuruşmayı düşün ... Hem de Truva düzlüklerinde! Herodot'u rehber alacağım kendime.

— Patrick Shaw-Stewart, şair ve Gelibolu'da asker

Üç küçük çocuk, on yaşında, koşturuyor mayınlar, torpidolar arasında,
Çimenlik Kalesi'nin yeşilliğinde, taş surlarında,
Fatih Sultan Mehmet'in yaptırdığı o surlarda, durdurmak için Haçlıları, Venediklileri,
koruyorlar Dardanel'i. Mimozalar tatlandırıyor silahların gri denizini. Kediotları çiçek
açıyor, pembe ve beyaz, yüksek duvarların çatlaklarında.
Turuncu tişörtüyle en uzun boylunun, top ağzından büyük bir gülücük
var ağzında.

Çelik ağları tırmanıyorlar uçlarına siyah beyaz oklar bağlı
müttefik denizaltılarını durdurmak için uçları kuma saplı.
Üçü de geçip ağın boğazından sarılsalar gövdeye eğer sığıp
çıkacaklar boşluğa. Objektifleri pek severler.
Korkusuzca sorup dururlar 'merhaba,' 'merhaba' diye selamlıyorlar.
Ciddi ol şimdi. Kaderine poz ver. Düşünülecek şey savaş ve kahramanlıklar.

Hemen yolun altındadır Truva. Kahramanların kemikten evleri.
Oğlum durup baktı, Akhilleus ve Hektor'u gördü,
orduları gördü, mızraklarının ucu kanlı yüz binlerce askeri.
Ben korkunun kokusunu aldım, telaş içinde gizledim kızları. Parçalanmış
o kapıda
Priamos oğlunun sürüklenip lime lime edilişini izledi atların ardında.
Tanrıya yakardım, oğullarım insanlığın yolundan gitsin savaşsız bir dünyada.

İngilizler, Agamemnon'un dalgalarında yelken açıp geldiler.
Her İngiliz subayı ve Beyefendisi ellerinde Homeros,
ufuklarında yıkılmamış bir Truva hayaliyle büyüdüler.
Ölümsüzlük düşlerinin hayat bulduğu bu topraklar
izlerini taşır Yunan tarihinin. Zenginlerin sahte kaleler
minyatürler inşa ettiği topraklardan gelip, eski çağlardan hamaset aradılar.

Klasiklerden beslenip, yeni bir Truva ihtirasıyla, karargâh kurdular
Tenedos kalesinde, gemilerini boğazlardan geçirip
göndermenin düşünü kurdular geceleri taşı toprağı altın şehre.
Bir ayakları geçmişte ve bir ayakları bugünde dururlar Yunanlıların
Truvalıların atı içeri aldığı işaretini beklediği kovukta,
uyanınca onların izini süreceklerini sandılar modern bir gururla.

Yanlarında taşıdılar imparatorluğu – yenilmiş, sömürgeleşmişti,
farkında değildi. Öyle istediler ki Constantinople'u, bir efsaneydi,
akıldan çıkmayan mücevherler, yasak meyve gibi, arzularını kabarttı;
o esrarlı şehir, puslu zenginlik düşleri; peçesi açılacak, baştan çıkarılacak
kadınlar. *Constantinople'a ve Haremlere*
diye bağırıyordu Avustralya savaş gemisinin coşkulu pankartı.

'Close'

Who can dig a sepulchre great enough for you?
History itself, say I, cannot contain you

— Mehmet Âkif Ersoy (1873–1936) *To the Martyrs of Çanakkale*
Trans. Prof. S. Tanvir Wasti

close in every sense, air humid and heavy in
march, freezing and snow-bound in november,
trenches stained red, oozing water then
flooding with bodies washed to the sea,
but nothing to drink. i'm so dry.

a sea once vivid blue, now claret mud,
its crust of white in the wind scarlet.
no use when my body, lice-ridden,
can barely crawl for hunger, not swim.
and the thirst. we can't drink it.

close, the enemy trenches, feet away
rattling bullets or worse the steel,
upward lunge of a bayonet driven home,
jugular spurt, no need for medics,
if they could be found.

we throw notes over a sandbag that separates our ditches.
one said 'you are too weak to advance, too strong
to retire, and we are the same, so what shall we do about it?'
i can smell his cigarette in the break
as if we have rest periods to breathe.

i can smell the squelchy corpses. our shared dead.
briefly a white singlet on bayonet tip rises.
stepping out to look into our eyes
that's when we know them, suddenly, smooth hands,
voices, smiles, they are boys like us, young.

after, we go back into our holes. it's harder now
close up, i see him carrying his wounded
enemy, lifting him gently, laying him down
carefully for us to collect and he will probably
be shot returning and our soldier die anyway

and still he does it because
bravery isn't to do with this but with finding
himself again in some small act, some care.
another note lands: 'if you don't surrender
in 24 hours, we will!' we have humour at least.

'Yakın'

Sana dar gelmeyecek makberi kimler kazsın?
'Gömelim gel seni târîhe' desem, sığmazsın.
— Mehmet Âkif Ersoy (1873–1936), *Çanakkale Şehitlerine*

her bakımdan yakın, hava nemli mart ortasında ve
ağır, dondurucu soğuk ve kar havası kasım,
siperler boyanıyor kızıla, sular sızıyor ardından
sel olup bedenleri taşıyor denize,
içecek bir damla yok oysa. kurudum susuzluktan.

bir zamanlar masmaviydi deniz, şimdi çamur kırmızısı,
dalgaların beyaz köpüğü kızıla boyandı rüzgarda.
neye yarar bedenim, bitler içinde kaldıkça,
ne sürünecek gücüm var açlıktan, ne de yüzecek. bir
de susuzluktan. içecek yok bir damla.

yakın, düşman siperleri, birkaç adım ötede
kurşunların çatırtısı ya da çeliktir daha kötüsü, bir
süngü hamlesi ile her şey apaçık ortada,
şahdamarı yırtılır, gerek yok sıhhiyeye,
eğer bulunabilirse onlar da.

hendeklerimizi ayıran kum çuvalının üstünden notlar atıyoruz birbirimize.
biri diyor ki: 'ilerleyemeyecek kadar zayıf, geri çekilmeyecek kadar
güçlüsünüz, biz de öyle, o zaman ne olacak bu mesele?'
sigarasının kokusu geliyor burnuma ara verince sanki
tekrar soluk almak için ara veriyoruz cephede.

çiğnenmiş cesetlerin kokusunu alıyorum. ortak şehitlerimizin. bir
ara beyaz bir atlet dalgalanıyor bir süngünün ucunda.
bir adım atıyor dışarıya biri bakmak için gözlerimize o
zaman tanıyoruz onları, aniden, yumuşacık ellerle,
sesleri, gülüşleri, bizim gibi genç birer çocuk onlar da.

sonra, dönüyoruz deliklerimize. daha zor her şey şimdi,
yaklaşıyorum, taşıdığını görüyorum düşmanının yaralı bir
askerini, onu usulca kaldırıp, yere yatırışını dikkatlice gidip
alalım diye şehidimizi o gidince
askerimiz çoktan öldü ve o da vurulacak dönüşte

yine de yapıyor bunu
yiğitlik savaşmak değil kendini bulmaktır çünkü
küçük bir eylemde, bir iyilikte.
bir başka not der ki: 'teslim olmazsanız eğer
24 saat içinde, biz oluruz!' en azından gülüyoruz birlikte.

we can hear them laugh sometimes, weep others,
call to us at night. we don't know the language but
we know song when we hear it, the sound of a joke.
their songs break your heart open, you can hear home in them.
one of us far away from home, the other not close enough.

close is what i remember of my son five, his smell,
my wife leaning from bed for her slippers, her dark hair
a lost photo. now i know him in the trenches best,
his ribs thin like mine, his bandaged foot,
that cough at night, the black sleepless shape of his death.

we all know each other both sides.
we know our towns, our cities, our families.
we share our breath here, sometimes our sad food,
inedible bully beef, grapes, tomatoes, hard biscuits, fresh bread.
they killed my friend relieving himself at dawn

blew him to pieces and he fell on us all like rain.
close, i love him now, my enemy. i know him. like me
he can't understand the way of it, the charging out,
the sure death, the way they tell us and we do it.
i feel his tremble at the boom of canon, the snipers' zip.

he knows death is here for us, no other way.
line after line of us both sides, one defending the place
he loves, the other knowing it. they don't want us killed,
we'd all be lonely here. we have no boundaries anymore.
we are killing ourselves in this intimate war.

bazen güldüklerini duyarız, ağladıklarını,
bize seslendiklerini geceleri. dillerini anlamasak da
şakalaşmaları ve şarkıları tanırız duyunca.
şarkıları yüreğini burkar derinden, memleketi duyarsın dinledikçe.
birimiz uzaklardadır evinden, diğerimiz değildir yeterince yakınında.

ne kadar da yakın oğlumun hatırası, beş yaşında, kokusu,
karımın yataktan terliklerine uzanışı, siyah saçları
kayıp bir fotoğrafta. en iyi siperlerde tanıyorum onu şimdi,
benim gibi zayıf kaburgaları, sargılı ayağı,
geceki o öksürüğü, ölümün kara uykusuz şekli.

her iki tarafta da iyi tanıyoruz birbirimizi. biliyoruz
kasabalarımızı, şehirlerimizi, ailelerimizi.
nefeslerimizi paylaşıyoruz burada, bazen kederli yemeklerimizi,
yenileyemeyecek etler, üzüm, domates, sert bisküvi, taze ekmek.
arkadaşımı öldürdüler benim idrarını yaparken şafakta,

paramparça olup bedeni yağmur gibi yağdı üstümüze.
yakınımda, seviyorum şimdi onu, düşmanımı. biliyorum onu. benim gibi
anlayamıyor bu işleri, ne işe yaradığını,
kesin ölümü, bize nasıl anlatıldığını ve nasıl yaptığımızı.
hissediyorum titreyişini mermiler vızıldayıp, toplar patladıkça.

biliyor, ölüm burada bekliyor bizi, başka yer yok.
sıra sıra bekliyoruz her iki tarafta, biri savunuyor
çok sevdiği ülkesini, öteki de biliyor bunu. istemiyorlar ölmemizi.
yapayalnız kalırız diye burada. hiçbir hudut tanımıyoruz artık.
bu yakın savaşta öldürüyoruz kendi kendimizi.

'Green Road'

This is the way that we went
to get here — past lochs in early dawn,
reeds so still they were painted in,
green shamrocks we'd sewn
into our jacket sleeves
never to match those shimmering Connaught fields
clotted white with sheep —
but travelling with us anyway. And out of Dublin's
grey light we came, out of the poor, the cold,
always hungry and now to be fed by our work.
And out of Trinity, the future of a new nation.
They would know us then —
our imperial overseers —
know our worth in battle,
pay the value in our freedom after.
That is honour. That is why we came.

The Fife band of the Irish Fusiliers played
The Wearing of the Green
as we sailed out to war from Devonport,
those of us coast-born, knowing the fear
of a rough sea and the want of swimming in it.
We had thought to save poor wee Belgium.
We knew it wasn't France when they
shaved our heads for the heat, lads
running anyways to avoid it.
We'd heard from the Irish gone before,
Gallipoli was hell, but when they landed us
under sheer cliffs, and no artillery, it didn't make sense.

We waited. We waited too long.
In heat I've never known. Shears your skin off,
peeling it back, sunburn red-raw.
Water now, I knew about water, and rain.
I lived on land that was watery earth,
it never went dry. But I never knew
how precious it really is, how alive
it brings you, how strong it makes you, and
what it can do to you — going without —
slit lips, mouth full of pebbles for the wet,
stumbling about so mad for it,
you don't care if anyone can shoot you.
Honest men made thieves, liars,
some gone so crazy they might kill for it.
Wild flowering plants over those hills,
there must have been clear springs somewhere —
if anyone in charge had a map.

'Yeşil Yol'

Bu yoldu gittiğimiz
varmak için oraya — gölleri geçip şafakta,
öylesine sakin ki sazlıklar, rengine boyanmışlar,
ceket kollarımıza diktiğimiz
yeşil yoncaların
asla eşleşmemek için rengiyle
koyunların beyaza boyadığı ışıl ışıl Connaught tarlaların —
ama bizimle seyahat eder yine de. Ve çıkıp geldik işte
Dublin'in gri ışıklarından, yoksulluğundan, soğuğundan,
her zaman aç ve artık işimizle beslenecek olan.
Ve Triniti'den, yeni bir ulusun geleceğinden.
Öğrenecekler bizi o zaman —
imparatorluk yöneticilerimiz —
savaşta anlaşılacak kıymetimiz,
özgürlüğümüzle ödeyecekler değerimizi sonradan.
Bu bir onurdur. Bu yüzdendir gelişimiz.

İrlanda Piyadelerinin Flüt Bandosu
Yeşilin Yıpranışı marşını çalıyordu
biz yelken açarken Devonport'tan savaşa doğru,
biz sahil doğumlular, hem korkusunu biliriz
fırtınalı denizin hem de denizde yüzme arzusunu.
Zavallı küçük Belçika'yı kurtaracaktık
Fransa değildi gittiğimiz anladık
sıcak hava için kazıdıklarında saçlarımızı
delikanlılar dört bir yana kaçışıyordu.
Önden giden İrlandalılardan duymuştuk,
cehennem gibiydi Gelibolu, ama indirdiklerinde bizi
sarp kayalıkların altında, hem de ağır silahsız, anlamadık ne olduğunu.

Bekledik. Çok bekledik.
Daha önce görmediğim bir sıcakta. Derini kabartan,
soyup, altından kıpkırmızı güneş yanığı çıkaran.
Su lazım şimdi, suyu bilirdim, yağmuru da.
Toprağı sulak bir ülkede yaşadım,
asla kurumazdı. Hiç bilmezdim oysa
bunun ne kıymetli olduğunu, nasıl hayat verdiğini
nasıl da güçlendirdiğini insanı,
neler yapabildiğini sana — dolaşma diye ortalıkta —
dudakların çatlak, sulandırmak için çakıl dolu ağzınla,
sendelerken su için çılgınca,
umurunda değildir hiç vurulsan da.
En dürüstler bile döner hırsıza, yalancıya,
kimi öyle döner ki çılgına, öldürebilirler seni onun uğruna.
Çiçek açmış yabani bitkiler var yukarıda,
su pınarları olmalı orada bir yerlerde –
kime yok mu gösterecek yerini haritalarda.

This is the way we went and nothing more to know.
Jumping from lighters and drowning,
the chuck of bayonet up the guts,
or hailed into with lead, 'riddled' such a true word.
Say it fast many times — *riddled riddled riddled* — that's it.
General Sir Bryan Mahon, a Galway man,
had a tantrum when he didn't get promoted, resigned and
headed off to an island, leaving his men under fire,
and no-one game to pull us back without command.
The Fife Band was swallowed by Suvla. One great bite.
Most of us were dead in the many ways of war.
Most of us wearing the green, never got back.

This is the way we left, in early dawn,
past the broken wire, small heaps of charred khaki —
wounded burned to death by gorse fires —
bodies heaped so you couldn't tell
what country they were from, scattered about,
half-buried, the smell of crushed thyme
never to leave the company of blood, of cinders.
We sailed over the ones that never made it to land,
never fired a gun, or saw the carnage,
drowning out of the *River Clyde.*
They were from my home-place and I left them there
in those razor ravines, too far from Irish earth.

I shake out of rage now as I did then, frustrated,
throwing stones when grenades were gone.
All I want to do is drink water, drink and drink,
drown in it, drink anything.
Will they pay that honour-price now,
do you think? Will I have my own country
when I get back to it? The Turks have theirs.

Buydu gittiğimiz yol ve bilinecek başka şey yoktu.
Dubalardan atlayıp boğuluyoruz,
dimdik süngüler karınlarımı
ya da mermi yağmuru altında, "delik deşik" olmuşuz en doğrusu.
Hızla söyle defalarca — *delik deşik delik deşik delik deşik* — işte bu.
General Sir Bryan Mahon, bir Galway'li,
sinir krizi geçiriyor terfi edilmeyince,
bir adaya gidiyor, bırakıp adamlarını ateş altında, ve
kumar oynamıyor emirsiz geri çekmek için bizi. Flüt
bandosunu Suvla Koyu yutuyor. Bir lokmada. Pek
çoğumuz öldü savaşın pek çok halinde.
Pek çoğumuz yeşil giyen, bir daha hiç geri dönmedi.

Buydu ayrıldığımız yol, erkenden şafakta,
geçerek kopuk tel örgüleri, yanık haki öbeklerini —
çalı yangınlarıyla yanarak ölen yaralıların cesetlerini —
öyle yığılmış öbek öbek bedenler ki bilinmez
kimin hangi ülkeden geldiği, dağılmışlar etrafa,
yarı yanık, ezilmiş kekik kokusu
bırakmıyor peşini kanın ve külün asla.
Karaya asla çıkamayanları üstünden sürüyoruz gemileri,
ne bir silah atabilmişler, ne de kıyımı görmüşler,
düşüp boğularak *River Clyde* gemisinden.
Hepsi de benim memleketimden ve bıraktım orada
o jilet gibi keskin çukurlarda, İrlanda topraklarından çok uzakta.

Sarsılıyorum şimdi o zaman olduğu gibi,
öfkeyle, taşlar fırlatıyorum el bombaları bitince.
Tüm istediğim su içmek, içmek ve içmek, içmek
ne olursa, boğulmak içinde.
Ödeyecekler mi bu onurun bedelini sence?
Benim kendi vatanım olacak mı
geri dönünce? Olduğu gibi Türklerde.

'When he was young, once'

She only knew his body when it was young.
Not this.
He rode wild horses, tamed everything, everything.
He prayed, or not.
He swept her into life.
His urgency was for her alone
not some idea of history, some vision of a hero.
Now this short year that seemed so long —
and she did not know this body now.

Not this.

Scarred, the leg gone, mind altered beyond
his being able to speak of it except to say –
'we did things we had to do'.
She had been so hungry. No food.
She had been so alone.
Everything changing, family dispersed,
confusion, no-one to underpin
all that was familiar, known.
She wanted him back.

Not this.

She only knew his body as husband.
She remembered the moustache they laughed about,
her lace veil trailing, her hennaed hands in his,
her happiness, certainty of a future —
never years passing apart, the place falling to dust,
death lists, the fear of news, the understanding
everything had gone now that she knew.
Everything changed.
She didn't want this.

Not this.

What country is this? Men full of strange energy
they call 'war'. They call 'necessary'.
She can see it in a trapped kind of way, that necessity.
But every young man from her town,
every station hand, every merchant in the market,
every father who had seemed so old then.
Now him. Old while young.
She wanted him back, real as the rocks and the sand,
lonely for the 'him' she knew in her heart, in her very loins.

Not this.

'Gençken, bir zamanlar'

Kadın sadece gençken biliyordu onun bedenini.
Bunu değil.
Vahşi atlara biner, ehlileştirirdi her şeyi,
her şeyi. Dua ederdi, ya da etmezdi.
Hayatın içine sürdü kadınını.
Sırf onaydı acelesi
tarihi bir fikre değil, kahramanlık hayaline değil.
Şimdiyse bu uzun gelen kısacık yıl —
ve kadının tanıdığı beden bu değil şimdi.

Bu değil.

Yaralı, bacağı kopmuş, aklını yitirmiş
konuşamayacak kadar, şuydu bütün söyleyebildiği —
'biz yaptık üzerimize düşeni'.
Kadın çok açtı. Yemek yoktu.
Kadın çok yalnızdı.
Değişiyordu her şey, aile darmadağındı,
kargaşada, dayanacak kimse yoktu
güvendiği, bildiği.
Geri istediği bu değil.

Bu değil.

Kadın sadece kocası olarak biliyordu bedenini.
Bıyığını hatırlıyordu her zaman güldükleri,
dantel peçesi sarkıyordu, kınalı elleri erkeğinin ellerinde,
mutluluğu, geleceğinin güvencesi —
yıllar hiç ayrı geçmezdi, darmadağın oluyordu her yer,
ölüm listeleri, haber korkusu, anlamak
bildiği her şeyin yok olduğunu şimdi.
Her şey değişmişti.
Bu değildi istediği.

Bu değil.

Hangi ülkeydi burası? Tuhaf bir enerjiyle doluydu erkekler
'savaş' diyorlardı adına. 'Gerekli' diyorlardı.
Görebiliyordu, tutsak bir halde, bu gerekliliği.
Fakat, her genç erkek onun kasabasından,
her istasyondan, her tüccar pazar yerinde,
her baba o zaman çok yaşlı görünen.
Şimdi de o. Gençken yaşlanan.
Geri istiyordu onu kadın, kayalar ve kumlar kadar gerçek,
'onun' için yalnızlığıydı bildiği kadının tüm kalbiyle, tüm varlığıyla.

Bu değil.

'Poppy-picking'

for Meral, Bozcaada island/Tenedos, 2013

Not the soft wrinkled skin of old men —
papery, easily torn — or the crumpled blooms in our town plots.
Upright as tulips, Turkish Red Poppies are firm and sure,
they need just four petals, bright scarlet,
red as red can get, each with its eye kohl-black.

We are laughing like children,
racing through fields-full, higher than our knees.
They crowd the narrow roads of your island
spilling across runnels, under fences
as if they were once water, spreading in a flood.

We are poppy-hunters, poppy-picking.
We run ahead of the other women,
driving to lane's end, friends' building sites,
competing for the best field to harvest.
You hold them hostage with talk while I grab and gather.

We pluck the four petals. Pollen-loaded stems are
shocked, naked, worrying how to attract bees.
Velvet along our fingers we recall our babies' skin,
filling bucket after basket, harvesting till your small green car
is loaded with the lightness of their feather-weight.

At the house we wash them outside in basins.
Small creatures emerge to be purged,
bits of grass, poppy seeds, perhaps enough
to charm a winged monkey, put a lion to sleep
on their trudge behind the rainbow.

Over and over we rinse them, the spring heat on our backs,
flowers ruffling and crinkling in our cool hands.
It's like washing silk shirts. The pot in the kitchen is
boiling its sugary clouds. Your secret ingredient
that I am to take with me 'to the grave' is wafting old Morocco in.

When the jam is ready it cools into dark-claret shades
ready to sit in my bags with poppy lokum, red-poppy syrup,
travelling back to a country where red poppies only ever meant
grief over fields full of the bodies of dead young men,
a generation of women left unmarried, alone.

Now — you say to me — when you see red poppies you will think of these —
friendship in spring; wild flowering and its fruit; *gelincik*,
which means lovely 'young brides' in their ladybird beauty,
black eyes shining with happiness; the touch of red velvet,
of sunshine, wet silk; the sweetness of jam on the tongue.

'Gelincikler'

Meral'e, Bozcada adası/Tenedos, 2013

Ne yaşlı erkeklerin kırışık yumuşak cildi —
kâğıt gibi kolay yırtılan — ne de park saksılarının buruşuk çiçekleri.
Laleler gibi dimdik, kendinden emindir Kırmızı Türk Gelincikleri,
alabildiğine parlak, kırmızı dört yaprak,
bir de gözlerine çekili birer kara sürmedir tüm istekleri.

Çocuklar gibi gülüyoruz koşarken,
boyu dizimizi aşan tarlalar dolusu gelincikleri.
Sokaklarını dolduruyorlar adanızın
saçılıyorlar dereler boyu, geçip altından çitlerin
sanki bir zamanlar yollara taşan seller gibi.

Gelincik avcısıyız biz, gelincik toplarız.
oşup başka kadınları geçer,
yolun sonuna varırız, inşaatların ardına,
en güzel tarlayı bulmak için yarışırız.
Ben demetleri toplarken lafa tutarsın onları arkada.

Dört yaprağını yolarız. Polen dolu kökler
şaşkın, çıplak, arılar nasıl gelecek diye bekler.
Bebeğimizin cildini andırır kadife yapraklar parmaklarımızda,
tüy gibi yükle dolana kadar o küçük yeşil araba
ardı ardına doldurur sepetleri gelincikler.

Eve varınca yıkarız doldurup küvetlere.
Küçük böcekler fırlar içlerinden,
otlar, gelincik tohumları, yeter belki de
uyutmaya bir aslanı, uçan bir maymunu eğlendirmeye
gökkuşağının ardındaki merdivenlerde.

Üst üste duruları, yakarken sırtımızı bahar güneşi,
çiçekler kırışır, buruşturur sular serinleyen ellerimizi.
İpek gömlekleri yıkamaya benzer. Mutfaktaki tencereden
tatlı bir buhar yükselir. Hoş bahar kokuları tüttüren
senin o eşsiz tarifin benimle 'mezara' gidecektir.

Reçel hazır olduğunda koyu gölgeler çöker üstüne soğudukça
hazırım artık gelincik lokumu dolu çantamla,
gelincik şurubumla hüzünlü bir ülkeye yolculuğa
gelincikler yalnızca genç ölen adamlar,
evlenmemiş yalnız kadınlar anlamına gelir o topraklarda.

Şimdi — diyorsun ki bana — şunları düşün gelincikleri görünce —
bahardaki dostluğu; yabani güzelliği ve onun meyvesini; gelincik,
'genç bir gelinlik' kızdır hanımböceği güzelliğinde,
mutluluktan ışıldar kara gözleri, kadife gibi dokunur,
günışığı, ipek gibi; bir reçel tadı dilinde.

Index

Note: Page numbers in *italics* refer to figures
Page numbers followed by 'n' refer to notes